GAME,SET,AND MATCH

GAME,SET,

AND MATCH

The Tennis Boom of the 1960s and 70s

Herbert Warren Wind

E. P. Dutton   o   New York

Copyright © 1962, 1964, 1965, 1967, 1968, 1970, 1971, 1972, 1973, 1975, 1976, 1977, 1978, 1979 by Herbert Warren Wind · All rights reserved. Printed in the U.S.A. ·
No part of this publication may be reproduced or transmitted in any form or by any means, electronic or mechanical, including photocopy, recording or any information storage and retrieval system now known or to be invented, without permission in writing from the publisher, except by a reviewer who wishes to quote brief passages in connection with a review written for inclusion in a magazine, newspaper or broadcast · For information contact: E.P. Dutton, 2 Park Avenue, New York, N.Y. 10016 · Library of Congress Cataloging in Publication Data · Wind, Herbert Warren, 1918– · Game, set, and match · "All the material . . . originally appeared in *The New Yorker* in slightly different form." · 1. Tennis—History. 2. Tennis players—Biography.
I. Title · GV995.W733 1979 796.34'2 78-26895 · ISBN: 0-525-11140-9 ·
Published simultaneously in Canada by Clarke, Irwin & Company Limited, Toronto and Vancouver · Designed by The Etheredges · 10 9 8 7 6 5 4 3 2 1 · First Edition

For Al Laney

CONTENTS

ACKNOWLEDGMENTS

Many people helped me a great deal in gathering material for this book and in giving me the benefit of their experience and insight. I would particularly like to acknowledge my appreciation to the following persons: George E. Alexander, who has unearthed so much valuable new material on Major Wingfield and the early days of tennis; Ed Baker, now in retirement from the U.S.T.A., but the friend everyone turns to when the record books do not have the answer; Sarah Palfrey Danzig, the last national champion from the frozen North—Massachusetts; Steven Flink, who, after imbibing two Transfusions, can reconstruct the head-to-head record of, say, Regina Marsikova and Linda Mottram; David Gray, formerly of the *Guardian,* now secretary of the International Tennis Federation; Ronald Howard, for many years a pillar of the Wimbledon pubs; William Mangold, an old colleague at *The New Yorker;* Dudley Sutphin, always a stimulating friend with whom to discuss the game; and Fred Tupper, who guided me around the Centre Court and other places for many years.

PREFACE

This book deals primarily with the nineteen-sixties and the nineteen-seventies, a period in which tennis underwent some radical changes. For example, the number of players in the United States increased from about five million to close to twenty million. Not only that, but the converts came from all classes of society and all walks of life. As the number of players grew, so did, among other things, the number of new tennis clubs and public facilities, the quality of instruction, the interest in international tournament tennis and the coverage of it. In fact, the whole position of tennis in American life was drastically altered.

The arrival of open tennis in 1968 played a very important part in the tennis explosion. While this book focuses on the leading players and the outstanding matches during this period of change, it has, I trust, another dimension. There are many flashbacks to the beginnings of the game and to the fascinating champions of earlier eras, such as the Renshaw twins, Hazel Hotchkiss Wightman, Bill Tilden, and the French Musketeers. My hope is that all the separate investigations and glimpses fit together like a rough mosaic and constitute, in effect, an informal history of tennis since the game's invention by Major Walter Clopton Wingfield in 1873.

H.W.W.

INTRODUCTION

In 1881, eight years after Major Walter Clopton Wingfield, a retired English cavalry officer, had devised the game of lawn tennis, this country set up its own governing body. It was called the United States National Lawn Tennis Association, and thirty-four clubs were affiliated with it. In 1920, no doubt tired of being accused of tautology, the association decided to become the United States Lawn Tennis Association, or, for short, the U.S.L.T.A. It was the U.S.L.T.A. that initiated the Wightman Cup matches, reprimanded Bill Tilden, mourned when Don Budge turned pro, and so on and so forth down through the years. Indeed, the U.S.L.T.A. made all the decisions, national and international, for American amateur tennis and eventually, in 1968, led us into the brave new world of open tennis.

A few years ago a startling communiqué was released from the U.S.L.T.A.'s main office on Forty-second Street, in Manhattan. In the future, we were informed, the U.S.L.T.A. would be the U.S.T.A., inasmuch as it had been decided to change the name of the organization to the United States Tennis Association. This made sense, for our national championships at Forest Hills were no longer played on grass but on a synthetic clay-like surface called Har-Tru. Moreover, while the old clubs, such as West Side, Longwood, Orange, and others, retained some grass courts (the Newport Casino still has nothing but grass courts) the day of grass has passed. There is no surface as conducive to fine tennis as good grass, but there is no surface as frustrating to play on as bad grass, and our grass had gradually deteriorated (due primarily, we have been told, to the increase in industrial pollution) until by the middle nineteen-sixties it could no longer stand up to the day-after-day beating of a week-long or a twelve-day tournament. Even the quality of the grass in Wimbledon's Centre Court, which, with rare exceptions, is used only during the fortnight of the championships, isn't what it used to be.

For another thing, after the arrival of open tennis, the television networks offered lucrative contracts for the rights to telecast tournaments. Since the TV show had to go on if it was at all possible, this was another potent reason for our tennis clubs to shift from grass, which drained slowly, to one of the many new composition surfaces, either gritty clay-type courts that drained quickly and dried quickly, or asphalt-type courts which were impervious and needed only to be mopped up here and there after a rain to be fit for play again. So the point was well taken: What with outdoor tennis being played predominantly on the new synthetic surfaces and indoor tennis on a large variety of mats and carpets, the moment had come to dispense with the *Lawn* in our national governing body's title.

Tennis, like golf and many other enduring games, was first played in Britain. In tennis' case, it was invented in the latter half of the nineteenth century when Britain, and England in particular, was hit by a craze for games that could be played on weekends, girls and boys together, on the spreading lawns of stately country homes. As is typical of the British, they called their lawn tennis association The Lawn Tennis Association. (They still do, as if there were no other.) Why, one asks, when for years and years nearly everyone who has played the game has referred to it simply as tennis, was it necessary to use the word *lawn?* There was a good reason. In the Middle Ages the game we today call court tennis was established in Europe. (Perhaps the only older game that is still played is polo, which the Persians may have originated four thousand years ago.) Some of the people involved in court tennis have always preferred to call it real tennis or royal tennis, if not court tennis, but for most people it was customary down through the centuries to call it tennis and let it go at that.

Major Wingfield, the founder of modern tennis, was the descendant of a very old English family. According to some sources, there may have been a court-tennis court in the ancestral home, Wingfield Castle, in Suffolk. In the major's day the castle had long since been in ruins, but the major—he was born in 1833—knew about court tennis from childhood and played it frequently. When at the age of forty he returned to Britain after a tour of duty in China, he consciously set out to create a new game that he hoped would catch on with the young men and women, who, as he observed, were exuberant about the new cult of games. Because of his background, he was careful not to call the imaginative adaptation of court tennis he devised just plain tennis. The court-tennis crowd still thought of their game as tennis and alluded to it as such, and they would not have liked the major's chutzpah one bit. Since his game was designed to be played on lawns, Major Wingfield opted for lawn tennis, and, no matter what surface it was played on, lawn tennis it remained throughout the world until just a few years ago. It was only when the U.S.L.T.A. decided that the grass at Forest Hills had seen its best days and when Har-Tru courts were installed in 1975 for our championships that here in America the climate became right to consider officially deleting the *lawn* from lawn tennis.

Over the last dozen years, tennis has enjoyed an incredible boom the likes of which, to my knowledge, no other game has ever experienced. Something like twenty million Americans now play it. Since one of the chapters in this book describes this phenomenon at length, at this time I wish to discuss only one phase of it—the rather widespread misconception that the boom transformed tennis overnight from a minor into a major sport. Assuredly, many more millions play the game and watch it nowadays, but throughout its lifetime, on certain occasions—and they go back as far as the eighteen-eighties when the Renshaw twins ruled Wimbledon—tennis has been of major interest to the hard core of informed enthusiasts in this country and sometimes even to the vast uncablestitched public that has always found it hard to distinguish between a rally and a volley. Every now and then, in the natural flow of things, tennis players of exceptional skill and personal appeal have opposed challengers of equal quality, and when these confrontations drew near, American sports fans became involved—not to the degree that they did at the prospect of a turbulent World Series, but, nevertheless, genuinely involved. One such occasion was the match at Cannes in 1926 between Suzanne Lenglen and Helen Wills—"our Helen." In my hometown—Brockton, Massachusetts, which was not a particularly tennis-oriented community—on the eve of that match it seemed that everyone was talking about it, and the next day the wire-service report appeared on the front page of the local newspaper. It was the same, I gather, throughout the country. The general interest was extremely intense also whenever Bill Tilden met one of the French Musketeers in a crucial Davis Cup match. In between these big occasions—almost invariably they were international clashes in which an American was up against a player of great reputation—tennis dropped back and became a minor concern of the average American sports fan. However, it should be noted, in the years before the Second World War professional baseball was the only truly major sport in this country and there was no close second. After baseball, the sport that commanded the most attention at that time was college football. In much the same way that was true of tennis, the other sports were of limited interest until a dynamic personality came along and seized the popular imagination. This was true, for example, of Dempsey and boxing. In Dempsey's era there were spirited debates on every veranda or in every den for a week before each of his title fights and for a week after it. The American public, which had historically viewed golf as a rich men's diversion—and the rich were welcome to it—began to follow it when Bobby Jones came along, for they sensed that he was the model American athlete. Accordingly, a big occasion for Jones, such as his extended pursuit of a grand slam of the four major championships in 1930, was a big occasion for them. Not many American sports fans burned with a hard, gem-like flame about track and field, but every four years when the Olympics loomed on the horizon, track and field mattered a lot. And so on. My basic thesis is that it is not entirely right to look upon tennis as being an inconsequential sport in this country until the boom when, thanks in the main to open tennis tournaments and the cornucopia of televised matches which gave it the audience it should have had long before, it jumped over the wall of the élite country club and became the raison d'être for nearly all the members of the new egalitarian tennis club. It had attained this position decades earlier in Britain where, up to a point, golf and tennis have long been "national sports." It had become one of the glories of France in the nineteen-twenties because of Suzanne and the capture of the Davis Cup by the Four Musketeers. In Australia, where the workingman's chief relaxation was playing sports, tennis was always important, and in the years following the close of the Second World War when the island continent produced the finest players in the world, it became, even in that country where the average man followed cricket and the various forms of rugby fanatically, *the* national sport.

This leads to a related subject that is worth our attention. If tennis was periodically transformed into a major sport in the old days when the big occasion came along, one reason this took place is that tennis is a remarkable game that at the championship level calls for superior athletic talent, marvelous hand-and-eye reflexes, power, speed of foot, intelligent study of one's opponent during the progress of a match, the ability to alter tactics when necessary, psychological equilibrium, fantastic physical stamina, and, along with all this, courage and determination. It is relevant to mention what it takes to play good tennis because for years and years, although they should have known better, many people tended to look upon it as a sissy's game. I suppose that the absence of physical contact in tennis may have had something to do with this, but then how does one explain the acceptance of baseball as our national pastime? At any rate, I honestly wonder if tennis, at the top level, may not require the highest kind of athletic coordination, laced with discipline and mentality, of any sport. What comes to mind first, because they are so recent, are the matches between Bjorn Borg and Jimmy Connors, the two of them going at each other without letup for two hours and more beneath a broiling sun, racing to the ball back and forth along the baseline, moving fast into the forecourt to volley or smash, grunting like football linemen as they throw nearly every ounce of energy they can marshal into their serves, somehow returning a serve hit with such speed that it is a feat just to get the racquet on the ball let alone play a controlled stroke, chasing a cross-court drive yards beyond the doubles alley and throwing up a desperate lob in the hope of somehow getting back into the rally, and on point after point after point watching the ball diligently, moving quickly to the ball and getting into position, and then swatting a good, sound, heady shot. Styles in tennis change, to be sure, but the leading players are always something to behold, and I have long wondered how anyone with a feeling for sport could watch a first-rate match—say, Tilden versus Lacoste, Budge versus Crawford, Kramer versus Sedgman, or Hoad versus Trabert—without becoming committed to tennis for life.

The great explosion, which arrived in 1968 or thereabouts, had been brewing for years. It surprised nearly everyone by its size, its spread, and its depth. Most old tennis hands I have talked with are quick to admit that it was three or four times bigger in every dimension than the explosion they had anticipated, and I think that very few people in the game were not flabbergasted when, for example, there were suddenly more tennis matches, both live and taped, available on television on Sunday than there were variations of "Meet the Press." Inevitably, a few exaggerations about the new tennis scene crept in. One went like this: Now, with people from all walks of life participating in the boom, for the first time one didn't have to come from a rich family to have a chance to play lots of tennis in his youth, and possibly make a career in the game. That was true only up to a point. Yes, the well-to-do families sometimes had had their own private courts and almost always had belonged to country clubs with splendid tennis facilities; and, yes, they generally had sent their children to colleges where it was a real feather in your hat to make the tennis team. However, it is wrong to deduce that, before the boom, tennis was played only by the very well-to-do— like polo. Shortly after the turn of the century, in most cities and many towns throughout our country there were public tennis courts, sometimes at the municipal parks and playgrounds, other times at the Y.M.C.A. or the high school athletic grounds. Just as good looks are not limited to girls and boys from well-heeled families, neither is athletic prowess, and as long ago as the period before the First World War fine young tennis players who had picked the game up on public courts went on to enjoy wonderful careers that carried them to Wimbledon and the other famous homes of tennis. Maurice McLaughlin, Bill Johnston, Ellsworth Vines, Alice Marble, Don Budge, Bobby Riggs, Frank Parker, Jack Kramer, Pancho Gonzales—let us stop there—are just a few of the many champions who came from middle-class or poor families and who necessarily were the products of public courts. Today, when many colleges, eager to gain recognition through their outstanding athletic teams, have quite a few tennis scholarships to hand out to young men and women with a deserving backhand, it is considerably easier for talented players to get the advanced instruction and the competitive experience they need than it was in the old days when the young whizzes off the public courts had to play up to the local tennis czar in order to get the backing necessary to keep improving and move ahead in the game. It has been much the same in every country. Most people would suppose that Fred Perry, for example, came from the same kind of upper-class background as did his Davis Cup teammate Bunny Austin. In fact, Perry, the son of a Labor M.P., actually came from a working-class family, and, as a rising player, got by purely on his capability before the men in authority at The Lawn Tennis Association and the All England Club were forced to notice his extraordinary talent and to extend a friendly hand. Most of the great Australians came from working-class families, and, if I remember correctly, many of the boys who developed into international stars had to leave school at an early age and go to work for the big tennis equipment companies, stringing racquets and the like in order to earn the support of these companies and to receive the instruction and the overall superintendence that brought them along surely.

On the other hand, the good old days were not so good for the people on the periphery of tennis. They had few opportunities to see the best players in action. The pro tour, that will-o'-the-wisp, seldom came to town. Just where the vagabonds were playing was often a mystery—maybe Mombasa, maybe Marseilles, maybe Mobile. As for the amateur game, it was the custom in America for the players to swing up the eastern seaboard in summer, following the tournament trail that wound, with some variations, from Merion to Seabright to Orange to Southampton to Nassau to Newport to Longwood and ultimately to Forest Hills. The members of the host club and their guests turned out en masse during the glamorous tournament week, but only a sprinkling of the other tennis players and fans in the vicinity attended the matches, principally because they felt that it was a club occasion and, in addition, because little was expended to let local non-club members know that they were indeed welcome. As a consequence, before the boom, a gathering of over three thousand on a weekday was regarded as a large crowd. In those days, though sports had long been a prime staple of television, there was no televised tennis to speak of. Tennis on the tube began and ended with the network coverage of the last two days at Forest Hills, the telecast lasting an hour and a half to two hours each day. (In Britain it was already the practice of the B.B.C. to provide nearly seven hours of coverage each playing day during the Wimbledon fortnight.) It came down to this: Considering the number of Americans who were attracted to tennis, only a comparative handful had the opportunity to see the champions in action until around 1970 when the advent of open tennis shook up the whole world of tennis and, among other things, opened up the whole tournament scene and revolutionized TV coverage. The essential interest, as I say, had always been there. For example, in December 1947, on the night when one of the biggest snowfalls in the history of the New York City area at length ended, something like fifteen thousand fans would not be deterred by the twenty-six inches of snow and fought their way to Madison Square Garden so that they could be present at the long-awaited match in which Jack Kramer made his professional début against the reigning king of the pro tour, Robert Larimore Riggs.

Of the many games we play and watch, baseball and golf perhaps have the finest literature. Some sports just seem to write better than others. It is not difficult to understand why golf is one of them. It is the only game that is played on natural terrain, with the wind and weather also having a critical role. It is also easy to understand why so many people have written so well about baseball from its formative years on. The game is an exquisite amalgam of checks and balances which the men who created it in the mid-nineteenth century somehow got absolutely right.

It is rather surprising, though, that tennis literature is both meager and somewhat mundane, because the game is such a superlative one. Aside from being a delight to play, it is a treat to watch, for no action on the court is hidden from the spectator. It has had a long succession of vivid and magnetic champions, both men and women. It demands as much technical skill as any game there is. Along with soccer and golf, it is a bona fide world sport. For illustration, since the Davis Cup competition was instituted in 1900, teams representing the United States, the British Isles, Belgium, Australasia (Australia and New Zealand), Japan, France, Great Britain, Australia, Italy, Mexico, Spain, India, Rumania, West Germany, South Africa, Sweden, Czechoslovakia, and Chile have reached the Challenge Round. It is a game that can dazzle you with its speed and beauty and that can leave you exhausted when you have watched a hard-fought singles or doubles match in which victory and defeat for both sides have hung in the balance on a good many points that could have gone either way. The structure of tennis can make for a whole series of such thrilling junctures. A number of excellent books, it should be stated, have been written about tennis. To name a few that I admire, there is Dame Mabel Brookes' memoir, "Crowded Galleries"; Bill Tilden's "Match Play and the Spin of the Ball," published in 1925, which many cognoscenti consider the best technical book on the game; René Lacoste's fastidious and absorbing "Lacoste on Tennis"; Al Laney's "Covering the Court," the brilliant evocation of his fifty-year love affair with tennis; and Frank Deford's recent biography, "Big Bill Tilden," a superb piece of work. Then, too, there has been a plenitude of gifted tennis journalists, from H. S. Scrivener and A. Wallis Myers, both of whom were English, down the years through Allison Danzig of the New York *Times*, Laney of the New York *Herald Tribune* and the Paris *Herald*, and John Tunis of the New York *Post*, to the contemporary era with its growing corps of able tennis specialists, in particular the peripatetic British battalion headed up by such veterans as Lance Tingay of the London *Daily Telegraph* and Rex Bellamy of the *Times* of London.

Where tennis books are concerned, the principal trouble has been that most of the champions with a real story to tell have neglected to take the time and pains that are required to bring off a worthwhile book, one that will mean something to future generations. More than that, a large percentage of these players, for some reason or another, have been less concerned with letting us know about themselves and their tennis than in calling attention to the socialites and celebrities they have become great friends with thanks to the wonderful game of tennis. As a result, we shall probably never know all that we would like to know about the champions and near-champions, the famous matches and the significant uncelebrated matches, the major and minor characters who have been part of the tennis world in every era.

Because there are so many gaps in the literature of tennis, one treasures the work that is of the first order. In my own case, I find that I regularly re-read my favorite articles and books. Here, for example, are three short passages from writing on tennis which especially please me. The first was written by Robert Gordon Menzies in 1955 when he was Prime Minister of Australia. He is speaking of Norman Brookes, the first Australian to win at Wimbledon, which he did in 1907:

> What a player! His long trousers perfectly pressed, on his head a peaked tweed or cloth cap, on his face the inscrutable expression of a pale-faced Red Indian, no sign of sweat or bother, no temperamental outbursts, no word to say except an occasional "well played." A slim and not very robust man, he combined an almost diabolical skill with a personal reserve, a dignity (yes, dignity), and a calm maturity of mind and judgement. I have sometimes suspected that a modern coach would have hammered out of him all the astonishing elements that made him in his day (and his day lasted for many years) the greatest player in the world.

The second is an extract from "Lacoste on Tennis" in which René Lacoste assesses his arch-rival Bill Tilden:

> Tilden always seems to have a thousand means of putting the ball away from his opponent's reach. He seems to exercise a strange fascination over his opponent as well as the spectator. Tilden, even when beaten, always leaves an impression on the public mind that he was superior to the victor. All the spectators seem to feel that he can win when he likes. Seemingly, in two steps he covers the whole of the court; without any effort, he executes the most various and extraordinary strokes. He seems capable of returning any shot when he likes, to put the ball out of his opponent's reach when he thinks the moment has come to do so. Sometimes he gives the ball tremendous velocity, sometimes he caresses it and guides it to a corner of the court whither nobody but himself would have thought of directing it.

And third, here is a passage from Al Laney's "Covering the Court." He is recalling the memorable match between Don Budge and Gottfried von Cramm in the 1937 Davis Cup Interzone Final. It is the fifth set, and Budge, having just broken von Cramm's serve to go into the lead 7–6, is serving for the match:

> And then, finally, after the sixth deuce point, Budge won the advantage and stood for the fourth time one point from victory. Three times Cramm had saved match point and seemed certain to save a fourth when Budge served weakly this time, giving the German a chance to step in and pound the ball to the forehand corner once more. Since Don could not come across court after such a ball, Cramm dashed in and crowded the other side. And Budge hit now the finest shot of the match, a truly gorgeous forehand as straight as could be down the line, swift, low, and certain. I can see the picture yet. The bending of the knees for the crouch—with Budge it was an ungainly squat—the lifting of the low spinning ball with all the weight going into the swing as the knees straightened and locked. Cramm lunged to his left, hiding the ball from me as it flew on its way to pitch just beyond the service court, where a little puff of white marked the spot as it fell. Cramm had fallen to the court in his futile effort to intercept. He rose quickly and, without looking back, came around the net to congratulate Budge. No need to look back. He knew and we all knew the moment the ball was struck that it was a winner and the wonderful match was over.

Since the advent of the boom, instruction books, with or without esoteric psychological overtones, have done well, but I have an idea that we may currently be on the verge of a period in which a number of tennis books of marked literary quality will be written. It strikes me that many of the talented young people now writing about tennis are completely interested in the players, the entourages, the coaches, the agents and the promoters, the changing trends, the different surfaces, the friendships and feuds, the colossal rewards and pressures—the whole intricate, enchanting fabric of this world within a world. Early this past summer I had a chance to read "Nastase," a biography written by Richard Evans, who doubles as a tennis administrator in Europe, and the book has the ring of distinction. So too has "Handful of Summers," an extended reminiscence by Gordon Forbes. A South African who for many years was a player of international class, Forbes, since his retirement from competition, has shown himself to be that rare bird, a serious humorist. As I say, I have the feeling that these two books are simply the first of a large number of superior tennis books that will be produced in the coming years and that will begin to give the game, at long last, the literature it deserves.

HERBERT WARREN WIND

New York, New York
September 1978

GAME, SET, AND MATCH

LAVER COMPLETES
HIS GRAND SLAM

(1962)

Rod Laver is the only player who has achieved grand slams of the traditional four major championships both as an amateur and a professional. As an amateur he reached an exceedingly high level before turning pro late in 1962. As a pro he was near his peak when the major championships became open competitions in 1968. His second grand slam came in 1969.

The 1962 United States Lawn Tennis Championships, which were concluded last week at the West Side Tennis Club in Forest Hills, were, for a number of reasons, the most memorable in years. To begin with, Rod Laver, the sturdy little Australian left-hander, added our national title to the Australian, French, and Wimbledon titles he had won in January, May, and July, respectively, and thus carried off all four major championships in one season—a feat that had been accomplished only once before, by Don Budge in 1938. Although an Australian victory in our men's singles is anything but novel (indeed, it is now seven Septembers since anyone *but* an Australian has won it), this year, for the first time ever, the women's singles also went to an Australian—to Margaret Smith, a powerful, equable Melbournian, who is now quite clearly the best woman player in the world. Miss Smith then teamed up with another of her talented compatriots, Fred Stolle, to win the mixed doubles. This unprecedented all-Australian sweep, furthermore, was scored against the most thoroughly international field that has ever assembled at Forest Hills—players from no fewer than thirty-five countries. This exceptional turnout was made possible by the enterprise of the People-to-People Sports Committee, which, among other things, arranged for seventy of the foreign players to be flown in by chartered plane from Amsterdam, the central collecting point. There were, by the way, ten empty seats on the plane. Six of them had been set aside for the Russian delegation, which chose to come over on its own but arranged to join the party on the return flight. The other vacancies were somewhat unexpected; four Italian players, without informing anyone, simply failed to show. It had been a tossup all along whether the most prominent of the absentees, the tightly strung Nicola Pietrangeli, would manage to be at the right airport on the right day, and his eventual explanation, from Rome, of why he wasn't was perfectly in character. It was a matter of "professional dignity," Pietrangeli said; he wasn't playing well.

The presence of so many players from other parts of the world gave our championships an aura that had been badly lacking in recent years. It might be well to point out, however, that the day is long past when a spectator, roving from field court to field court in the early rounds and getting acquainted with dozens of new faces, can tell a player's nationality simply from his appearance or from some helpful clue like the nice cut of the Englishmen's flannels, the berets of the French, or the square-faced racquets the Australians used to favor. Today, tennis players, wherever they come from, dress very much alike, usually speak English on the court, and have basically the same kinds of strokes and mannerisms, so until you have seen them in a match (as opposed to practice), where their identities are revealed by the scoreboards at courtside, there is no guessing just who it is you're watching. Early in the tournament, for example, as I was admiring all the tanned and handsome young men and women sitting around the club-house, my attention was captured by a pretty, animated black-haired girl in a long white woollen cardigan—a Wellesley sophomore, if ever I saw one. A day or two later, I wandered over to the grandstand court, where Margaret Smith was scheduled to play the Russian ladies' champion, Anna Dmitrieva, and was stunned to discover that the Wellesley girl was Miss Dmitrieva. She is a left-hander, and while she is not in Miss

Smith's class—she took four games in the two sets—she is a very respectable player, with a lovely natural manner on the court. Later that afternoon, when Alexander Metreveli, the Russian junior champion, came out to play Gordon Forbes, of South Africa, it was much the same story. Just why one still expects Russian sports stars to be ponderous and phlegmatic I do not know, but Metreveli turned out to be neither. Instead, he was a fluidly coördinated young athlete with enormous élan. He took the first set from Forbes, and had a fine chance to take the second as well, when he succumbed to a sudden attack of anxiety, like any other seventeen-year-old boy, and lost the set, 8–10, and in effect the match. Metreveli is more than a good prospect—he is an outstanding one. Another of the Russians, Sergei Likhachev, was eliminated in the first round by Jim McManus, of Berkeley, California, but he, too, was quite impressive, carrying the match to five sets and holding his own in the fifth until a debatable call by a linesman at a critical moment went against him. This was the first time Russia had sent its players to our championships, and to judge by their surprisingly strong showing it may be only three or four years before they become a power of some consequence in the tennis world. This year's pioneer group was shepherded by the president of the U.S.S.R. Tennis Federation, Dmitri Gosudarev, who, it might be added, differed from his players in that he looked more or less the way one expected him to—like a younger, ruggeder Sam Goldwyn.

The pronounced international atmosphere at Forest Hills not only gave the championships a definite glamour but gave them substance as well. In earlier years, when the number of foreign entrants was comparatively small, the draw was filled out by the American players with the best regional records. Since, for the most part, they were really only top-level "club players," there was seldom anything worth the watching until the quarter-final round, when the seeded players bumped into one another. This year it was different, completely. From the opening round on, there were extremely good, hard-fought matches, since a seeded star, instead of having mere walk-throughs, would find himself up against, say, the second-ranked German player in the first round and the first-ranked Belgian in the second. If Forest Hills made one point clear, it was that there are many more competent tennis players in the world than had been generally appreciated. Take Gordon Forbes, for example. In the first round, Forbes, a tall, bespectacled fellow, barely edged out Nicola Pilić, of Yugoslavia, in five tough sets. In the next round, he came up against Stolle, who had won the Pennsylvania and Eastern Championships earlier this summer and was seeded fifth.

Forbes upset him in straight sets, 6–1, 8–6, 11–9. He then moved on to defeat Metreveli, and, in the fourth round, made a wonderful comeback against Billy Knight, of England, to win in five wearing sets, 4–6, 5–7, 6–4, 11–9, 6–4. All this tennis eventually took its toll, and Forbes proved no match for the agile young Mexican Rafael Osuna when they met in the quarter-finals. Nonetheless, Forbes—and the same could be said of quite a number of unheralded visitors—leaves Forest Hills a much more highly regarded player than he was when he arrived.

There were a few moments early in the tournament when Osuna's chances of being among those present on the day of the quarter-finals looked very dim indeed, for in the third round, facing Whitney Reed, our first-ranked player, he became involved in a fierce and tremendously entertaining battle that had the large gallery in the stadium cheering and applauding almost without letup. Like most dramatic matches, Osuna vs. Reed brought together two extremely dissimilar personalities. Osuna, who led Mexico's Davis Cup team to its victory over the United States in August, is a limpid-eyed terrier of a youngster who can run all day and is forever digging for the forecourt, where he can exploit his talent for volleying and his sound overhead smash. He has had a fine season. Reed has not. He has been playing poorly all year and was so far off form this summer that he suffered the ignominy of being dropped from our Davis Cup squad before the match with Mexico. A native of Alameda, he is tall and blond, like many of his colleagues from California, but there his conformity to the mold ceases. He is the picture of awkwardness and unorthodoxy. He plays many of his strokes with a stiff wrist, shovelling the racket around with odd gyrations of his torso and arm. Since he is slow on his feet and, additionally, is not fond of the Spartan life (he is affectionately known to the other members of the live-it-up tennis crowd as Our Leader), he has evolved a singular style of play. In order to get to shots that are a couple of steps away, he flings himself through the air, so that he hits a high percentage of his returns while he is tumbling toward the grass. Few players in the long history of tennis can have spent as much time on the ground as this unacrobatic acrobat, and certainly no player has hit as many winning shots while hopelessly out of position and off balance. For example, in his match with Osuna, Reed's best forehand of the day, a blazer down the line that passed Osuna cold, came at the end of a long rally, and Reed, exhausted, was down on one knee and one elbow when he hit it. Against Osuna, Reed dropped the opening two sets, the first a gruelling one, and then confounded everybody by somehow summoning the energy and the shots to take the next two, both at 6–3. He continued to play well in the final set, scoring a succession of placements by hitting exactly the shot his opponent was not expecting, but when he fell behind, 0–40, with Osuna leading 5–4 and serving, the end was apparently at hand. Not at all. Reed saved three match points, the last on a sliding-falling-sprawling crosscourt forehand that left him spread-eagled on the turf over on the next court. He pulled out the game and went off on a terrific spree to take the eleventh game on his service and to lead, 0–40, in the next. Then it was Osuna's turn to show his mettle, and show it he did, fighting off three match points with forcing volleys and ultimately saving the game. In the fifteenth game, Osuna fought off still another match point, and that was it for Reed. He could go no further. He failed to hold service in the next game, and Osuna quickly ran out the set, 10–8. The epilogue to the match had just the right touch. Osuna leaped the net to slap Reed's back, and the next thing you knew, Reed had hoisted himself into Osuna's arms, so that he could be carried off the court.

The Osuna-Reed match, coming about halfway through the ten days of play, gave the championships an extra lift at an appropriate time, and from that point on the intense interest in the progress of the two favored Australians, Rod Laver and Margaret Smith, sustained the high pitch. For decades now, the tennis world has been wondering when Australia, which came up with the first of its almost continuous line of men champions back in 1907—that was the year Norman Brookes won at Wimbledon—would produce its first great woman player. Miss Smith, a soft-spoken girl with reddish-brown hair and a pleasant manner, is perhaps a little short of being a genuinely great tennis player at the moment, but she is far and away the most talented player of her sex ever to come from the Antipodes, and since she is only twenty and has all the physical requisites, as well as a stable temperament and the kind of earnestness that borders on dedication, she may very well leave quite a mark on the game before she is done. This season, prior to coming to America, she had been beaten only once in serious competition—ironically, at Wimbledon, the tournament that counts most, where Billie Jean Moffitt, one of the young Californians, put her out in the first round. At Forest Hills, Miss Smith was clearly determined not to let the second-most-coveted title elude her, if attention to the task at hand would count for anything. In racing through her first four matches, she lost a total of only twelve games, and showed herself immensely improved since last year, when, in her American début, she was defeated in the semifinals by Darlene Hard, the defending champion. A big, strong, rangy girl whom you would not call graceful but who moves athletically and well, Miss Smith now has a wide repertoire of strokes, and they all bear a considerable resemblance to those of her coach, the well-remembered Frank Sedgman. There is a lot of width to her forehand and backhand drives, her service is fundamentally sound, and she is an adroit, emphatic volleyer. Everyone was wondering how well her game would stand up to continuous pressure from a first-class opponent, and her semifinal match with Maria Bueno provided the answer. Miss Bueno, the Brazilian girl who has twice won at Wimbledon and who had the look of a lesser Lenglen about her until she had the misfortune to be stricken with hepatitis a year and a half ago, played extremely well all the way, and, in streaks, with utter brilliance. Miss Smith at length won out, 6–8, 6–3, 6–4, the scores giving an accurate picture of the closeness of the match, which was a stirring one, and a rare one, too, in women's tennis, both girls serving with power and attacking from all over the court. What eventually saw Miss Smith through was not so much superior physical stamina as patience and resolution. She is an unusually hard worker, this girl, and she could almost always force from herself the extra effort that would enable her, say, to get to and handle a stop-volley that seemed to have her beaten, and so turn a pivotal point completely around. The final, in which she defeated Miss Hard, 9–7, 6–4, was a definite letdown. Miss Smith played spottily and without any apparent tactical plan, and Miss Hard's service was tragically erratic. She double-faulted sixteen times in all, five of them in the third game of the second set. This final, moreover, was marred by a most regrettable emotional display on the part of Miss Hard. Down 3–2 in the second set and intent on breaking her opponent's service and getting back on even terms, she received what looked like a bad call on a drive down the line by Miss Smith. On the heels of this, she got a very late call by a back linesman on a drive of her own, which *was* out by the barest of margins, but which, because of the linesman's long delay in making his call, she had been led to believe was good. She thereupon broke down, retreating to the back wall of the stadium and leaning against the canvas with her hand to her eyes.

If the 1962 championships belonged to any one player, they belonged to Laver, the twenty-four-year-old redhead from Queensland, who is called Rod the Rocket by the press and is addressed simply as Rocket, in a wonderfully matter-of-fact way, by the whole Australian squad. It is a fitting sobriquet. Laver, who stands about five feet eight and weighs about a hundred and fifty pounds, probably hits his serve harder than any player his size before him, and it is questionable whether any player of any size has ever hit forehand and backhand drives of greater velocity. Very little purpose would be served by recounting in any detail his march to the final, in which he defeated his friendly rival and countryman Roy Emerson, 6–2, 6–4, 5–7, 6–4. It is sufficient to say that at no time during the tournament was there any doubt that Laver would be successful in his quest of his grand slam. En route to the final, he did drop one set—the third, at 4–6, in his quarter-final match with Frank Froehling III, a twenty-year-old Floridian who has a thunderous service and needs only a backhand and more experience to become a player of the top class. However, it was typical of Laver that he immediately broke Froehling's service at the start of the fourth set to regain command. Against Emerson, after losing the third set he got back on the right foot in exactly the same way, breaking service in the first game of the fourth. This year, Laver is, to say the least, a far better and more devastating player than he was when we saw him last. Heretofore, I gather, most American experts had rated him several notches below such earlier Australian paragons as Frank Sedgman, Lew Hoad, and Ken Rosewall, and perhaps a notch below Neale Fraser at his best. All this will now have to be revised, drastically, and so will the formerly prevalent opinion that Laver is a dullish, uninteresting fellow to watch. No player could have been more arresting than he was at Forest Hills. To begin with, there was the incredible speed with which he was hitting everything, his balance and timing so superb that the ball was exploding off his racquet. He finished his semifinal match with Osuna, for example, by leaping into four good first services and cracking each of them back with his magnificent backhand for an untouchable winner. The next day, against Emerson, he started right off with three backhands of the same species. Moreover, Laver executes his strokes with great deception. He has an unusually flexible wrist, and with a minute twist of it at the very last moment, just before he hits the ball, he can change what has all the earmarks of a whipped drive into a delicate lob, or hit the ball with underspin instead of topspin. He is rather like the best pitchers in baseball—Whitey Ford is one of those who come to mind—who throw an assortment of pitches with the same basic motion and never let you know what to expect. In short, Laver showed himself to be the complete player. He had his large variety of spin services so well under control that he dropped only two service games until the third set of the final, when his own rapid pace got to him a little. In perfect condition, he was all over the court and seldom out of position. He dispatched the most difficult volleys with amazing positiveness. He was always placid, the same unaffected and likable young man he is off the court. Sir Norman Brookes's contention on the eve of the tournament that Laver had become the best tennis player in the world, amateur or professional, seemed quite extravagant at the time. It doesn't now. He may possibly *be* the best, and if he isn't, he is not far away from it.

THE DAVIS CUP
GOES SOUTHWEST

●

(1964)

Harry Hopman had his detractors during his long and extremely successful career as captain of Australia's Davis Cup team, but it is difficult to think of any other captain who could bring his players into a Challenge Round as well prepared physically, mentally, and psychologically for that pressure-filled test. Of course, it never hurts to have someone like Roy Emerson around to play a key match for you.

On the eve of the recent Davis Cup Challenge Round match, in Cleveland Heights, Ohio, between the United States and Australia, the two names, apart from the players', that came up most frequently were Harry Hopman and Teniko Royal. Hopman has been well known to tennis fans for quite some time. A trim, sandy-haired man, now fifty-eight, with an un-Australian fondness for oblique verbal maneuver, he was in Cleveland Heights as non-playing captain of the Australian team —a function he has filled without interruption for fifteen years. In that time, Australia has become *the* tennis nation—from 1950 through 1963, its teams won the Davis Cup eleven times to our three—and Hopman has come to be considered just about the shrewdest mind in the game. (This holds true even in Australia, where there are almost as many tennis experts as there are players, and where second-guessing Hopman is now a minor national pastime, like collecting aboriginal art.) Although he is in some ways prone to overcaptain his teams—I think he is wrong, for example, in ordering his players on many occasions to let him do the talking to the press—I admire the controlled ardor and efficiency he brings to his work. The last two times before this year's visit that he came to this country with challenging Davis Cup teams, in 1955 (with Lew Hoad, Ken Rosewall, and Rex Hartwig) and in 1959 (with Neale Fraser, Rod Laver, and Roy Emerson), Australia won the Cup back immediately—an impressive trick to pull off on foreign soil. As he prepared his 1964 team at Cleveland Heights, Hopman appeared to be extremely confident of making it three successful visits in a row, and not without reason. Last year, when Dennis Ralston and Chuck McKinley took the Cup by defeating the Australians at Adelaide by the score of 3–2, neither won his singles against Emerson, but both beat John Newcombe, the No. 2 Australian singles player, and in addition they won the doubles, in which Emerson was partnered rather feebly by Fraser, the aging hero of the 1959 Challenge Round. This year, with Fred Stolle set to play the second singles, Australia was obviously fielding a much stronger team. Stolle had been a finalist this year against Emerson both at Wimbledon and at Forest Hills, and at Wimbledon he had defeated McKinley in four sets in the semifinals, and at Forest Hills he had defeated Ralston in five memorable sets in the quarter-finals. For all this, Hopman was not taking things easy, and he was concentrating particularly on improving Stolle's handling of certain situations and shots he was bound to face in the doubles.

Teniko Royal is the brand name of a fast-drying composition clay surface for tennis courts put out by the F. C. Feise Company, of Narberth, Pennsylvania, and at Cleveland Heights a Teniko Royal court had been expressly constructed for the big event on a strip of land next to a junior high school. Patently, this was not at all like old Davis Cup times; we always used to defend the trophy at such stately homes as the West Side Tennis Club in Forest Hills and the Germantown Cricket Club outside of Philadelphia, and the match was always played on grass. As a matter of fact, the only times since Davis Cup competition began, in 1900, that the Challenge Round was not played on grass came during the six-year French supremacy (1928–33), when Lacoste, Cochet, Borotra et Cie. met the invaders on the clay-type courts of Roland Garros Stadium, in Auteuil. Anyway, the idea that one day we would be playing a major international match in this country on anything but good old patrician grass did not enter anyone's mind until last February, when, to general amazement, the Executive Committee of the United States Lawn Tennis Association voted to award the 1964 Challenge Round of the Davis Cup to a group of Cleveland civic leaders—mostly members of the Cleveland Skating Club—who had formed Davis Cup in Cleveland, Inc., for the purpose the name of the corporation implied and had presented the U.S.L.T.A. with the most attractive financial proposition. The other principal bidders—a group speaking for Forest Hills and a group speaking for southern California—offered the participating teams all the profits; the Cleveland people guaranteed a fat sixty thousand dollars in *addition,* and, as part of their offer, agreed to build whatever type of court the Cup Committee requested. Vic Seixas, captain of this year's American team, naturally had as much say about this last matter as anyone, and he wanted a hard court—an all-weather one, with an asphaltic surface, specifically created for tennis. On a hard court, the ball bounces faster, and with less slide, than it does on a clay-type court, and performing on one is in general more like playing on grass than performing on any of the other fabricated surfaces is. However, under Davis Cup regulations the host nation can use a hard court in the Challenge Round only if the visiting team agrees. No such consent is needed for a gritty surface, and the idea of a hard court was at length abandoned in favor of a fast-drying clay-type court called Teniko Royal. Everyone, naturally, was wondering what effect this surface would have on the outcome of the match.

A Davis Cup Challenge Round involves, as we all know, two singles on the first day, the doubles on the second, and two more singles on the third. Determining who plays whom and in what order in the singles is worked out like this: Two envelopes, each containing the name of one of the two players nominated for the singles by the defending nation, are placed in the Davis Cup itself on one side of a central divider, and two envelopes, each containing the name of one of the two players nominated by the challenging nation, are placed on the other side of the divider. One envelope is selected from each side, and the two players drawn oppose each other in the opening match; the remaining two meet in the second match. A second draw determines which of the singles on the third day, when the pairings are switched, will go on first. Sometimes the draw can decisively influence the winning or losing of the Cup. The French players thought it did in 1927, when they scored their historic breakthrough at Germantown. Going into the match, they were fairly certain that Lacoste and Cochet would win their singles with Bill Johnston, but they felt that the only real chance of picking up the critical third point lay in Lacoste's meeting Tilden on the third day. A fresh Tilden probably would beat Lacoste, but a tired Tilden probably would not. They got just the draw they hoped for. Cochet, selected to play against Tilden on the opening day, lost to him, but only after extending the great man to four brisk sets. Lacoste defeated Johnston. In the doubles, Borotra and Brugnon lost to Tilden and Hunter, but Tilden was forced to go five more hard sets. As the third day began, France trailed, 1–2, but Lacoste squared the score by defeating a conspicuously enervated Tilden in four sets, and Cochet then made it 3–2 by beating Johnston. This year, neither of the two teams in the Challenge Round considered the draw important. To the Americans, however, something stood to be gained if Ralston, a high-strung twenty-two-year-old Californian who hates to sit around, played the opening singles. The Australians obviously were hoping that Emerson, the finest amateur in the world and a wonderful competitor under Davis Cup pressure, would play the concluding singles, just in case the outcome of the Challenge Round should hang on that match.

The draw was held with suitable Midwestern splash at noon the day before play began, in the Grand Ballroom of the Sheraton-Cleveland Hotel. Two hundred people turned up, and while they were arriving a cocktail pianist and a bass player bounced through "Let There Be Love" and "Getting to Know You." Then the duo struck up "Waltzing Matilda," and on this cue Hopman led his team to the dais. The duo then segued into "Yankee Doodle Dandy," and Seixas and the American players moved to the dais. Seven or eight reasonably brief speeches were made by local and visiting dignitaries, and then came the draw. The First Minister of the Australian Embassy in Washington plucked an envelope from the American side of the Davis Cup, and the Mayor of Cleveland plucked an envelope from the Australian side. McKinley and Stolle! Then came the draw to decide which of the two final singles— McKinley vs. Emerson, and Ralston vs. Stolle—would be played first. Ralston vs. Stolle! The Australians had undoubtedly gained a bit more from the draw, but nothing of consequence. Months ago, it was clearly appreciated that our chances of retaining the Cup depended on whether McKinley and Ralston could win the doubles and defeat Stolle in the singles, and this attitude still obtained.

When the ceremony was concluded, Hopman predicted a 4–1 victory for Australia, Seixas predicted a 3–2 victory for the United States, and the pianist and bass player slid into "I'm Gonna Sit Right Down and Write Myself a Letter."

On Friday, September 25th, a blustery and overcast day, McKinley defeated Stolle, 6–1, 9–7, 4–6, 6–2, and Emerson evened things by defeating Ralston, 6–3, 6–1, 6–2. I had never seen Emerson play so spectacularly well. He was getting to the ball even faster than usual, hitting it crisply, keeping it low, and keeping it deep. Yet it should be brought out that this match was not the runaway the score suggests until midway through the second set, when Ralston, after just failing to break Emerson's serve in the fourth game, dropped his own serve for the second time in the set; then he *was* finished. From the outset, it was apparent that Emerson, the marvellously conditioned black-haired Queenslander, intended to play the continuously attacking, net-rushing game he does on grass. This is risky business on a clay-type court, for the surface takes a good bit of the speed and spin off the ball, and this gives the opponent a higher, easier bounce to handle and appreciably more time to do things with the ball. Emerson is one of the few people with the coördinated quickness of foot, hand, and eye to get away with such an audacious strategy. On several occasions, after dashing into the forecourt behind an only moderately forcing stroke, he appeared to be cleanly passed by Ralston's down-the-line drives, but time after time, with those stupendous reflexes of his, he managed to get his racquet on the ball—a feat in itself—and then to angle a crosscourt drop volley that Ralston could not come close to reaching. A good measure of Emerson's superiority lay in the difference between services. Ralston's serve is the most vulnerable part of his game; Emerson's is first-class. He starts his service stroke by rotating his racquet hand and his ball hand twice on the way back, like a man shaking a Bacardi, but this curious takeaway evidently helps him to regulate his timing. In any event, he gets everything he has into his serve and he is exceedingly accurate, particularly when he is serving to the backhand court.

McKinley employed an altogether different strategy in his conquest of Stolle. His plan was to give the tall, angular Sydneysider, who thrives on hard hitting, no pace whatever on the slow court. He put this basically defensive plan into operation handsomely in the opening games, looping and chipping a succession of soft, spinning shots close to the baseline, and he won point after point on Stolle's errors. Stolle, who was playing in his first Challenge Round match, was jumpy, and as McKinley continued to keep him off balance with a gallimaufry of spins he found it difficult to settle down. Had Stolle been able to get his big service working as well as it did during the national championships at Forest Hills, he might have been able to collect his poise, but even in winning the third set he had trouble getting his first serve in, and his second had very little on it. Accordingly, there was never really any serious pressure on McKinley to alter his tactics. In the fourth set, as in the first three, he continued to concentrate on Stolle's forehand, a wristy stroke that is effective only when Stolle is up against a straightaway player who allows him to stabilize his somewhat fragile timing. In the fourth set, with victory in sight, McKinley kept urging himself, sotto voce, "Wait for the error. Wait for the error." He did, patiently, and it invariably came. Fabius Cunctator would have been proud of him.

What had we learned from this split in the opening singles? Really, only two things we had known before, I suppose. First, if the Americans could now win the doubles they had an excellent chance of retaining the Cup, for even in defeat Ralston looked like a man who could take the jittery Stolle in their singles on the third day. And second, Emerson's performance made it plain that if the Challenge Round hinged on the last singles match the Cup would go back to Australia.

On Saturday, a warmer day, but still gusty, the United States went out in front, 2–1, when Ralston and McKinley, after falling behind in the doubles, staged a wonderful comeback to win, 6–4, 4–6, 6–3, 6–4. Several times, the match came close to being a story of opportunities wasted by the Americans. Stolle and Emerson are not as yet a smoothly knit team (they had played together in competition only three times— against Mexico, Chile, and Sweden in Davis Cup matches in August), so it was most important that Ralston and McKinley, after winning the first set, keep right on top of the Australians. Instead, McKinley and Ralston contrived, in the second set, to toss away four game points on Emerson's service—three in the fourth game and one more in the eighth—and eventually the set that might well have been won was lost when McKinley was broken through in the ninth game. (When a team drops service in a doubles match, sometimes it is the server who is primarily at fault and sometimes it isn't.) After this, it was a vastly different match. Stolle, who had started off shakily again, had steadied down by this time, and he supported Emerson adequately the rest of the way. In the vital fifth set, after Ralston and McKinley had battled back to take the fourth set and square the match, they once again threw away several hard-earned openings that could have given them command of the match. Just when it seemed that they might even find a way to lose the match, they won it with a burst of great tennis. This came in the ninth game, the score 4–4, Stolle serving. The first point went like this: Stolle served to Ralston's forehand; Ralston hit a sharp crosscourt return, which Stolle was forced to take low and volley up; McKinley, cutting toward the center of the court, intercepted the ball and put it away with a fast forehand volley. 0–15. The second point went like this: Stolle served to McKinley's backhand, off which the Australians had been scoring regularly on service; this time, instead of chopping the ball back, McKinley drove a hard, flat-top spin backhand across the court; Stolle, taking it on his backhand, attempted to pass Ralston down the line, but his volley was weak and Ralston slapped it back through Stolle for a clean winner. 0–30. Stolle next tried to serve to Ralston's backhand, but Ralston ran around the ball, took it on his forehand, and sent a low, ducking shot crosscourt; Stolle tried to play it down the line, but once again his volley was high; McKinley stepped into it and walloped a vicious backhand drive-volley that neither Emerson nor Stolle could touch. 0–40. This time, there was no faltering by the Americans. Stolle tried to serve to McKinley's backhand, but McKinley ran around the serve and clubbed a strong forehand drive crosscourt; Stolle let the ball bounce and tossed up a tentative half volley down the middle; Ralston took it on his backhand and smashed it between the two Australians. Game. McKinley then held service for the set and match. In that decisive break-through at love in the ninth game, McKinley and Ralston, it should be underscored, played four absolutely classic doubles points. Each point was set up by an almost perfect crosscourt return of service that Stolle had to take low and volley (or half-volley) in an upward arc. Each point was then concluded by a smash or a volley that was utterly unreturnable.

Footnote: It should be added that Emerson's play, though solid, was nowhere near as dazzling as it was on the first day. Had it been, it might have tipped the balance. Anyhow, it wasn't and it didn't.

Several times on Sunday, it looked as if those four perfectly engineered points in the ninth game of the fifth set of the doubles would turn out to be the shots that won the Challenge Round for the United States, for in the fourth match Ralston came very close to getting that vital third point for us. In the end, however, he lost to Stolle in five gruelling sets, 7–5, 6–3, 3–6, 9–11, 6–4. Because of a heavy rain that began at noon, play was delayed almost three hours, and this, plus the length of the Stolle-Ralston duel, made it necessary to put the second singles over until Monday. Had the surface been grass, this day's program would have been completely washed out, but the Teniko Royal court did its stuff well. It not only dried quickly but was eminently playable.

So the winning of the 1964 Challenge Round came down to the fifth match. As was expected, Emerson won comfortably, 3–6, 6–2, 6–4, 6–4. After the first set, McKinley could not keep him in the back court and was never again in the match. It was not that Emerson played with the brilliance he had displayed against Ralston. He was, instead, in that more typical Emersonian mood in which he wears his man down by pressing him unrelentingly, point after point, shot after shot. In dealing with McKinley's only moderately good service, he did not hit the ball with the sharpness that scores placements, but he regularly got it back deep enough to permit him to come tearing into the forecourt and volley away McKinley's return. Following in to the net behind his own much severer service, he so dominated the play that in the third set McKinley was able to win only five points in the five games Emerson served. On match and Cup point, Emerson watched a drive by McKinley carry just over the baseline, and when he heard the linesman's cry of "Out" he stretched his long neck back in relief and closed his eyes for a tiny moment. This, for Emerson, is an emotional outburst, at least on the court. He is not a studied, poker-faced type, but he always sticks to business, like a Reese or a Rote. He is foremost a *player* rather than a thrilling shotmaker. His service and his first volley cannot compare with Hoad's. His backhand is far inferior to Rosewall's—whose isn't?—and Rosewall returns service better. Sedgman had a much surer forehand and a more powerful overhead. Laver is just about as fast afoot and produces much more exciting passing shots. Emerson merely does everything pretty damn well, or—closer to the point—there is nothing he does poorly. I can think of no player since the war—and there have been far greater stars—I would rather have on my side and playing the fifth match in a Challenge Round with everything riding on it.

In the dressing room after the match, Harry Hopman peeled out of his woollen sweatsuit and climbed into slacks and blazer for the presentation. During the Challenge Round, he had had to do no fancy masterminding. He had let Emerson take care of himself, which was wise, and his most significant contribution was to straighten out Stolle's game and to renew his confidence after his defeats on the first two days. Hopman had done this very well. He seemed quietly pleased with himself, and he had a right to be. He has now captained twelve victorious Davis Cup teams in the last fifteen years. Emerson is only twenty-seven, Stolle is now blooded in combat, and several fine young players are coming along nicely, so there is no knowing how many more victories await him in the years directly ahead. It could be a long, long while before we see the Cup again.

HORSESHOE PIAZZA, HORSESHOE STADIUM

●

(1965)

The Horseshoe Piazza refers to Newport, the Horseshoe Stadium to Forest Hills. In 1881, the year our national championships were inaugurated, they were held on the grass courts of the Newport Casino, and they continued to be until 1915. They were shifted then to Forest Hills. It was argued that Newport, the pearl of Narragansett Bay, was too hard to get to and that the spectators were indifferent to the importance of our championships. These days the Casino puts on a good summer invitational tournament, but it deserves a more substantial event, if for no other reason than that the grass courts at the Casino are probably the finest in our country.

The summer of 1965 marked the golden anniversary of the selection of Forest Hills as the site of our national championships. It also marked a half century since the championships were held at the Newport Casino, their original home, and since I had never before visited the Casino, it seemed the perfect time to rectify this omission.

The Casino, which covers an area of about a city block, stands in the center of town, its main building, a two-and-a-half-story gabled structure, fronting on Bellevue Avenue, the principal thoroughfare. At the present time, the ground floor of this building is rented to the La Forge Casino Restaurant and five shops—Peck & Peck, E. Braun & Co. (linens), Thompson-Forbes (sportswear), Jack's Shoes, and Bellevue Liquors—and I would guess that most tourists who visit Newport walk past the Casino without really noticing it. One enters the interior quadrangle through an archway of dull-red brick and comes out into a strange, vanished world that suggests such pre-World War I stars as R. Norris Williams and Maurice McLoughlin less than it does that eminent mixed-doubles team of Edith Wharton and William Dean Howells. It is a placid world of blue and white hydrangeas, English elms and copper beeches, and, in particular, old wooden buildings faced with weather-beaten, ornately patterned shingles and trimmed in old-fashioned New England colors like dark green and raspberry. A huge yellow-faced clock in a shingled turret shaped like a London bobby's helmet looks down on the upper court, which is separated from the lower court by the quadrangle's dominant architectural feature, the graceful Horseshoe Piazza, which was the center of social activity when the Casino was at its height, in the years before the First World War. The building that originally housed the Casino's ballroom has long since been converted into a summer theatre, and the court-tennis court in the clubhouse building, at the far end of the lower court, was destroyed by fire some twenty years ago, but, for the most part, the general aspect of the Casino is probably very close to what it was when the place was built, eighty-five years ago. Scattered around the grounds are thirteen grass tennis courts and three clay courts, but it takes a while for a first-time visitor to turn his attention to the anachronistic young people in shorts bounding over them.

The founder of the Casino was James Gordon Bennett, Jr., the publisher of the New York *Herald,* and—as is so often the case in matters of this kind—his motivation was a giant-sized pique. In the summer of 1879, one Captain Candy, an English polo player who was Bennett's guest in Newport, was riding his pony up Bellevue Avenue past the ultra-conservative club known as the Reading Room when a member, rocking on the veranda, challenged him to ride into the club. Captain Candy proceeded to maneuver his pony neatly up the stairs and into the main hallway, and, for his artistry, was forthwith banned from the club. Indignant at this treatment of his guest, Bennett resigned from the Reading Room and commissioned McKim, Mead & White to design buildings for a rival club, to go up on a plot opposite his home, also on Bellevue Avenue. He entrusted the operation of the

Casino, as the new club was called, to a corporation composed of a number of his dependable Newport friends. The Casino was opened in the summer of 1881, a month or so after the United States Lawn Tennis Association had been formed, and it occurred to the new organization that here was the ideal place to stage its first championships. They were held in August, before a sparse gallery seated in a row of chairs alongside the court. The winner of the singles was Richard D. Sears, a Bostonian with a sprightly net game, who successfully defended his title for the next six summers and then retired. By then, the championships had become one of the gala occasions of the Newport season, and they remained so until 1915, when the West Side Tennis Club, which had been founded in 1892 on Central Park West and moved to more ample quarters in Forest Hills in 1913, managed to persuade the U.S.L.T.A. that tennis had outgrown Newport, and that the championships deserved to be held at a club that, like the West Side, was readily accessible to fans from all sections of the country who wanted to see the famous champions and challengers. The Casino substituted an invitation tournament and quietly went its way until 1938, when its plant suffered heavy damage in the terrible September hurricane of that year. The big change came the following season, when the Spouting Rock Beach Association (Spouting Rock Beach is the official name of what is usually called Bailey's Beach) rebuilt its clubhouse, which the hurricane had destroyed, and decided to put in four clay courts alongside it. The new courts caught on immediately, for after taking a swim the members of the tennis set no longer had to go to the bother of changing into their white flannels and driving to the Casino—not when they could play right there in their bathing suits.

After the Second World War, the Casino entered upon a serious decline. In its halcyon period, it had been standard practice for residents of the summer colony to call in at least once a day, but now only a few ever dropped by. In 1947, the board of governors, tiring of their white elephant, sold off a couple of acres of the club property, where an A. & P. supermarket and a couple of other stores now stand, and it was generally assumed that the governors were only waiting for a handsome, unrejectable offer before selling the rest of it for a shopping center or a public school. The man who saved the Casino was James H. Van Alen, a fourth-generation Newporter and three-time United States court-tennis champion. Van Alen has been closely identified with lawn tennis since 1924, when he was captain of the Cambridge University team, and it is typical of him that he utilized that office to set up the first Oxford and Cambridge vs. Princeton and Cornell tennis match, for he is an incurable idea man and organizer. Some of his projects have been a little far out. At one time, for example, feeling that the native American robin was "disgustingly bosomy," he sought to introduce the svelter English robin to this country. This attempt was a failure, and so, to date, have been his efforts to persuade some wealthy foundation to endow the Newport home of Clement Clark Moore, the author of "A Visit from St. Nicholas," as a "museum of Santa Clausiana." Where the Casino was concerned, however, Van Alen was all sureness and acumen. His first move, in 1954, was to get the U.S.L.T.A. to sanction the Casino as the official home of the National Lawn Tennis Hall of Fame —the equivalent of baseball's Valhalla in Cooperstown. In 1957, he became president of the Hall of Fame Corporation and soon succeeded in inducing some of the largest shareholders in the Casino to donate their shares to the Hall; by 1959 the Hall had acquired fifty-four per cent of the shares and held a controlling interest in the Casino. Since then, Van Alen has been gradually revitalizing the old place. Among other things, he has bought back the old ballroom-theatre, which had been sold to a summer-theatre group in 1948, and has greatly improved accommodations for the tennis spectators by constructing a grass bank for box seats on three sides of the Centre Court and canopying not only these new installations but the old Centre Court grandstand. He has also built a new court, called the Hall of Fame Court, and he has kept in motion the machinery whereby a board of twenty-five directors annually elects a number of past heroes and heroines for enshrinement in the Hall of Fame. The Casino has not yet come all the way back, and the Hall has a long way to go before it is fit to carry Cooperstown's bat, but things are moving and the grass is greener.

This year, the Casino's tournament went extremely well, with several thousand fans turning out for the semifinals and finals. During the week of the tournament, Van Alen, a chirrupy, boyish, haberdashing man of sixty-three, was all over the place, attired in a wide-brimmed straw hat with a club band—the Casino's colors are green, silver, and yellow—and such coördinated outfits as apple-green shirt, olive-green trousers, chartreuse socks, and forest-green suède shoes. At a dinner for the players and officials held on the Horseshoe Piazza on Wednesday evening—the third day of the tournament—he introduced the speakers, played the ukulele, and recited a few poems of his own composition. On Thursday, the whole cast was invited to a cocktail party and buffet given by his mother, Mrs. Louis S. Bruguière, at Wakehurst, a pre-Breakers villa built by Van Alen's grandfather in 1884. On Friday, Van Alen made a television tape for the National Broadcasting Company, in which, as Emerson and Stolle played a sample set, he explained VASSS, which is short for the Van Alen Simplified Scoring System. (In VASSS, to put it briefly, the server stands three feet behind the baseline—a change that minimizes the importance of the serve—and the first player to win thirty-one points wins the match, eliminating the possibility of tedious marathons. Early this summer, Van Alen put on a VASSS tournament for the professional troupe at the Casino, and while the galleries and some of the players seemed to find it very enjoyable, general acceptance of the system doesn't appear likely.) Then, on the afternoon of the finals, James H. Van Alen himself—along with the late Ellen Hansell, our first women's champion; Watson Washburn, a star of the pre-Tilden era; Don McNeill, national champion in 1940; and Pauline Betz Addie, national women's champion from 1942 through 1944 and again in 1946—was inducted into the National Lawn Tennis Hall of Fame.

Forest Hills, with its abundance of sun-tanned blondes, its neo-Tudor clubhouse, its polyglot galleries, and its concrete horseshoe stadium seating almost fourteen thousand, presents a far more contemporary and animated picture than the Newport Casino. Months before the first ball was served at Forest Hills this year, it was practically assured that the golden-anniversary championships would be the best attended and most lucrative ever, for instead of waiting until practically the eve of the event, as most of his predecessors had done, J. Donald McNamara, the new president of the West Side Tennis Club, began to promote the championships as early as last October, and on an unprecedentedly intensive scale. As a result, on the opening day of the tournament, a good-sized crowd streamed into the stadium and around the field courts, although few matches of any consequence were on tap that early, and over the Labor Day weekend there were long queues at the ticket booths and the general-admission section of the stadium was sold out. All that was needed was some interesting tennis. There was a good deal of it in the early rounds. However, traditionally, the quarter-finals are usually considered the round when a tournament really begins. Two of the most highly regarded Americans, Dennis Ralston and Charlie Pasarell, were ousted in the quarters by Cliff Drysdale, of South Africa, and Rafael Osuna, of Mexico, respectively, but their departure was somewhat ameliorated by Arthur Ashe's magnificent conquest of Roy Emerson (13–11, 6–4, 10–12, 6–2) in the last quarter-final match. It should be stated at the outset, I think, that the Emerson that Ashe beat was not the best Emerson—certainly not the stonewall defender, the ever-harrying attacker we saw in the 1964 Davis Cup Challenge Round. Just before his meeting with Ashe, in defeating Pierre Barthes, of France, in three rough sets (6–4, 13–11, 6–4), Emerson had looked sluggish, and had missed what was for him a large number of shots when he had control of the court. Against Ashe, he was similarly erratic. He double-faulted an incredible seventeen times, and his ground strokes were hurried and uncertain. On the other hand, in a game like tennis, as everybody knows, it is difficult to ascertain to what degree a man is playing below par because he is somewhat off form that day and to what degree he is playing below par because of the pressure exerted by his opponent—and Ashe put enormous pressure on Emerson. Ashe, the best young black tennis player we have produced in America, is a tall, slender athlete who stands six feet and weighs a hundred and fifty pounds. He is exceptionally agile for a man of his build and has very fast hands. Under the tutelage of Pancho Gonzales, he has developed a sound all-court game, but his service is generally regarded as his strongest point. His first serve, an authentic cannonball, really explodes off his racquet, and following its flight is no easy matter. (I would hate to be a linesman charged with calling the service line in one of his matches.) However, it was not his service that saw him home against Emerson. It wasn't that he served poorly—he served very well, in fact—but fairly early in the first set, after he had been having trouble getting his first serve in, he switched to a slower, spin service and, when it proved effective, stayed with it until the fourth set, by which time his cannonball was working again. Rather, it was his return of service that proved to be his most formidable weapon. This was no accident. Several times in the days preceding the match, which, by the way, was Ashe's first encounter with Emerson since he lost to him, 6–3, 6–2, 7–5, at Wimbledon in 1964, Ashe had consulted with his friend Dick Savitt, the 1951 Wimbledon champion, on the best way to play the Australian. Savitt's counsel had been firm and explicit: "Crack those returns of service. Everyone just chips them back against Emerson. Don't you. Hit them, hit them, hit them. Put four of them in and you've got the game." Most of the time, Ashe uses a 16-gauge gut, but for his match with Emerson he had some racquets strung with thinner, more resilient 17-gauge, expressly to increase the velocity of his return of service. In the extended first set—it was a great set, too, producing some of the boldest, sharpest tennis since the duels between Hoad and Trabert in the mid-nineteen-fifties—Ashe's robust returns put a severe strain on Emerson's service and indirectly led to two double faults that cost him the twenty-third game and the set. At the beginning of the second set, with Emerson obviously concerned about his inability to get his service functioning properly, and Ashe a notch more confident that he could continue to match Emerson's speed of foot, speed of reflex, and speed of stroke, Ashe became even more aggressive in returning service. He belted the ball back with an abandon one rarely sees except in informal warmups, and time after time his returns—particularly his topspin backhands, hit crosscourt like a shot—went for outright placements or forced Emerson into volleying errors. Even in the third set, when Ashe's game suffered a slight but noticeable letdown, Emerson remained on the defensive during most of his service games, and, to tell the truth, it was not Emerson's play so much as his wonderful pertinacity, plus that elusive quality which derives from experience, that enabled him to pull out the third set in the twenty-second game and prolong the match. During the ten-minute intermission that followed, everyone I talked with agreed that if Emerson could manage to take Ashe to a fifth set the odds would be in his favor. When play was resumed, however, Emerson was surprisingly slow getting started. He dropped his first service at 30. Ashe moved quickly to 3–1, and then broke Emerson again, this time at 15. Three games later, Ashe served out with spectacular ease for the set and the match, and walked off the court to one of the most vibrant ovations ever heard at Forest Hills.

The following day, after Drysdale had defeated Osuna in four sets in the first semifinal, Ashe met Santana. In repose, Santana, who stands five feet eight inches tall and is chunkily built, looks more like a soccer player than a tennis player. He is twenty-seven, brown-haired, and, for a Spaniard, comparatively soft-eyed, and when he smiles his prominent smile he brings Fernandel to mind. With the possible exception of Rod Laver, he has the most flexible wrist of any player today, and on clay, where the slower, higher bounce of the ball gives him more time to get set for his shots than he has on grass, the variety of his spins, his changes of pace, and the acuteness of his angles can be dazzling. On grass, he is usually far less intimidating. Last year, when he made one of his rare appearances at Forest Hills, he was put out in the third round by a journeyman player. This year, he was in much better form, and improving with each match, but it was felt that Ashe could beat him if he could summon the kind of game he had played against Emerson. Ashe started out in brilliant form. He took the opening set, 6–2, overwhelming Santana with his power and allowing him only three points in the last four games. Early in the second set, the two pivotal games of the match took place. In the third game, Santana dug in hard to see if he could find a way to handle Ashe's cannonball, for Ashe had been getting it in regularly and had already ripped through three service games at love. In this third game, whenever Santana read from Ashe's delivery that a cannonball was coming, he backpedalled a few quick steps behind the baseline and took it much better; then he remained at the baseline or came in a step to receive Ashe's less fiery second serve.

A series of solid returns and Santana moved out in front, 15–40, in this game. On the next point, Ashe blew a big first serve by him for a clean ace, then pulled up to deuce with a backhand drive off a weak return of service. Advantage Ashe, the point set up by a fine serve. Then deuce again, Santana winning a flurry at net. A netted return by Santana— advantage Ashe. A beautiful backhand return of service down the line for a perfect placement—deuce again. A crosscourt forehand return of service that Ashe couldn't touch—advantage Santana. Another clean ace by Ashe—deuce once more. An error by Ashe on a low volley— advantage Santana. A marvelous forehand right at Ashe's feet—game Santana. The second pivotal game followed immediately. Inspirited by this breakthrough, Santana, who had been serving spottily, poured in four fast deep serves and won four quick points. After that, he never lost his service again. Indeed, after that he was in full command, for his whole game began to bloom with assurance and, as it did, Ashe's declined correspondingly. The effort he had expended in his long match with Emerson had patently taken a lot out of him, and he could no longer stay with Santana as the Spaniard, shrewdly keeping the ball low when Ashe came in to volley and keeping him off balance with his ducking topspin forehand, his down-the-line backhand, and his variety of touch shots, ran out the last three sets, 6–4, 6–2, 6–4.

I hasten to add that, for all the conclusiveness of Santana's victory, Ashe remained a hero in defeat. His match with Emerson had not been an unduly burdensome assignment; he had had everything to gain and nothing to lose. The Santana match was different. Then everyone expected the world of him, and that was a little more than the young man, up against the world's two most accomplished amateurs on consecutive days, could carry off. The important point, though, is that Arthur Ashe has arrived—no question about it—as a player of the very top order. He has improved immensely over the past three years, moving from eighteenth to sixth to third (and now, presumably, to first) in the national rankings, and since he is a sound and diligent as well as an altogether engaging young man, he should continue to improve in the next few seasons. In his twenty-two years, he has come a long way. He grew up in Richmond, Virginia, where his father is now a probation officer. Barred from entering that city's tournaments, he transferred, with the assistance of his tennis adviser, Dr. R. Walter Johnson, of Lynchburg, to an integrated high school in St. Louis. There he won the National Schoolboy Championship once and the National Indoor Junior Championship twice, and also won a tennis scholarship to U.C.L.A. He is a very attractive player, with superb court manners—a welcome change from some of our recent hot shots who outsulk Jackie Searl whenever the going gets rough. He is a bright young man, too, and it is a pleasure to hear him say, with a little smile, as he did on the eve of the Emerson match, that he was "quasi-confident of winning," or, as he said after that match, that a certain racquet of his "had passed the optimum point of resiliency." All other things being equal, he could develop into our finest player since Pancho Gonzales. It is something to look forward to.

Santana and Drysdale met on a gray, windy Sunday afternoon, following the women's final, in which Margaret Smith, of Australia, had just enough to edge past Billie Jean Moffitt, of California, 7–5, 8–6. (Maria Bueno, of Brazil, Miss Smith's regular vis-à-vis in championship finals, had gone down before Miss Moffitt the day before.) While Santana and Drysdale had both reached the semifinals at Wimbledon—Santana in 1963, Drysdale this year—neither had previously been a finalist in a major grass-court championship, and the immense importance this match held for them undoubtedly accounted for the tentativeness and overdeliberateness of much of their play. Nevertheless, it was not a dull match, largely because of the prepossessing qualities of the two men. Santana, who began his career at ten as a ball boy in Madrid, plays with the flair that, in any sport, only the self-taught seem to possess. Drysdale, the son of a stationer in Port Elizabeth, is, at twenty-three, perhaps the handsomest man in tennis today—a sort of cross between Richard Chamberlain and John Lindsay. Cool and poised and articulate, he has the pleasant habit on the court (as quite a few South Africans have) of patting the face of his racquet to applaud an opponent's good shots. Now and then, he uses this gesture mockingly to register his displeasure at what he feels has been a bad call by a linesman, but basically he is a most agreeable young man and a much tougher and more talented player than he looks to be—particularly when he is given a chance to paste the ball with his extraordinarily strong two-handed backhand. He and Santana split the first two sets and were locked at 5–5 in the third when a rain squall forced a forty-minute interruption. Upon the resumption of play, Drysdale had lost his touch completely, and Santana, who had been playing moodily, as if he wanted to win his points exquisitely or not at all, rediscovered his resolve and took eight of the next nine games to run the match out, 6–2, 7–9, 7–5, 6–1. Coasting home in the last set, he cut loose with his full repertoire of fluent, imaginative shots and, for good measure, threw in a delicate backhand lob volleyed with overspin. He was extremely modest in victory and seemed especially delighted at having performed so much better here than he had last year. He said that he thought the difference lay in the fact that in

1964 he had come over only two days before the tournament, allowing himself far too short a time to adjust his game to grass, whereas this year he had had two full weeks of practice. To be at his very best, he would need six weeks, he said. He added apologetically that while he likes our grass, he honestly prefers the surface at Wimbledon, where the turf is harder and faster.

The championship, by the way, ended on a wonderfully happy note. As Santana left the stadium, he was hoisted on the shoulders of proud and excited countrymen. Then there materialized out of nowhere a troupe of entertainers from the Spanish Pavilion at the World's Fair—about a dozen men and women in native costume, complete with guitars and castanets—and Santana was carried in triumph to the club-house to the strains of "Aragonesa." On the clubhouse terrace, which is seldom used for such things, the troupe serenaded their hero—the first Spaniard ever to win an important championship in an important sport in this country—with a colorful ten-minute floor show. Everyone loved it, but, of course, it may have set a dangerous precedent. If an American, say, wins at Forest Hills next year, I suppose we can expect the dancers from "Hullabaloo" and "Shindig"—or, at least, James Van Alen and his ukulele.

MRS. WIGHTMAN
AND MR. NEWCOMBE

(1967)

One of the people in sports I have most admired and liked is Hazel Hotchkiss Wightman, our national champion in 1909, 1910, and 1911. As a player, a coach, and a friend to young men and women, she always struck me as epitomizing the spirit of sport at its best. The fiftieth anniversary of the playing of the United States Doubles Championships at the Longwood Cricket Club gave me an opportunity to go up to Boston and look in on Mrs. Wightman at her home up the street from the club. It also afforded me a chance to catch up on the progress of John Newcombe. Earlier that summer this up-and-coming young Australian had scored his first major triumph, at Wimbledon. At Longwood he won the doubles with Tony Roche and then went on to win our singles championship at Forest Hills.

The week before Forest Hills, I went up to Longwood, in Chestnut Hill, primarily to watch some of the play in the United States Doubles Championships, now in their fiftieth year at Longwood, which itself is in its ninetieth year—the oldest tennis club in the country. Before the Second

World War, I hardly ever missed a Longwood, but since then my visits have been few. Old homes of tennis don't change much, though, and Longwood least of all. Chicory stalks still break through the cracks in the sidewalk in front of the clubhouse, and, inside the grounds, the dirt walk leading past the battered tool shed to the stadium courts is as bumpy and untended as ever. I made a sentimental pilgrimage one afternoon to the field courts where, thirty-odd years ago, I saw the best (or, at least, the most attractive) mixed-doubles match of my life—Kay Stammers and Gregory Mangin versus Alice Marble and Gene Mako— and I would have sworn that the identical spectators were gathered around the court. It is a nice, unhurried, unself-conscious old Yankee world. Overhead, the gulls still flap along so slowly it is a wonder they stay airborne, and at the start of each afternoon's schedule of matches the national anthem is played. (In one department, though, Longwood —I should say Boston—has jumped ahead of New York and the other sleeker centers of tennis. Each night during the tournament, starting at seven during the week and at eight on the weekend, WGBH-TV, Boston's enlightened educational-television station, presents a taped rebroadcast of the entire day's play. The photography is good, and the commentary, by Bud Collins, of the Boston *Globe*, is crisp and in-formed, so even when the show runs well past midnight thousands watch until the last point has been played.)

In this summer of the Great Reassessment, I had a special reason for going up to Longwood. I wanted to talk with Hazel Hotchkiss Wight-man, the famous old champion, the donor of the Wightman Cup, and a guiding beacon still for young players, in order to learn her ideas on the subject. On the Saturday, when the matches were rained out, I visited her at her home on Suffolk Road, close by Longwood. Mrs. Wightman is now eighty, but her blue eyes are as bright as ever and there is the same old bounce in her step and in her thinking. (Earlier in the week, seven hundred people attended a luncheon in her honor at the club, and seven hundred more would have come if there had been room in the tent.) During the hour and a half we chatted, she said so many good things that I can't begin to remember them all, but here is the essence of her remarks: "The youngsters today put entirely too much emphasis on the serve, the only stroke played from a stationary position. They don't work on the other strokes sufficiently, so, as a consequence, they are not on balance either running to the ball or when they arrive at the ball. They should be there a little sooner. Then they'd have the time to play the right shot to fit the situation, and not just any old shot that comes into their head. . . . Most of our young players want to be too flashy. They don't realize that nine good shots will always beat one sensational shot. They don't think enough about preparing each point—setting up the winning shot with two or three shots that draw your opponent out of position. Billie Jean King is an exception. That girl has a purpose behind every shot she plays. . . . I don't know why our players don't understand defensive tactics better. They've all seen Roy Emerson often enough, and he lives by defending and having that wonderful nice disposition of his. . . . A good many of our players are inclined to develop artificial strokes, sometimes through overinstruction. Everyone, you know, hits the ball a little differently from anyone else. You can't just copy a stroke; you must build better strokes that are extensions of your natural style. The old-timers did, and that's one of the reasons that a McLoughlin or a Tilden or a Johnston didn't play flop matches. For that matter, nobody taught Kramer or Gonzales. We've gone too far in the other direction. The best tennis teacher is the player himself."

As I walked back to the clubhouse after my visit with Mrs. Wightman, I couldn't help thinking what a different America it was back in 1902, when she took up the game in Berkeley, California, as a girl of fifteen. She and two of her brothers—Marius and Homer—got up every morning at five, awakened by a neighboring boy, the fourth for doubles, who yanked at a piece of string that was tied to Homer's big toe and trailed out a window. The four ate apples for breakfast as they trotted a mile to Berkeley's one available court, where they played till six-thirty. This gave Hazel time to get in an hour's practice at the piano before she headed for school. Industriousness—that's what lay behind her record of forty-four national titles.

At Longwood, the Australian team of John Newcombe (the new Wimbledon champion) and Tony Roche won the doubles, taking the final from their countrymen Bill Bowrey and Owen Davidson. Newcombe then went on to win the singles at Forest Hills—the ninth Australian since 1951 to do so at least once. He defeated Clark Graebner in a rather dull final, 6–4, 6–4, 8–6.

Newcombe, a chiselled-featured giant who looks as if he should be on television leading the wagon train to Alice Springs, serves a very heavy ball that has about the same velocity as Graebner's. In the final, fearing that he wouldn't be able to control it in the wind, he took a little off his serve and concentrated on getting it in, and his success would suggest that these were the correct tactics. An experienced internationalist at twenty-three, Newcombe has now mastered Emerson's old knack of lying doggo during the early rounds of a long tournament; then, as he faces more formidable opponents, his serve gradually grows heavier, the loop comes out of his ground strokes, and, moving much more swiftly on his sorties into the forecourt, he becomes all adeptness at handling the difficult low volleys he was just waving at before. Newcombe's game still has a certain unimaginative, prosy, mechanical quality, but he has learned how to win, and that is the big thing. Since his victory at Wimbledon, incidentally, he has won seven of the nine tournaments he has played, and today many experts would rate him above Santana and Emerson as the best amateur in the world.

THE FIRST
OPEN WIMBLEDON

(1968)

Thanks to the stubborn stand of the British Lawn Tennis Association, which had had its fill of fake amateurism, the International Lawn Tennis Federation at length voted to replace the old amateurs-only championships with championships open to both amateurs and professionals. In June 1968, all of the top players in the world assembled for the first Open Wimbledon, and this in itself was thrilling—for the first time in years such great players as Laver, Rosewall, Gonzales, and many other outstanding champions who had become professionals were back in action in the event that has long been regarded as the heart and soul of tennis. Although the first Open Wimbledon was not a dream tournament—it had its dull stretches—it did produce an excellent men's final that was won most appropriately by the best player in the world: Rod Laver.

There is a good chance that December 14, 1967, will go down as one of the significant dates in the history of sports. On that day, the

British Lawn Tennis Association, having tried unsuccessfully for almost a decade to persuade the game's top governing body, the International Lawn Tennis Federation, to sanction open tournaments —that is, tournaments open to professional players as well as to amateurs—took the bull by the horns and voted (295–5) to conduct the 1968 All England Championships at Wimbledon as just such an open event. This move by the British came as a vast surprise, to say the least, since no one supports tradition in sports more zealously than they do. It was a daring move as well, because by their decision they risked expulsion from the International Lawn Tennis Federation. In the end, however, it was the I.L.T.F. that backed down. When it became clear to the tennis associations of other countries that the British were determined on an open Wimbledon, a good many of the associations that had regularly opposed open tennis or had been lukewarm about it locked arms with the British, and in a special general meeting of the I.L.T.F. in Paris, on March 30th, forty-seven member nations ended up by voting unanimously to endorse open tennis. It was a great victory for the British, and a heartwarming one. In this day, when the impetus behind almost every radical change in sports is financial, the British Lawn Tennis Association had no such motive. While the upsurge of professional tennis following the Second World War had cut deeply into the box-office receipts from the national (amateur) championships in most countries, Wimbledon had not suffered at all. Every year, the reserved seats were sold out six months in advance, and something like four hundred thousand dollars in ticket applications usually had to be returned. However lustreless the field and however murky the weather, Wimbledon continued to prosper. (In 1967, the championships drew a record attendance, the legendary queues stretching longer than ever as three hundred and one thousand spectators poured in during the twelve days of play.) Instead of simple greed for profits, two genuinely idealistic concepts fomented the British revolution. First, the British L.T.A., under the leadership of its chairman, Derek Hardwick, wished to end the so-called "shamateurism" that had plagued amateur tennis for years—the hypocritical system under which a tournament had to shell out, under the table, to the ranking amateurs sums of money far exceeding their expenses in order to assure their appearance. And, second, with the most gifted of the recent amateur champions having all turned professional, the British L.T.A. was convinced that the time was overdue for tournaments proposing to present the best tennis in the world to open their doors to the world's best tennis players, especially since there was no moral reason to exclude the pros and since their presence would give the game a vitality and meaning it had long needed.

When the first open Wimbledon began, on June 24th, the galleries were at a high pitch of excitement, as well they might have been. They were in on a historic occasion. For the first time since 1927, when Suzanne Lenglen became the first of the great champions to turn professional, not a single one of the world's outstanding players was missing from the lists; the men and women who carried off the titles would be authentic world champions. Interest had been building up for months. In April, in the first sanctioned open tournament —the British Hard Court Championships, at Bournemouth—the spectators had hardly settled down to see how the amateurs would make out against the pros when Mark Cox, an English amateur who had shown sporadic promise, defeated Richard (Pancho) Gonzales, who had been the cool, tough overlord of the professional world in the nineteen-fifties and, in the opinion of many observers, the finest player over the last quarter of a century. Right on top of this, Cox knocked out Roy Emerson, of Australia, a two-time Wimbledon champion who had turned pro this spring. In the final, Cox was stopped, by Rod Laver, of Australia, currently the No. 1 player among the professionals, but Cox's exploits had made it quite clear that the pros were more vulnerable than one would have guessed. A week before Wimbledon, on the grass courts of the Queen's Club, in London, this lesson was brought home again, even more forcibly. Clark Graebner, the fourth-ranked American amateur, eliminated both Emerson and Emerson's fellow-countryman Fred Stolle, the 1966 United States champion, who is now in his second professional season. Even more to the point, Marty Riessen, our fifth-ranked amateur, defeated Andres Gimeno, of Spain, who for several years now has stood behind only Laver and Ken Rosewall in the professional hierarchy, and the rout was completed when Tom Okker, a young Dutch amateur, trounced Laver himself in the final. This lèse-majesté at the Queen's Club established the theme for the Wimbledon fortnight: Would the amateurs continue to treat their illustrious elders with so little respect?

The general feeling was that, having waited so long for an open Wimbledon, the pros—certainly the top-class pros—would be bearing down all the way and would be rough to beat. (The committee charged with seeding the favorites apparently had felt much the same way, for Manolo Santana, of Spain, who was seeded sixth, was the only amateur placed among the first ten.) At the same time, the galleries were prepared for the form to be exploded every which way—in fact, were rather anticipating it. During the first three days of play, nothing really untoward occurred, but on Thursday, in a second-round match, Rosewall came up against Charlie Pasarell, our first-ranked amateur, and barely survived a tremendous battle: 7–9, 6–1, 6–8, 6–2, 6–3. On Friday, more excitement: Lew Hoad, a pro since 1957, was ousted by an amateur, and so was Gonzales—Hoad in five sets by Bob Hewitt, an Australian who now lives in South Africa, and Gonzales in four sets by Alex Metreveli, a twenty-three-year-old Russian with a good, hard-hitting game. On Saturday, in a third-round match, another shocker: Ray Moore, a twenty-one-year-old South African with a Mark Twain hairdo and mustache, defeated Gimeno, the third-seeded player. Of these unexpected early departures, there is no doubt that Gonzales' was the most dramatic. Nineteen years ago, when he was a young star on the way up, he had made his only visit to Wimbledon as an amateur and had been beaten in an early round. Now, at forty, he was back, a legend, well past his tennis prime, with a touch of silver streaking his black hair, the smooth, feline elasticity gone from his legs and the thunder gone from his serve, but determined to do well and counting on his experience and his savoir-faire to contain his opponents. For one set, these worked against Metreveli. Slicing one return and spinning the next, keeping the ball down low, he controlled the play and took the opening set, 6–4. Near the end of the second set, however, he served a weak game and lost it, and after that Metreveli, seeming to be no longer inhibited by the awareness that he was up against the Old Master, took charge. As I watched Gonzales sweating in the breeze, arriving a half step too late for his volleys and finessing his overheads instead of smashing them away, all I could think of was that I was witnessing the tennis version of some old Anthony Quinn movie—the aging champion struggling vainly against the laws of nature in an attempt at a comeback. When Metreveli had moved to within two points of victory, serving at deuce with games at 5–4, Gonzales managed a last gasp of bravado: for some reason, the ball boy hesitated in throwing a ball he had retrieved toward Metreveli's end of the court, and Gonzales told him, in his deep gravel voice, "Throw him the ball, son. He'll need it." Metreveli did, but two games later he was home, 4–6, 6–4, 6–3, 7–5. The beaten Gonzales left the court to a considerable ovation. In this match, and in others in which an old champion returning as a pro was pitted against a rising young amateur, the galleries during the early stages invariably pulled for the underdog and for an upset, but once it became evident that the old champion was in serious trouble they rooted hard for him and hated to see him lose. Wimbledon galleries have nice long memories.

At the start of the second week of play (Wimbledon rests on Sunday), the men's singles was down to the round of sixteen—eight amateurs, eight pros. This meant that the matches were running about a day behind schedule in this division, and in the four other divisions—the ladies' singles, the men's doubles, the ladies' doubles, and the mixed doubles—even more ground had to be made up. This state of affairs had been occasioned by frequent rains during the first week, which interrupted many matches and forced the postponement of others. (On Friday, when the skies were still oyster gray but the rain had stopped, and I was watching the ground crew remove the tarpaulin from the Number One Court, a middle-aged lady seated next to me turned and remarked, with the ineffable cheerfulness of the English, "The forecast is better. 'Showers.'" I must have looked puzzled. "It could have been 'Steady showers,'" she explained.) On the second Monday, however, the weather turned warm and dry, and by Tuesday evening the tournament had made up the lost ground and was back on schedule.

It is difficult to think of any international sports fixture that is organized as splendidly as Wimbledon is, and functions as fluently. Of course, it starts with a peerless tennis plant. At its heart is the famed Centre Court, a rectangle of perfect tennis grass surrounded by a high, roofed, twelve-sided structure, which holds slightly over fourteen thousand spectators. Just to the west of the Centre Court is the beautiful Number One Court, whose stands (three roofed, one open) can accommodate around seven thousand. And to the south of these two courts —just across the club's main artery, the wide South Road—are fourteen other grass courts, arranged in a sort of grid pattern, separated by walkways about four yards wide. With so much going on in different places at the same time, the ideal way to see the championships is to leave your reserved seat in the Centre Court stands, or in the Number One Court, at the conclusion of a featured match and wander around for a while, catching the action on the field courts. Wimbledon has thought of everything you'll need to orient yourself, even if you have left your daily program behind in your seat. A large scoreboard on the South Road posts the scores of matches in progress and the results of completed matches. Across the road, on the outside wall of the Number One Court, electric scoreboards flash the point-by-point scores of the matches in progress on that court and on the Centre Court. (Naturally, there are also electric scoreboards on the inside walls of the two principal courts.) Since the days at the championships are long, with play customarily starting at two o'clock and often continuing past eight, ample facilities have been provided for patrons to stoke themselves up between matches. For the inner set, there is the Members' Enclosure, a green-purple-and-white striped marquee (purple and green are the All England Club's colors) that opens onto a garden where tables are shaded by straw umbrellas. For the public, there is a small refreshment area off the Number One Court, and a large one fronting on a lawn east of the Centre Court, at both of which drinks, buffet lunches, and teas are available and separate counters under orange-and-green striped awnings offer hamburgers, sundaes, fruit ades, and, of course, strawberries and Devonshire cream, which have been as closely identified with Wimbledon over the years as the mint julep with the Kentucky Derby. At several points along the South Road, you bump into that lesser Wimbledon tradition, the open-air bonbon stand, where customers help themselves to an assortment of hard candies, caramels, and toffee from three dozen tins—a shilling and sixpence for a quarter of a pound. For decades now, the men who run the championships have kept their eyes open for any flaws in the mechanism, and today there is no part of the complicated operation that hasn't been carefully attended to. Adjoining the grounds are seventeen acres for parking. The ushers in the Centre and Number One Courts are members of the armed forces on leave. The ball boys come from Fortescue House, a school in Twickenham, where they are trained for the job. Above all, the needs of the players are understood and provided for. They have their own restaurant, where they can escape from their fans, and foreign players are ferried to and from their hotels in chauffeur-driven limousines. There was no stinting here. Everyone had a limousine: Don Budge, Doris Hart, Pancho Segura, and the other old familiar faces who had returned to play in the veterans' doubles or the mixed doubles, and also Gussie Moran, whose spectacular lingerie brightened some of the drabber championships after the war. The first open Wimbledon was, among other things, a tennis reunion on a grand scale.

I spent part of every day watching the crowds—always well upward of twenty thousand, and some days near thirty. A fairly high percentage of the Wimbledon regulars are foreign visitors who have converged on London not only for the tennis but also for the three other gala sports occasions that make up the Season: Ascot, Henley, and the cricket test match at Lord's. Nowadays, with people from all corners of the globe dressing more nearly alike than they used to, the Wimbledon crowd is not the romantic sight it once was, but it remains vigorously polyglot, and one's ear is constantly surprised. The bulk of the crowd, though, is English—very English. It is not a true cross-section of English society, few workingmen being on hand, but it is quite an assortment nonetheless: regional tennis officials in their blazers and association ties, schoolgirls and schoolboys in their uniforms, middle-class matrons in their best millinery, shopgirls and clerks who have saved up for the occasion, a sprinkling of long-legged "birds" in microskirts, lots of county types, and, in large numbers, the silvered and the grizzled—folks who haven't missed a Wimbledon since the Relief of Mafeking. They all know their tennis. (So do the English who follow the championships at one remove, on television. Just about the whole country does, and no wonder, considering the thoroughness of the coverage. For example, B.B.C.2, the color channel, goes on the air daily from Wimbledon at one-forty-five and stays with the tennis until seven-thirty. Then, at ten every night, a program is presented featuring the "Match of the Day" and filled out with random highlights.) I am not a lover of crowds, even sports crowds, but the Wimbledon regulars are an exception. I admire them for their polite orderliness, their obvious pleasure in the occasion, their knowledge of tennis, their unquenchable enthusiasm, their effort to be fair to all competitors, and even for their bias toward their British players. I learned to admire them in 1939, when I first attended the championships. Like everyone else that June, the people who had gathered in the Centre Court recognized the imminence of war, but when, in an early round of the men's doubles, the German team of Roderich Menzel and Raul Goepfert came up against the French team of Jean Borotra and Jacques Brugnon—a great team, then ten years past its peak—the fans tried hard to dissociate tennis from the world situation and to applaud the two sides equally for their winning shots. They succeeded in maintaining this equilibrium when the Germans took the first two sets, but when Borotra and Brugnon, their old favorites, their allies, rallied to win the third set, 6–3, and the fourth, 6–4, it was too much for them. No French gallery could have made its support more keenly felt than that English gallery did when Borotra and Brugnon completed their stirring comeback by taking the fifth set, 6–2. But, above all, I love the Wimbledon crowds for the quiet, deep pride they take in Wimbledon. In 1877, when the championships were launched, Victoria had been Queen for forty years and Empress of India for one, England was at the zenith of its power and glory, and London was the great city of the world. That England vanished a long time ago, but at Wimbledon it lives on. During this fortnight, the Centre Court is the center of the world—the world of sport, anyway—and it is as clear as the Crystal Palace that, at least in this one area, nothing has changed and the show England mounts is in a class by itself, the envy of all other nations.

By the second Monday, as I mentioned earlier, the men's singles had reached the fourth round—the round of sixteen. Perhaps the most effective way of bringing out the remarkable depth of the field in this first open Wimbledon would be simply to list the lineup of those eight matches. Proceeding from the top of the draw down, it went like this: Laver vs. Cox; Metreveli vs. Dennis Ralston, the sophomore American pro; John Newcombe, of Australia, the defending champion and a freshman pro, vs. Arthur Ashe, our second-ranked amateur; Okker vs. Emerson; Stolle vs. Graebner; Tom Edlefsen, an amateur from California, vs. Moore; Earl Buchholz, a seasoned American pro, vs. Hewitt; and Tony Roche, another freshman pro, vs. the veteran Rosewall, the second seed. The point is that any of these matches would have made an acceptable final in most tournaments. The two men who eventually did get through were a pair of left-handed Australians —Laver, the odds-on favorite, and, quite unexpectedly, Roche, the fifteenth seed. The match that cleared the path for Roche was his surprising conquest of Rosewall in straight sets, 9–7, 6–3, 6–2. Despite the one-sidedness of the score, this was a gripping duel, for even when Rosewall is not producing his best stuff—and he wasn't that day —it takes first-class tennis to get on top of him and stay there. This match took place on the hottest day of the fortnight, with the temperature well over ninety degrees, and this may have been to Roche's advantage, since he is only twenty-three—ten years Rosewall's junior. Indeed, under the burning sun Rosewall took to wearing a cloth cap and knotted a handkerchief around his neck. However, Roche was the superior player on this particular day. A rugged, rawboned, longjawed fellow who loves to patrol the net, he won his own service games without undue exertion, coming in behind his wide-swerving delivery, and he was so successful in attacking Rosewall's service that he commanded the net almost continuously during those games. In the quarter-finals, he got by Buchholz without very much trouble, but he got by Graebner in the semis only after a very tough battle—9–7, 8–10, 6–4, 8–6. Graebner, incidentally, had a splendid tournament. In defeating Santana in straight sets, he played the finest match of his career, and he was almost as impressive in beating Stolle and Moore, also in straight sets. There was little to choose between him and Roche, but the Australian was the sounder tactician. He muffled Graebner's awesome power most of the way by shrewdly changing his pace, and his mobility in the forecourt at length suggested to Graebner that his best countering weapon was the lob, which probably wasn't. It is the stroke he plays least skillfully.

As for Laver's route to the final, it was a lot bumpier than people had imagined it would be. Cox took a set from him, and Ralston took two sets. In these matches, and in his earlier ones as well, Laver was in nothing like his best form, and there was some question whether he would ever get himself untracked and begin whistling those high-speed placements into the corners from all over the court, as he does when he's in full flight. In eliminating Ashe, 7–5, 6–2, 6–4, in the semifinals (Ashe had accounted for both Newcombe and Okker in a most encouraging showing), Laver started to come on a bit. For the first time, he began to get his fizzing first serve in regularly, and, also for the first time, his second serve had consistently good depth. The rest of his game then picked up noticeably, and there were some bursts in which the ball came back so fast to Ashe that he hardly had time to contrive even a hurried stroke. In the final, Laver rose to the occasion, and what we were treated to, at last, was real vintage Laver. The outcome was in doubt only for seven games. Over this stretch, while Laver was experiencing some difficulty with his serve, Roche won each of his three service games at love. Laver, though, has a way of slipping through and busting a set open before you realize it, and, at 4–3, he did this in the eighth game, breaking Roche with a sudden fusillade of sharply hit service returns. He then served out for the set, 6–3. The decisive moments in the second set arrived in the sixth game, which Laver came within a hair of losing. He saved himself with two incredible stop volleys; each time it looked as if he would be cleanly beaten by a severely angled forehand drive that Roche had blistered crosscourt, and each time, racing frantically to his left and lunging out at full stretch, he managed to get his racquet on the ball and stab it over the net. He went on from this to break Roche in the very next game, and took the set, 6–4. Then he began to move faster and faster to the ball, and to hit it harder and harder, and the third set was his, 6–2, in no time at all. The whole match, in fact, was over in exactly an hour, and the odd thing about it was that Roche had played more than respectable tennis. Everyone had been hoping, naturally, that the first open Wimbledon would be climaxed by a classic match, but if that wasn't to be, we had the next best thing—a classic performance.

This was Laver's third victory in the Wimbledon championship, for he had won in 1961 and 1962 as an amateur. Following the 1962 season, in which he swept the four major championships, he turned professional. Now twenty-nine, he has become a far more assured young man, but in repose he still does not look like much of an athlete.

Small and almost scrawny in physique (five eight, a hundred and forty-five), a bandy-legged redhead with a quiet eye, he ranges alongside the husky Adonises who people Australian tennis like the ugly duckling who made good. In action, he doesn't appear to be fast afoot, but he is, and, what is more, he has such wonderful balance that he can recover from a "get" in an instant and be well positioned to return his opponent's next shot. He doesn't appear to be strong, either, but with his supple wrist he generates terrific racquet-head velocity. Along with this, he has astonishing control of his speed. For example, against Roche, who is so strong in the forecourt, Laver frequently had to thread the eye of a needle to bring off a passing shot, and time after time he did. Historically, left-handed tennis players have excellent serves, forehands, and overheads, and they volley well off the forehand, but their backhands are weak—a chip instead of a full-bodied stroke. Laver is an exception; his backhand is as solid as his forehand. He plays it just like his forehand, taking the ball on the rise and whipping over it to impart maximum topspin. When he is right, he has only one weakness—the low backhand volley, which is not a very bad weakness to have. In rating the champions since the war, some tennis scholars put Jack Kramer at the top and others put Gonzales or Rosewall there, but a growing number believe that this distinction may properly belong to Laver. I do not know about this, but I do know he is a truly great player, a kind of Ben Hogan of the court. It was appropriate that he was the man to carry off the first open Wimbledon.

In the ladies' singles, Billie Jean King, from Berkeley, California, won her third straight title. It was a triumph of perseverance more than of brilliance. In the semifinal, her opponent, Ann Jones, of England, took the first set, 6–4, and stood at 5–4 in the second, with her own serve coming up, when she succumbed to Centre Court tension, which, understandably, afflicts the English even more than it does the visitors; she tossed away thirteen straight points, and with them the set and, ultimately, the match. In the final, Mrs. King faced Judy Tegart, a big, hearty, likable Australian audit clerk who looks more like the canoeing councillor at a girls' summer camp, and who had trained for the championship by giving up beer for a month. In six previous tries, Miss Tegart had never reached the semifinals at Wimbledon, but she made it this time, by upsetting Margaret Smith Court with some beautiful free-hitting tennis. Then she came on even stronger against Nancy Richey and overpowered her. If Miss Tegart had been able to hold that form for a third consecutive match, we might have had a memorable final, but two foot faults called against her early in the match weakened her verve, and what we had instead was just a good scrap. With her surer volleying, Mrs. King was a shade steadier in the clutch, and won, 9–7, 7–5. As for the other titles, the men's doubles went to Roche and Newcombe, the ladies' to Mrs. King and Rosemary Casals, and the mixed to Ken Fletcher and Mrs. Court, who defeated Metreveli and Olga Morozova, the first Russians ever to reach a Wimbledon final.

Though the pros dominated the championships in the end, there is bound to be a good deal of discussion in the weeks ahead about why the amateurs fared so well against them. Was it because the amateurs had nothing to lose and could shoot the works, while the pros were under strain? Was it because the pros had been confined for too many years to playing against the same small set of opponents? Was it because the pros, long accustomed to a short-match format, lacked stamina when carried to five sets? Or was it only that youth must be served? There will be lots of discussion, too, about "registered players"—players not under contract to a promoter or agent who compete for prize money —and whether they are pros or amateurs or simply players, which is how the British L.T.A. views them. It will all come out in the wash. The big thing is that finally, after all these years and all these detours, tournament tennis is where it should be.

SEPTEMBER SONG – GONZALES AND ROSEWALL

(1968)

Pancho Gonzales and Ken Rosewall were unfortunate in that they were just too old to take home satchels full of the ample new prize money that arrived with open tennis. For their ages, though, they were still marvels, and their play in our first Open at Forest Hills may well have been the highlight of the tournament. For me, as for so many other fans, Rosewall stands as perhaps the most attractive of all the postwar champions.

About midway between the first open Wimbledon, which ended shortly after the Fourth of July, and the first United States Open Tennis Championships, which began shortly before Labor Day, it became clear to me, as I thought ahead to our championships, that my major concern was whether Ken Rosewall and Richard (Pancho) Gonzales would come through with good, solid performances at Forest Hills. I expected neither of them to win. For Gonzales, that was simply out of the question. He is forty years old—an age when an extraordinary athlete can flout the laws of nature on isolated afternoons now and then but certainly not throughout a seven-round championship in which a contestant must play a series of matches with, at most, a day between them to recuperate in. Rosewall's case is somewhat similar yet somewhat different. At thirty-three—he will be thirty-four in November—he is physically capable of standing up to the rigors of a protracted championship, but the hard fact of the matter is that the years have also begun to catch up with this brilliant Australian and he is now a discernible shade past his tennis peak. While he can still hold his own against anyone on a slow surface, he is a lot more beatable on a fast surface, like grass, than he was two or three years ago. At Wimbledon, for example, where he was seeded second, he was defeated by Tony Roche in straight sets in the fourth round—the round after Gonzales was eliminated by Alex Metreveli. As I say, I didn't expect Rosewall to go all the way at Forest Hills—like almost everyone, I thought that Rod Laver would repeat his Wimbledon triumph without much trouble—but I wanted both him and Gonzales to be in much better form than they had exhibited in England, so that, however long they lasted, they would leave an imprint on our first Open befitting two exceptional champions, each of whom had reigned for years as the best player in the world (Gonzales, roughly, from 1954 to 1960, and Rosewall from 1960 to 1965) but had had the misfortune to be past his prime when open tennis finally arrived.

Gonzales' story is fairly well known. In brief, he came out of the Mexican section of Los Angeles; survived a difficult period as a junior star; won our national title in 1948, at twenty, and won it again the following year; was thoroughly laced (ninety-six matches to twenty-seven) when he then turned professional and made the usual coast-to-coast tour with the incumbent champion, Jack Kramer; got another crack at the tour—then the only game in town for a professional—in 1954, and after defeating Frank Sedgman and Pancho Segura that year, dominated all his subsequent challengers until he went into partial retirement, in 1960. No one who ever saw Gonzales in his heyday was likely to forget it. It was not only that he combined power and touch and tennis sense as few players before him had done but that he projected one of the strongest personalities in all of sport. Saturnine and disputatious, an unrepentant loner, this tall, graceful man who moved like a panther seemed forever to have a chip on his shoulder. When the galleries rooted for his opponents (galleries invariably attach themselves to the underdog), Gonzales seemed almost to welcome it, as if to say, "Who needs you?" During his reign, he didn't change an iota.

Rosewall is quite a different person and he has quite a different story. Born and brought up in the Rockdale section of Sydney, he was the only child of tennis-playing parents. While he was still an infant, his father, a grocer, bought a piece of land with three clay tennis courts on it. He supplemented his income by renting out the courts, and his son grew up bashing the ball around on them when he wasn't bashing it against a wall or a fence. The father made one significant change in his son's game. Convinced that a two-handed player imposed unnecessary limitations on himself, he was displeased when he saw that the boy had fallen into the habit of using both hands on the racquet for certain strokes, and he asked him to decide whether he wanted to play left-handed or right-handed, and to stick with that one hand. Rosewall threw left-handed, batted left-handed in cricket, and did most other things left-handed, but he chose to play tennis right-handed. He became very good very quickly. Interestingly, his backhand, because of his unusual control of the movements of his left side, was from the outset his soundest and most natural stroke—essentially the finest backhand since Don Budge's. (Australian tennis players are a strange lot when it comes to port and starboard. Rosewall plays golf left-handed, and so does the right-handed star Mal Anderson, who won at Forest Hills in 1957. Laver, Neale Fraser, and Mervyn Rose, who are left-handers on the court, are right-handed golfers.)

Rosewall's first big moment in tennis came in 1946, shortly after he had turned twelve. Jack Kramer and Ted Schroeder, who were in Australia for the Davis Cup Challenge Round, appeared in Sydney for an exhibition match, and Rosewall was selected to play a curtain-raiser set against another precocious Sydneysider, Lew Hoad, who was just three weeks younger than he was. The two had met before, but this was the first time they had played each other. From that afternoon on, the careers of Rosewall and Hoad were closely intertwined. The first time we saw them at Forest Hills was in 1952, when Harry Hopman, the captain of the Australian Davis Cup team, brought them over for a little seasoning. One afternoon early in the championship, some of the Forest Hills officials got the bright idea that the spectators might enjoy watching an exhibition set by the two seventeen-year-old Australians. Onto the stadium court came a husky blond boy, Hoad, and a small, trim black-haired boy. (As I remember it, Rosewall had not then reached what was to be his full height, five-seven, or his eventual playing weight, one-forty.) They hit a few warmup shots, and then proceeded to flabbergast the gallery with the beauty of their strokes and the cohesive maturity of their games. No one who saw them that afternoon was exactly surprised when, on the day of the fourth round, the two kids—they were entered in the singles—turned the tournament upside down: Rosewall defeated Vic Seixas, the No. 1 seeded player, and Hoad defeated Art Larsen, the 1950 champion. (In the quarter-finals, Gardnar

Mulloy stopped Rosewall, in five sets, and Sedgman put out Hoad.) In December 1953, when the Davis Cup Challenge Round was held in Melbourne, Rosewall and Hoad, a month past their nineteenth birthdays, were called on to replace Sedgman and Ken McGregor, who had won the Cup for Australia three years in a row but, having turned pro, were no longer available. Up against the potent American pair of Seixas and Tony Trabert, the kids successfully defended the Cup, three points to two, with Rosewall beating Seixas in the deciding match. The Americans took the Cup the next year (and Seixas took Rosewall), but in 1955 Rosewall and Hoad won it back, and they retained it the following year with no trouble at all.

Shortly after the 1956 Challenge Round, Rosewall turned professional. For a twenty-two-year-old, he had compiled an astonishing record: he had never won at Wimbledon (though he had reached the final twice), but he had captured the three other major titles—the French in 1953, the Australian in 1953 and 1955, and the American in 1956, when he defeated Hoad in the final. (Hoad, incidentally, did not turn pro until July of 1957.) Rosewall had accomplished much, but how he had accomplished it was at least as important. In a period in which just about every other player of world class was an exponent of the so-called big game—the big serve followed by the big volley or smash—Rosewall was that comforting anachronism, the baseliner with superb ground strokes who won his points by outmaneuvering his opponents. A cool, neat, economical workman with an extremely pleasant court personality, he prepared his points carefully. When the structure of a rally suggested it, he did not hesitate to move up to the net—he was a very deft volleyer—but he concentrated on the forecourt only in those rare matches in which he was making no headway against a determined opponent and felt he had to change his pattern of play. (He did this in winning a marvellous five-set match with Dick Savitt at Forest Hills in 1956, for example.) For all his ability, however, there was some doubt whether he would enjoy equal success as a pro, because most of the time he would be facing Gonzales and the other serve-and-volley virtuosos on fast indoor courts that favored their style of play. There was increased doubt, and not a little sadness, when Rosewall himself, as soon as he turned pro, went over to the serve-and-volley game. With the least powerful serve of any of the great players since René Lacoste, he seemed ill-equipped for this, and few people were surprised that Gonzales had little difficulty with him on their coast-to-coast tour in 1957, winning fifty of their seventy-six matches. Then Rosewall amazed everybody all over again. Gradually, he became adept at the big game. ("I felt I had to try to play that way, because, under the conditions, it was the easiest way and the most certain way to victory," he told me recently. "Indoors, the percentages for making good passing shots are very low.") He improved his forehand, which had a tendency to be loose, by cutting down the length of his backswing. This put his return of service in a class by itself. He beefed up his own serve a bit, but what really made it click was his incredible quickness in getting to the return and dispatching an aggressive volley. Before too long, he was beating Gonzales as often as not, and after Gonzales went into semi-retirement Rosewall succeeded him as the world professional champion. (That title is not determined by a victory in one special championship but goes to the player who amasses the highest point total in half a dozen stipulated tournaments, a certain number of points being allocated to the winner, a lesser number to the defeated finalist, and so on down the brackets.) Rosewall held the championship until 1965, when Laver took over.

One of the most grievous drawbacks of professional tennis—and, it follows, one of the most valuable rectifications of open tennis—was that one got to see the great players so seldom; they always seemed to be in Ponca City, Wollongong, or Spa. In the spring of 1963, however, they did assemble at Forest Hills for one of their infrequent tournaments on grass, and this enabled me to catch Rosewall when he was just about at his zenith. He was so far superior to all his opponents, Laver included, that none of his matches were even remotely close. That week, by a happy chance, I discovered the secret of one aspect of Rosewall's skill that had always fascinated, and mystified, me: How come he was always perfectly positioned for each shot when men of comparable agility weren't? During the final, when Rosewall was on the far side of the court, I had the inspiration of holding up my hand in such a way that it blocked off the near side and I could focus wholly on how Rosewall moved to the ball from shot to shot. My guess was that I would find he took quite a few more steps than the average player—maybe fifteen on some shots. What I found was that he often took as many as thirty. The instant after he had executed his stroke, he began repositioning himself, with a series of quarter and half steps, and all the while that he was studying the stroke his opponent seemed to be planning, he continued to shift his position, with a dozen or so noodling little steps; then, when the return was on its way—and he was already darn close to where it was coming—he went on adjusting, with a succession of tiny sidesteps. No wonder the ball arrived so regularly in his "strike zone." And since he was always on balance, no wonder he had such exquisite timing that the ball exploded off the face of his racquet.

In sum, Rosewall, thanks to his inherent artistry, made even the serve-and-volley game a delight. How Rosewall at his peak would have fared against Kramer, Gonzales, and Laver at *their* peaks I cannot say, but I do know that for me, as for many others, Rosewall stands as the most attractive player of the postwar era. Certainly no other player has given me nearly as much pleasure. For these reasons, and for the additional one that he is now starting down the far side of the slope, I wanted him to have a very good Forest Hills.

Although Forest Hills can't compare with Wimbledon as a spectacle, an occasion, or as an institution, there was little to choose between the two history-making Opens in terms of straight tennis. The only player of renown who appeared at Wimbledon and not here was Manolo Santana. If Wimbledon gained a special evocative aura from the high number of former champions who returned either to play in peripheral events or simply to be on hand, this was equally true of Forest Hills. In the Senior Men's Doubles, for instance, nostalgia flowed like wine when Bobby Riggs and Pancho Segura confronted Don Budge and Frankie Parker in the quarter-final round. (They all looked pretty good, and Parker, at fifty-two, appeared indecently untouched by time. He weighed not a pound more than he had back in 1947, when he played Kramer in the championship final, and he seemed to be wearing the same pair of shorts—the ones with the blue stripe down the side.) The first open Forest Hills also resembled the first open Wimbledon in its unpredictability. From the moment, early in the tournament, when Fred Stolle fell before young Peter Curtis, of England, the seeded players were treated roughly. To say the same thing in a slightly different way, no fewer than thirteen professionals were ousted by amateurs, and even if this statistic is qualified by the observation that two-thirds of the players who have turned pro in recent years had not been colossi in their amateur days, it does indicate the prevalence of the unanticipated. Whatever the reasons, tennis, long the most form-abiding of sports, isn't that way at the moment. The most startling upset took place in the fourth round, when Laver, the heavy favorite to win the championship, was put out by Cliff Drysdale, of South Africa, 4–6, 6–4, 3–6, 6–1, 6–1. (Note the decisiveness of the scores of the last two sets.) In the second round, Laver had barely avoided elimination at the hands of Tomas Koch, of Brazil. When, after losing the first two sets, he pulled that match out despite his inability to control his serve, most of us were inclined to view his escape as an almost classic example of a champion's grit and resourcefulness, and we expected that Laver, a notoriously slow starter, would gradually come onto his game as the tournament progressed. Well, we couldn't have been wronger. In the fifth set of his match against Drysdale, when it was do or depart, Laver failed three times to hold serve and, if I can trust my notes, amassed a grand total of three points during Drysdale's three service games. Indeed, he played so utterly unlike the Laver we know that there was rather widespread speculation as to whether he was still hampered by the wrist injury he suffered in late July. Laver flatly denied that he was, and remarked only that he had found it hard to serve with the official tournament ball. Inexplicably, the ball selected for Forest Hills—one sold by Macy's and manufactured in England by Slazenger, but not the Slazenger ball used at Wimbledon—has very little fuzz, is heavy to begin with, and becomes as heavy as a rock after four or five games. Laver was by no means the only contestant who felt that he might have played somewhat better with a better ball.

One man who coped with the ball fairly well—though he didn't much care for it, either—was Gonzales. After a bye and an easy second-round match, he came up against Mal Anderson, who, at thirty-three, is still a redoubtable player. The Gonzales we saw against Anderson was an entirely different Gonzales from the tired old man of Wimbledon. His pride had obviously been wounded by his performance there, and he meant to do something about it. Having got his weight down to a hundred and seventy-five pounds, he looked years younger and he moved years younger. Against Anderson, he played an almost perfect match, expending his limited reserves of energy at just the right moments. In each set, when he had his chance for the pivotal service break he seized it, and he wrapped up the match quickly, 6–4, 6–4, 6–4. On the court, he was uncharacteristically pacific, and after the match was over he positively radiated bonhomie. (On being asked if he had noticed that the gallery was solidly behind him, he broke into a big smile. "Sure, I'm an old man now," he said. "When I was the champion, I was the villain. I had both my opponents and the crowd against me. I think I like the change.") In the next round, when Gonzales met Roche, the young Australian who was a finalist at Wimbledon and was seeded second at Forest Hills, the stands were so passionately pro-Gonzales that on several occasions they went too far, even applauding Roche's double faults. In truth, though, Gonzales did play a rousing match. In winning the first set, 8–6, he fought off four set points in the tenth game, broke through Roche in the thirteenth with two bravura forehands, and then held his service at love. In the second set, when Roche, leading 4–1 in games and 40–15 on his serve, became a little careless, Gonzales pounced on his errors like a cat on a mouse, and before you knew it he had broken Roche's service twice. That was it, really: Gonzales, 8–6, 6–4, 6–2. There are a lot of men who can hit a tennis ball with authority but very few who are gifted match players, like Gonzales. What it requires, at bottom, is true resolution and infinite care. You give nothing away cheaply yourself, but you are poised to exploit every cautious serve by your opponent, every shallow return, every imprecise volley, and every lob that is out of context, not to mention every little edge—a moment of flagging concentration on your opponent's part, the fact that the sun is in his eyes, his awareness that he has muffed two backhands in a row, and so on. Only a man who wants terribly to win can work so hard and steadily at the task of winning.

Gonzales' victory over Roche took him to the quarter-finals, where he opposed Tom Okker, a twenty-four-year-old Dutchman, who is currently the fastest man in tennis. Again, Gonzales gave it everything, but this time it wasn't enough, and he went down, 14–16, 6–3, 10–8, 6–3. The first set was the key. Since Gonzales played this match the day after he played Roche, his one chance of winning lay in avoiding a drawn-out battle; if he had to go five sets, or even four, he couldn't hope to stay with a beautifully conditioned young athlete like Okker. Accordingly, although Gonzales won the first set, it was a Pyrrhic victory, for he was forced to play thirty games—only two fewer than his entire match with Roche had taken. After that, he was simply too weary to do what he wanted to do. Though patently irked by his powerlessness to defy the gods, Gonzales was pleasant in defeat, and not unhappy. The impression he gave me was that he felt that, all things considered, he had atoned for Wimbledon and done himself justice.

In the semifinals, Okker met Rosewall in the lower half of the draw, and in the upper half Arthur Ashe, Jr., who had eliminated Roy Emerson and Drysdale, met his fellow-American amateur and Davis Cup teammate Clark Graebner. En route to the semis, Rosewall had had a relatively quiet journey. His only uncomfortable moments had come in the fourth round, against that perennial ranking enigma of American tennis Ron Holmberg, a player of immense talent who invariably finds a way to lose. Down two sets to one, Holmberg was outplaying Rosewall in the fourth set and seemed likely to win it, but, only too typically, he allowed himself to become upset when, at a comparatively uncritical point, he hit a first serve that he thought had ticked the net but that wasn't called a let. Rosewall then coasted home. His opponent in the quarters was Dennis Ralston, but what would ordinarily have been a very good match turned out to be no match at all. Handicapped by a torn stomach muscle, Ralston could serve only at half speed and, in general, offer little more than token resistance. From Rosewall's point of view, a tougher match might have helped him sharpen his game but would have taxed him more physically. At least, he would be fresh and rested for Okker, and against the Flying Dutchman, as Okker has inevitably been labelled, he would need to be.

Until this year, Okker was just a respectable internationalist. Then he suddenly blossomed. He won the South African and Italian championships, and in the Queen's Club tournament, prior to Wimbledon, he knocked off three professionals, Laver among them. A slim (five-ten, one-forty) young man with a handsome, Ivy League face, Okker is what is currently called in this year of change a "registered player"—that is, he is registered with his national association and has its sanction to compete both in amateur events, where he is paid expenses, and in open events, where he plays for prize money, just as the pros do. It is like having the best of both worlds. (The British Lawn Tennis Association approves heartily of this new category. Ours doesn't, so no American can be a registered player.) Anyhow, Rosewall vs. Okker proved to be the finest match of the championship—crisp and entertaining tennis, filled with dramatic exchanges. In the ninth game of the first set—games 4–4, Okker serving, and the score 30–40—we had just such an exchange. The Dutchman raced in behind a good fast serve, volleyed the return deep, and smashed Rosewall's hurried lob into the backhand corner —an apparent winner; because this was an important point, Rosewall was giving it that extra something, and as he lunged across the baseline he managed to get his racquet on the smash and block the ball back over the net; Okker then played a rather tentative forehand to the backhand corner, and Rosewall not only got to it but pasted such a severe backhand down the line that Okker's off-balance volley carried over the baseline. Point and game, Mr. Rosewall. Up to this juncture, the trim little Australian—he seemed hardly altered from the boy we had seen trotting out with Hoad sixteen years before—had had a slight edge in the play. He was keeping the ball away from Okker's dangerous topspin forehand, he was making Okker do a lot of running, and he was moving very well himself. However, in the tenth game, when Rosewall was serving for the set, we had the first adumbration of the course the match was to take. Down 30–0, Okker fought his way to deuce with two placements— hit while he was running at full tilt—and a forehand drive that Rosewall volleyed into the net. He went to ad on another volley error by Rosewall, and took the game by whipping a forehand down the line off Rosewall's first service. Four games later, he broke through Rosewall's service again, to win the set, 8–6. The rest of the way, except for a shaky passage in the third set, Okker was just a little too much for Rosewall to handle. His speed afoot was something to behold. For example, there must have been a dozen rallies that Rosewall controlled yet ultimately lost when Okker not only caught up with an angled volley that would usually have terminated the point but added insult to injury by hooking a stunning winner into the distant corner of the court. In addition, Okker possesses terrific reflexive speed in handling a racquet, and I think that what may, more than anything else, have convinced Rosewall of the impossibility of his task was finding that in those rat-tat-tat volley exchanges at close quarters the shot that should have won for him kept coming back. Okker in four sets: 8–6, 6–4, 6–8, 6–1.

In all this there was, of course, a lavish splash of irony. Rosewall had played very well—well enough to have won most matches—but he was up against the one type of opponent he could not contain: a young Rosewall.

As finals go—they are generally anticlimactic—the men's final between Ashe and Okker was a superior one. Ashe won it in five sets, 14–12, 5–7, 6–3, 3–6, 6–3, and, as the scores indicate, it was closely fought all the way. However, it was a decidedly less interesting match than the Okker-Rosewall duel. It produced a paucity of rallies, for one thing, and, for another, Okker was not in such dazzling form. Both of these phenomena—an absence of rallies and a less than glittering performance by his opponent—occur in just about every match that Ashe plays. They are curious affairs, Ashe's matches, often boring and exciting at the same time. Ashe, you see, hits a tennis ball harder and faster than anyone else has for years. He simply blows it past his opponents. On a good day it goes in a lot, and on a bad day it goes out a lot. As a result, you can have long successions of points that are over almost before they have begun. That is what makes for the boredom. What makes for the excitement, of course, is the sheer velocity of Ashe's strokes. The odd thing is that he has a rather wispy build for a power hitter. The secret of his power is fantastic coördination. For example, on his crosscourt backhand—his best stroke, apart from his serve—he doesn't appear to swing especially hard at the ball, but it travels like a shot. His method of serving is simplicity itself. He bounces the ball twice, tosses it about a yard above his head, leans forward, and cracks it. It goes like a blur. In the first set alone against Okker, he scored fifteen aces.

Ashe's admirers have long speculated about the heights he might reach if he modified his all-attack style by adding to his repertoire some more restrained strokes on which he could rely during those afternoons when his control is off—and on which he could call during his good afternoons, too, in those tactical situations that require a whisper rather than a thunderclap. Ashe is only twenty-five, and in time he may develop a more complete tennis vocabulary and move closer to Rosewall and Gonzales than to Ellsworth Vines and the other outright cannoneers.

MARGARET COURT'S
BIG YEAR

(1970)

There is a reluctance in some quarters to place Margaret Smith in the very top class of women tennis players, largely, I would suppose, because of her occasional lapses on the big occasions. At the same time, the rangy young woman from New South Wales put together a tremendously impressive record, headed by eleven Australian singles titles, seven in our championship, five in the French, and three at Wimbledon. In 1970 she got it all together and scored the first women's grand slam since Maureen Connolly's sweep in 1953.

There were several occasions this past year when I would not have been at all surprised if I had opened a reference book and stumbled across the following entry:

> Carroll, Lewis. 1832–98. Pseudonym of Charles Lutwidge Dodgson, lecturer in mathematics at Christ Church, Oxford. Author of "Alice's Adventures in Wonderland" (1865) and "Through the Looking-Glass" (1872). Invented lawn tennis (1873).

In so many words, the world of tennis, instead of settling down and making sense, as we all thought it would after "shamateurism" was routed and open tennis arrived, in 1968, has become curiouser and curiouser, and today it is such a plexus of contradictions that, as often as not, up is down, forehand is backhand, and to be is not to be. Here are a few examples of the way things have been going:

1. The largest chunk of prize money in the history of tennis—$35,000—was won by Rod Laver when he defeated Ken Rosewall *indoors* (at Madison Square Garden) on July 16th. They were playing the final of the Champions' Classic, a strung-out tournament that had started in January.

2. In late August, the United States team retained the Davis Cup, which is emblematic of supremacy among the tennis-playing nations, by turning back West Germany in the Challenge Round every bit as impressively as it had turned back Rumania in 1969. Australia, our old Davis Cup nemesis, was eliminated fairly early this year, losing to India in the final round of the Eastern Zone. The top five seeded players in the recently concluded United States Open at Forest Hills —Laver, Rosewall, John Newcombe, Tony Roche, and Roy Emerson— were all Australians, but since they were "contract pros," they were ineligible for Davis Cup competition. In today's jargon, a contract pro is a player who is under contract to a "pro promoter," a commercial outfit that sets up its own tournaments for its stable of players and charges a healthy management fee for their appearance in other people's tournaments. (Until this summer, there were two main pro promoters—the National Tennis League and World Championship Tennis —but in July the former was absorbed by the latter, which is owned and operated by Lamar Hunt, a Dallas millionaire whose aboveground assets include the Kansas City Chiefs football team.) Mind you, the players on our successful Davis Cup team were professionals, too, but the distinction is that they were "independent pros"—meaning that their business affairs were handled by individuals or groups who, unlike the pro promoters, respected the suzerainty of the various national lawn tennis associations and were happy to work with them. (As a matter of fact, the captain of our Davis Cup team for 1968 and 1969 was Donald Dell, the same fellow who for the past few years has acted as business agent for four members of that team—Arthur Ashe, Stan Smith, Bob Lutz, and Charles Pasarell.) Some people have charged that the United States, in effect, bought the Davis Cup, the implication being that the United States Lawn Tennis Association made it worthwhile for Ashe, Smith, Lutz, Pasarell, and Cliff Richey, the fifth member of the team, not to become contract pros, but, of course, in an edgy, vindictive microcosm like the world of tennis you have to expect that kind of talk. Anyhow, that's ancient history now: the week after Forest

Hills, Ashe, Lutz, and Pasarell signed with World Championship Tennis.

 3. Harry Hopman, the great Australian coach who for so many years was the scourge of our Davis Cup ambitions, spent a delightful summer at a tennis camp in Amherst instructing young American players.

 4. In 1969, you will remember, Laver scored a grand slam of the four major championships—the Australian, French, Wimbledon, and United States Opens, to list them in the order in which they are played. This year, Laver didn't even get a chance to defend the first two of these titles. The pro promoter he was affiliated with couldn't come to terms with the Australian L.T.A. and, accordingly, would not allow its players to participate in the Australian Open. As for the French Open, there wasn't a contract pro in the field, for the French L.T.A. held firm and refused to pay a management fee to either of the two big pro promoters.

By and large, this is the way it went all year—a paucity of news about the actual game of tennis, a plethora of news about the business of tennis. What has happened, I gather, is that open tennis has brought a sizable amount of new money into the sport, plus the prospect of a real gold mine, and, as a result, in this present period of flux everyone is chasing the buck, the quid, the gaj, and the girsh as hard as he can, and when he is not doing that he is jockeying to be in the right place when and if the huge financial breakthrough does occur.

To fire the enthusiasm of its followers, a sport—and particularly a worldwide sport, like tennis—must have a sense of continuity about it. This past year, with men's tennis in such arrant disorder, the big story was Margaret Smith Court's attempt to duplicate the grand slam of the four major championships achieved by the late Maureen Connolly in 1953. No woman had won a grand slam before—the thought of invading Australia in the winter months never occurred to Suzanne Lenglen, Helen Wills Moody, or Alice Marble—and no woman had done it since.

 Miss Connolly, far and away the finest exponent of the baseline game since Mrs. Moody, was in jeopardy only twice en route to her slam. The Australian Championship had been no bother at all: only one of her opponents won as many as three games in a set, and that was Julie Sampson, a touring Californian, whom Miss Connolly defeated in the final, 6–3, 6–2. In the French, though, she had a slight scare in an early round: Susan Chatrier took the first set from her, 6–3, before Miss Connolly got down to work and sped through the next two sets, 6–2, 6–2. In the final, she defeated Doris Hart, 6–2, 6–4. At Wimbledon, in excellent form, Miss Connolly only once yielded as many as three games in a set until the final, but there, up against Miss Hart again, she had to summon every last ounce of ability to pull out a tremendous battle, 8–6, 7–5. Forest Hills was relatively easy: after marching through her earlier matches she confronted the unfortunate Miss Hart once more in the final, and this time she was well in command all the way—winning 6–2, 6–4. The astounding thing about Miss Connolly's slam was that she was only nineteen when she brought it off. Unfortunately, two weeks after she captured her third Wimbledon Championship, her leg was broken in a freak riding accident and she never competed again in the championships.

Where grand slams are concerned, Margaret Court starts with one advantage: she is usually in Australia when the Australian Championships are held. She was born and grew up in Albury, New South Wales, a town on the main Sydney-Melbourne railroad line, where her father worked as a foreman in a dairy-products plant. In 1960, when she was seventeen, she won her first Australian Championship, two days after she had been beaten in the final of the Girls' Junior Championship. When she began her campaign this past winter, she had won the Australian title eight times, the French three times, Wimbledon twice, and the United States three times, not to mention countless other national singles titles and just about all the doubles and mixed-doubles titles you could name. Despite this awesome record, many tennis authorities have been a little leery about placing her on a level with Lenglen, Moody, Marble, and Connolly, and have been reluctant to describe her, without qualification, as a "great player." The most likely explanation is that the people in and around the game have always expected even more of Margaret Court than she has produced, because probably no woman has ever been so well equipped physically to play tennis. A big-boned, smoothly coördinated, attractive girl who stands five feet nine and weighs around a hundred and fifty pounds, she could pass for a sister of either Frank Sedgman or John Newcombe, those ruggedly handsome specimens of Australian manhood. She has a lot going for her. Her serve, though not in the same class as Marble's, comes in hard and fast. Her ground strokes are sound—the forehand biffed with exceptional power, the backhand executed with a touch of elegance. She has a fine instinct for volleying, and, what with her long arms, is very difficult to pass when she comes to net. She covers the court swiftly and can run all day; when she was starting out she came under the influence of Sedgman, who is a fanatic on physical fitness, and she has since made it a point to do some roadwork and weight lifting every day. However, the experts have always had a tendency to write her off as just a marvellously effective player, and to note, in passing, that both her court manner and her strokes lack the style, the fluency, the panache, and the excitement that distinguish the top champions. Curiously, the Court match that Americans seem to remember most vividly is her defeat in the 1963 Forest Hills final by Maria Bueno. (After winning the first set, 7–5, Miss Bueno was trailing, 1–4, in the second when, suddenly, she began to race around the court like Lenglen, getting to the ball in a flash and dispatching it in a flash, and she swept the next five games with the loss of only six of the last twenty-seven points.) Though it was not true on that particular occasion, Mrs. Court has lost a number of matches (some of them to rather ordinary players) by suffering—for no apparent reason, since she is a player of courage—strange attacks of nervousness, during which she would hit forehand after forehand yards out of court and serve streams of double faults. Sometimes she was able to regain control of herself and sometimes not. "The underlying fact about Margaret is that she didn't have true confidence in herself," an Australian tennis writer told me recently. "She is basically an extremely shy girl. People meeting her for the first time are always surprised by the way she speaks. They expect the assertiveness of a celebrity, and out comes this small little London voice."

At the close of the 1966 season, Margaret Court—she was still Margaret Smith at the time—decided to quit tennis. She had ceased to enjoy it. From this point on, her story reads like one of those Hollywood films of the nineteen-thirties in which "nice people solve nice problems." In an effort to get away from it all, she became a partner in a boutique in Perth, the beautiful city on the Indian Ocean, twenty-five hundred miles west of Sydney. There she met Barry Court, a wool broker and the son of a politician who currently holds two portfolios in the West Australia government—Minister for Industrial Development and Minister for the Northwest. The young Court was a sailor, not a tennis player. He had twice won the Skate Class (fourteen-footers) in the West Australia Championships, and he had competed in the 505 Class (sixteen-and-a-half-footers) in the World Championships at Adelaide in 1966, racing against Jim Hardy, who skippered Gretel II at Newport last month. Miss Smith and Mr. Court were married in the autumn of 1967, and the following year, accompanied by her husband, Mrs. Court returned to tournament tennis. She has been a splendid advertisement for the benefits of a happy marriage—conspicuously more relaxed, far less subject to those old *crises des nerfs* on the courts, surer of herself in all respects. Last year, she won three of the four major championships, losing her chance for a grand slam when Ann Jones upset her in the semifinals at Wimbledon. This year, she meant to do better.

In January, she got off on the right foot, taking the Australian

Championship without losing a set or allowing an opponent more than four games in a match. In the French (it is amazing how closely her fortunes this year paralleled Maureen Connolly's seventeen years before) she had a very rocky moment: in the second round she lost the opening set to Olga Morozova, the charming Russian girl, and was in deep trouble in the second set before surviving it, 8–6, but she won the third decisively, at 6–1. After that, no worries at all. In the final, she defeated Helga Niessen, of Germany, 6–2, 6–4. The women's ranks today are not especially strong to begin with, and at Wimbledon, since the defending champion, Mrs. Jones, had chosen not to defend, the field was the weakest in years. If form held—and it did—Mrs. Court's only real opposition would come from her old and fervent rival Billie Jean King, of California, a three-time Wimbledon champion. They met in the final on a coolish afternoon under an oyster sky, and a remarkable match ensued. From the start, neither player hit the ball with maximum pace or tried for blazing winners. Each had a more defensive strategy. Mrs. Court was out to take away Mrs. King's exceptional volleying game by pinning her in the backcourt. Mrs. King was out to keep Mrs. Court away from her net, too, and was working to keep the ball away from her forehand. Both women were succeeding. I have never seen a match in which two adversaries maintained a higher level of concentration. Game after game went by with neither playing a careless stroke. It was a battle of attrition: most points were won only after a fairly long rally. The feeling one got as one stared down at the court was that, more than anything else, each player was determined not to let the other beat her. In the first set, for instance, Mrs. King broke Mrs. Court's service four times, and each time the set was hers for the taking, but each time Mrs. Court broke back immediately. The set moved on, to 9–9, to 10–10, the atmosphere fiercely quiet, neither player speaking a word or moving an eyebrow. At length, in the twenty-sixth game, Mrs. King's concentration wavered. She lost her serve at love and, with it, the set, 14–12. It had taken eighty-eight minutes. The spectators in the Centre Court leaned forward for the second set. There was no letdown. Game after game, the two women persevered with their vigilant tennis. When the score reached 7–7, Mrs. King, who had just staved off a match point, changed her tactics. Her right knee was beginning to bother her, and, with her mobility impeded, she decided to stay near the baseline and see if she could break up Mrs. Court's game with an artful mixture of deep drives and drop shots. Mrs. Court, however, with her speed of foot, got to just about everything. In the twentieth game, after holding three match points, she finally broke Mrs. King's serve to take the set, 11–9. In all, the match had lasted two hours and twenty-eight minutes and required forty-six games, exceeding by two the previous record for a women's final, established in 1919, when Suzanne Lenglen, making her début at Wimbledon, at the age of twenty, defeated Mrs. Lambert Chambers, a seven-time champion, 10–8, 4–6, 9–7.

Three down and one to go—Forest Hills, the first two weeks in September. It was hard to see how Mrs. Court could fail to win there. First, Mrs. King, the one opponent she had reason to fear, was *hors de combat,* convalescing from a knee operation she had undergone after Wimbledon. Second, the week before Forest Hills, Mrs. Court had a piece of good luck: in the semifinals of the Marlboro Open, at East Orange, she had run into one of those old jittery spells and had been beaten by Patti Hogan, an erratic young Californian. This defeat, Mrs. Court's first in forty-two matches, eased the pressure that had been building up, and made it less likely that she would defeat herself at Forest Hills. There, on her way to the final, she lost a mere thirteen games in five matches, among them a 6–1, 6–1 victory over Miss Hogan. The final was different. Up against Rosemary Casals, a talented, spunky twenty-one-year-old San Franciscan, who is Mrs. King's doubles partner and closest friend, she won the first set, 6–2, but she dropped the second by the same score. The crucial point of the match came in the fifth game of the third, and deciding, set. Mrs. Court, serving, was leading, 3–1. The first point of this game went to Miss Casals when she hit a forehand return of service down the line for a placement. On the next point, Miss Casals, after driving deep to Mrs. Court's backhand, volleyed the weak return crisply crosscourt for what appeared to be a clean winner. Flying up from the baseline and flinging herself toward the ball, Mrs. Court somehow got her racquet on it and batted it across the net. I happened to be sitting near Judy Tegart Dalton, the veteran Australian player, and as the rally continued she chirped up excitedly, "You wait and see. Margaret will win this point." Sure enough, after an extended exchange from the baseline, Miss Casals netted a forehand. Had Mrs. Court lost that point, she would have been down 0–30 and in danger of being broken. As it was, from 15–all she swept the next three points for the game. "On that second point, no one but Margaret could have got to that volley," Mrs. Dalton said. "That's a perfect example of why she's so hard to beat. She takes away your winning shots." A few minutes later, the match was over. Mrs. Court had won the third set, 6–1, and had completed her grand slam.

TEXAS AND THE
NEW ENTREPRENEURS

(1971)

In the midsummer of 1971 I made a trip to Texas to talk with two people who, as tennis continued to expand, had become increasingly important forces. The first was Gladys Heldman, a native New Yorker, who had moved to Houston when her husband was transferred to that city. The founder of World Tennis *magazine, Mrs. Heldman had in 1970 organized the first separate tour for women players with marked success. I wanted to see her in action on her new non-native heath. I also wanted to go up to Dallas and meet Lamar Hunt, a healthy, wealthy, and wise native son who had established W.C.T.—World Championship Tennis.*

The story of the Women's Pro Tour is largely the story of Gladys Heldman, an energetic, strong-minded, peppery New Yorker, now in her late forties, who has been a considerable force in tennis since 1953, when she founded *World Tennis,* a monthly magazine that quickly became the leader in its field. During the 1970 championships at Forest Hills, a group of prominent women players who had long felt that most tournaments did not allot a big enough share of the prize money to the distaff side of the proceedings decided that the time had come to do something about it. What had set them off was the prize-money ratio in the Pacific Southwest Open, scheduled to be played in Los Angeles two weeks after Forest Hills. The usual prize-money ratio between the men and the women in European tournaments is two and a half to one, and in American tournaments it is about five to one, except at Forest Hills, where it is about three to one. In the Pacific Southwest, though, the purse for the women—seventy-five hundred dollars—was less than one-eighth of the men's purse. (The way things were set up, a woman player had to reach the quarter-finals to receive any prize money at all. The tournament, furthermore, was paying no travel fares or other expenses.) At Forest Hills, Billie Jean King and Rosemary Casals, representing the dissident group, approached Mrs. Heldman and asked her if she would talk to Jack Kramer, the tournament director of the Pacific Southwest, about increasing the women's prize money. Mrs. Heldman was the logical choice for the group's spokeswoman. As the editor and publisher of *World Tennis,* she had long been at the heart of the game, and, as the mother of Julie Heldman, then the second-ranked American-woman player, she was particularly close to women's tennis. As it turned out, Kramer proved to be unbudgeable, whereupon Mrs. Heldman swung into action with her characteristic briskness and arranged for a tournament with a field of eight of the insurgents to be held at the Houston Racquet Club the same week as the Pacific Southwest. She chose Houston because her husband, a vice-president of the Shell Oil Company, had recently been shifted to that city from New York and she was then in the process of moving her household and her magazine there.

Despite the speed with which things had to be done, the Houston tournament worked out well. It was able to offer seventy-five hundred dollars in prize money, five thousand of it from the sale of a hundred fifty-dollar tickets that entitled the purchaser to attend special instruction clinics, and the rest from Virginia Slims cigarettes. (With a field of only eight, the first-round losers received three hundred dollars—enough to cover expenses.) To protect the Houston Racquet Club from suspension by the U.S.L.T.A. for putting on an unsanctioned tournament, the eight players—Nancy Richey, Kerry Melville, Judy Tegart Dalton, Valerie Ziegenfuss, Peaches Bartkowicz, and Kristy Pigeon, along with Mrs. King and Miss Casals—turned Contract Pro, signing with *World Tennis* for a dollar each. (At that time, a club that put on a tournament only for Contract Pros did not require official sanction.) On the second day of the tournament, the players were informed by telegram that they had been suspended by the U.S.L.T.A., but by that time several encouraging things were happening. Most important, Barry MacKay, the chairman of the Pacific Coast Championships, scheduled for Berkeley following the Pacific Southwest, called Mrs. Heldman to tell her that the tournament, which had originally offered twenty-eight thousand dollars in prize money for the men and two thousand for the women, had raised the women's share to forty-four hundred. He was informed that the women would be delighted to appear if their prize money was raised to eleven thousand dollars, a figure in keeping with the minimum standards that the group had established. When MacKay rang back to report that he had been able to round up the eleven thousand, the Women's Pro Tour—Women's Lob, it inevitably came to be called—had scored a major victory.

Mrs. Heldman arranged for only one other tournament in 1970, but this year, with more and more players joining the tour, she was able to set up a whole new circuit for the women. During the first four months alone, they played thirteen tournaments offering prize money of between ten and fifteen thousand dollars—in San Francisco, Long Beach (California), Oklahoma City, Milwaukee, Chattanooga, Philadelphia, Fort Lauderdale, Winchester (Massachusetts), Birmingham (Michigan), New York, San Juan, St. Petersburg, and San Diego—as well as a thirty-thousand-dollar tournament in Las Vegas. Local corporations sponsored about half of these events, and where this wasn't possible Virginia Slims stepped in and put up the necessary money. When you reflect on the tensions traditionally believed to be endemic to all-girl orchestras or all-girl anythings, the tour has done amazingly well. To begin with, the players have been happy because they have made out much better financially than they had ever hoped to. As early as May —by which time just about all the top players in the world except Margaret Court, of Australia, and Virginia Wade, of England, had gravitated to the Women's Pro Tour—four of the nomads had earned over twenty-five thousand dollars each: Mrs. King, Miss Casals, Ann Jones, of England, who had been the 1969 Wimbledon champion, and Françoise Durr, the best French player. (In the past, only the most outstanding women players could ever hope to make as much as twenty-five thousand a year, either above or below the table, but as of this writing Mrs. King has won over ninety thousand dollars in prize money in 1971 and is sure to go over the hundred-thousand mark.) For another thing, the regular presence on the tour of Philip (Pip) Jones, Ann's husband, gave the tour just the balance wheel it needed. A sound and amiable man, Jones retired four years ago, upon reaching the age of sixty, as the director of sales for a worldwide British paint company that has its headquarters in Birmingham, England, and he has since travelled with his wife on her tennis campaigns. Fretful this past winter at the amount of free time on his hands, he volunteered to take on the duties of tour coördinator, and he has performed them superbly. Moreover, since all but two of the winter and spring tournaments drew well and made money, the sponsors were extremely pleased, and Mrs. Heldman consequently found it no trouble to set up a full post-Wimbledon summer circuit, which featured a twenty-thousand-dollar Ford Capri tournament in Venice and a forty-thousand-dollar Virginia Slims International in Houston—the richest women's tournament in history.

The fact that the separate women's tour, for which many tennis insiders had predicted outright disaster, has fared so well is really not surprising when one recalls Gladys Heldman's astonishing record of achievement. A slim, dark-haired woman who is the daughter of the late George Z. Medalie, a New York lawyer and judge, she graduated from Stanford in 1942 and shortly thereafter married Julius Heldman, a former national junior tennis champion who was then an instructor in chemistry at the University of California at Berkeley. Mrs. Heldman took a master's degree at Berkeley in medieval history, and went one up on her husband by becoming a full professor of mathematics at Williams Institute, a small college in Berkeley, where she taught calculus and differential equations. Although she did not take up tennis until after the birth of her two daughters, Carrie and Julie, she quickly became proficient at the game, and in 1951—by this time her husband had accepted a position with Shell and the family was living on the outskirts of Houston—she won the women's division of Houston's famous River Oaks tournament and was ranked No. 1 in Texas. She has played at Wimbledon once—in 1954. In 1953, a month after the first issue of *World Tennis* came out, Mr. Heldman was transferred to New York. Mrs. Heldman brought the infant magazine along, and quickly established herself as the city's ranking tennis hostess, but it wasn't until 1959 that the scope of her executive ability became apparent. That year, after the U.S.L.T.A. had voted not to hold the national indoor championships, an inveterate money-loser, she and two friends got permission from the organization to put on the tournament, rented the Seventh Regiment Armory, and made a profit of eight thousand dollars, which they turned over to the Association. In 1962, when the U.S.L.-T.A., as poky as ever, was undecided whether it would be financially worthwhile to bring over a contingent of foreign players for the championships at Forest Hills, Mrs. Heldman had a bright idea. She and nine friends put up seventeen hundred dollars apiece and chartered a jet, which collected some seventy international players at Amsterdam, flew them to New York for the tournament, and then flew them back. Under the terms of the deal, the U.S.L.T.A. was obliged to recompense the ten underwriters only if the gate receipts for the championships broke the old record; they did. Despite all these outside activities, Mrs. Heldman's primary commitment has always been to *World Tennis.* She has made it the most successful tennis magazine of all time, with sixty-five thousand subscribers and a newsstand sale of approximately twenty thousand.

My visit to Houston coincided with the Virginia Slims International, and I naturally spent a good deal of time watching the tennis. Because of the oppressive humidity and heat of August along the Gulf of Mexico, the matches were held in the University of Houston's new Hofheinz Pavilion, an air-conditioned auditorium with ten thousand seats—all of them brilliant red—which serves as the home court for the school's basketball team. The tennis was of a very high order, with Billie Jean King defeating Kerry Melville, a much improved player, in the final. The matches were well attended, and I was struck by the fact that many of the patrons' cars were adorned with blue-and-chartreuse bumper stickers, supplied by the Houston Tennis Association, which proclaimed "Houston, Tennis Capital of the World." Houston has not yet attained quite that eminence, but it is a lively tennis town, having been exposed to competition on the best international level since 1931, when Ellsworth Vines won the first River Oaks tournament.

The Heldmans live on Timberwilde, an extraordinarily beautiful street that curves its way through a residential district of Houston called Hunter's Creek Village. Whenever I visited the house, I found a swirl of activity, but I especially remember one late breakfast I looked in on there. Gathered around the table, and all in full conversational flight, were Mrs. Heldman, her husband, their daughter Julie, and their house guests: Pip and Ann Jones; Joseph H. Cullman III, the chairman of the board of Philip Morris (which puts out Virginia Slims), and Mrs. Cullman; and the London couturier Teddy Tinling, who—after interrupting his career to serve for four years of the Second World War as the personal assistant to General Kenneth Strong, Eisenhower's G-2—became an international celebrity in the late nineteen-forties as the designer of tennis clothes for Gussie Moran and many other celebrated players. There was a good deal of spirited, knowledgeable tennis talk that morning, and two passages in particular linger in my memory. The first was an iridescent biographical sortie by Tinling in which he touched on (a) his boyhood years in southern France, when he served as the umpire Suzanne Lenglen insisted on in a hundred and six matches; (b) the years in which he competed at Wimbledon and also acted as the tournament's official liaison with the "overseas players"; and (c) the dress he designed for Evonne Goolagong, the sensational young Australian, to wear in the final at Wimbledon this summer. The second passage, a brief dissertation by Pip Jones on some of the problems that tennis is currently facing, was remarkable for its frankness and its progressive outlook: "Nothing should ever stand still—not even Wimbledon, with all its excellent points. The time has come, I believe, for Wimbledon to adopt a more modern approach to advertising in order to produce a larger revenue. Of course, this must be handled intelligently. The main reason behind such a move is *not* to have the funds to pay the star players large guarantees. No, the reason is that we need money to develop young players in Britain, and this would provide it. You see, our boys and girls cannot practice indoors during the winter months. We don't have the facilities. If we had some modern indoor arenas—and some *good coaching*—I think we could find a champion."

Lamar Hunt, the man behind World Championship Tennis, is the youngest of the six children of H. L. Hunt, the Texas oilman, the others being H. L., Jr., Margaret, Caroline, Nelson Bunker, and William Herbert. Another Texas oilman, J. Paul Getty, whom many people believe to be the richest man in the world, himself believes that this distinction belongs to Hunt, a native of Illinois, who started his empire by trading in oil leases around El Dorado, Arkansas, in 1920, and really hit it big ten years later, when he bought four thousand acres in Rusk County in East Texas, and it turned out to be the richest oil field that had ever been discovered in this country. Today his income is reputed to be more than a million dollars a week. Achieving a separate identity when you are "H. L.'s boy" and are further saddled with a modest, sensible nature is no easy thing, but Lamar Hunt has managed to do it. A founder of the American Football League and the owner of the Kansas City Chiefs, he was responsible, more than any other individual, for the A.F.L.'s survival and its eventual successful merger with the National Football League. Football is just one of several ventures he has made into professional sports. He is a part owner of the Dallas–Fort Worth Spurs, a baseball team in the Texas League. "Tommy Mercer, a friend of mine from Fort Worth, got me interested in that about eight years ago," Hunt told me when, at the conclusion of the Houston tournament, I called on him in his office in Dallas. "Behind it was the idea of trying to get a major-league franchise for Dallas–Fort Worth." Hunt is also co-owner of the Dallas Tornado, of the North American Soccer League—an eight-team league, now in its fourth year. "I went into that because soccer is a truly international sport and, as such, an excellent sport for our country to be involved in," Hunt explained. And then there is World Championship Tennis—W.C.T. for short. Hunt got into that in 1967, the year before open tennis arrived. That year, in preparation for the new era, George MacCall, who had been a captain of our Davis Cup team, had formed a group called the National Tennis League by signing up the game's top professionals—Rod Laver, Ken Rosewall, and Pancho Gonzales—and a small supporting cast. At about the same time, Dave Dixon, a New Orleans promoter, had created W.C.T. by signing eight young players who stood a rung or two below the top: John Newcombe, Tony Roche, Dennis Ralston, Butch Buchholz, Nikki Pilic, Pierre Barthes, Cliff Drysdale, and Roger Taylor. (This second group came to be called the Handsome Eight, or, sometimes, the Handsome Seven and Tony Roche.) In any event, Hunt, who had become interested in tennis through a nephew of his, Al Hill, Jr., at one time a nationally ranked junior player, bought a half interest in W.C.T., and later, when Dixon wanted out, took it over completely. Last year, after the National Tennis League disbanded, he acquired its best players, thus becoming *the* professional-tennis entrepreneur. "My brother Herbert likes to say, 'Lamar doesn't work. He's in sports,'" Hunt said to me, in his light Texas drawl. "I see it somewhat differently. I approach sports as a business. I've always been fascinated by sports, so most of the time I find my business relaxing and enjoyable. When it gets wearing and I need a change of pace, then I fall back on my hobbies—antiques and working around the yard."

Hunt runs his sports enterprises from an office on the twenty-ninth floor of the First National Bank Building, a fifty-story skyscraper. It is the tallest building in Dallas and is trimmed with nine stripes, running from top to bottom, that light up at night. (Members of the Hunt family rent nine floors of the building for their various business interests.) On a clear day, you can see the purlieus of Fort Worth, thirty-five miles away, from Hunt's office, and almost every day you are aware of airplanes roaring by overhead—one about every five minutes —on their way to or from Love Field, the airport for Dallas and Fort Worth. What you are most conscious of, however, is the unpretentiousness of Hunt's setup. There is a small reception room, decorated with a few subdued paintings, among them a watercolor of "Penrod Rig No. 32 Drilling for Sinclair McElroy Ranch, Upton Co., Texas, May, 1951." In the office proper, which is about eighteen feet by twenty, Hunt works at a large antique wooden desk of the type called a partners' desk, whose two opposite sides are identical, drawer for drawer. It came from a bank in London. The rest of the furnishings are a bulky overstuffed tan couch, two small leather-covered chairs, and an ornately carved wooden chest that appeared in several M-G-M movies and was acquired when the studio auctioned off a selection of old props and costumes. Hunt is an incorrigible collector and non-discarder, and the walls and shelves of his office are crammed with books, photographs of his wife and their children, team portraits, plaques, cups, citations and proclamations and awards, and autographed footballs that were used in important games. Hunt's secretary thinks that the best word for the office décor is eclectic, and he is inclined to agree with her.

Hunt, who is thirty-nine, is a stockily built, thick-necked man about five feet ten. His face is round, his hair dark brown, his forehead high, his eyes gray-blue, his nose snubbish, and his mouth wide, and he wears glasses that give him the owlish, ministerial look of a young Branch Rickey. He is a good athlete himself. At The Hill School, in Pennsylvania, he was a halfback on the football team, but when he went on to Southern Methodist University he was shifted to end. He played third base on The Hill baseball team and on the S.M.U. freshman team, but then gave up baseball. Although he is a fairly accomplished golfer, he has been playing less golf than tennis the last few years, because his business affairs have kept him busy and it takes so much less time to get in a couple of sets of tennis than a round of golf. He has a court at home. For a rich Texan, he is a very conservative dresser. On the day I met him, he had on a gray suit, a plain blue shirt, and a plain maroon tie.

His style as an administrator is similarly quiet. For example, when W.C.T. has an important announcement to make, Hunt usually stays in the background while Mike Davies, the executive director, confers with the press or faces the television cameras. I found Hunt not only a very likable man but a far more impressive one than anything I had heard about him had led me to expect. Like the Rockefellers, who believe that not much gets done when money is handled loosely, and who try to make a fair return on even their essentially altruistic enterprises in order to insure their effective operation, Hunt is out to make money from his sports businesses. It pleases him that today all of them except the soccer team are in the black. At the same time, if making money were his main concern, he would not be frittering away his time with the likes of tangential sports. "What attracts me is building something up," he said during our talk. "If I were offered a chance to buy, say, the Cincinnati Reds or the New York Giants, I wouldn't be interested. My pleasure is starting from scratch and building something into both a financial and an artistic success."

Hunt has found it a lot tougher than he thought he would to build professional tennis into a significant, flourishing world sport. The crux of the difficulty has been that his view of what professional tennis is all about is entirely different from the view held by the I.L.T.F. and its component national associations. As Hunt sees it—and here the I.L.T.F. would agree with him—there was no professional tennis to speak of before the coming of open tennis, in 1968. Up till then, the pro game just about began and ended with "the tour," the annual safari that was run after the Second World War, first by Jack Kramer and later by a short-lived coöperative called the International Professional Tennis Players Association, in which a handful of name players moved across the United States and the other tennis-minded countries playing one-night stands before sparse crowds in shabby halls. Occasionally a formal tournament was arranged, but neither the prestige nor the prize money came to much. (At least one of these tournaments, the 1963 United States Professional Championship, went bankrupt, and the two finalists, Rosewall and Laver, received nothing for their brilliant performances beyond the plaudits of the gallery.) Looking at this comparative wasteland, Hunt felt that it offered a great opportunity for the creation of a new business. In the eyes of the officials of the I.L.T.F., however, all tennis is their preserve, and this includes professional tennis if they choose to make it their business—and since 1968 they have chosen to. Consequently, they have tended to regard Hunt, as they would any outside promoter, as an intruder, an interloper.

To touch briefly on the key points of its complicated operations, W.C.T. has thirty-three players under contract this year and is conducting twenty forty-five-thousand-dollar tournaments, spread around the world from Teheran to Toronto, with about half of them in this country. The eight players who amass the highest point totals in these events qualify for a hundred-thousand-dollar tournament in November that will decide the world's professional champion. The top W.C.T. players, such as Arthur Ashe, receive substantial annual guarantees from the organization. After all, Ashe, who joined W.C.T. last autumn, had been doing nicely as an Independent Pro (the new term for a Registered Player); his earnings from prize money alone in 1970 exceeded a hundred and forty thousand dollars. In addition to guaranteeing its contract players a certain income for the year, W.C.T. pays for their air travel. As you would expect, it helps organize the various tournaments on its schedule, usually contributing a percentage of the prize money but in a few instances contributing all of it. It shares in the gate receipts in proportion to its degree of participation. When its players appear in "outside" events, like Wimbledon or Forest Hills, where they receive from the tournament's expenses fund an amount equal to one-third of the prize money they win there, that money goes to W.C.T. This year, in competition with W.C.T.'s million-dollar tournament tour, the

I.L.T.F. has been running a far-flung million-and-a-half-dollar circuit, consisting of thirty-five tournaments and featuring a two-hundred-and-fifty-thousand-dollar Pepsi (Cola) Grand Prix, in which the players with the largest point totals at the end of the year will take home the largest checks and qualify for the Pepsi Masters tournament. This battle between W.C.T. and the I.L.T.F. has, of course, been wonderful for the players; some fellows who couldn't carry Tilden's racquet press are raking in more than he ever did. However, it has been a very expensive rivalry for the two organizations, reminiscent of the bonus battle between the two professional football leagues which led to their merger. The realization that this was bound to be the case prompted the I.L.T.F. and W.C.T. to undertake a series of meetings last November and December, first in London and then in Dallas, to see if they could iron out their difficulties. The meetings were resumed at Wimbledon this summer, and one of the chief items on the agenda then was the feasibility of setting up a unified world schedule that would permit W.C.T. and the I.L.T.F. to run their separate circuits and would also make the players with both groups available for the major championships and a number of other tournaments. The meetings continued to the last day of Wimbledon and then broke down utterly, leaving each party embittered and determined to go its own way, W.C.T. confident that it would survive the power struggle because it controls the world's best players, the I.L.T.F. equally confident of its future because it controls the big prestige championships and also because attractive young players of talent are always coming along.

What caused the collapse of the negotiations? "The I.L.T.F. really doesn't have any idea of what we're trying to do," Hunt said, with vigor, at one stage of our talk. "They're very much behind the times in certain ways. For instance, they feel that a player like Laver should be delighted to make twenty-five thousand dollars a year and should automatically play in all the traditional events. They want to protect all those traditional events whether or not they mean something anymore or have a chance for growth. If there's no reconciliation, the I.L.T.F. can keep us out of the tennis clubs of France, England, Sweden, and so on, but our organization, I believe, will do well here in the United States. This is where the arenas are. We may have to think, though, about building a modern outdoor tennis complex suitable for a great championship. Through it all, we must never lose sight of our goal, which is to hold a series of top-class professional tournaments around the world."

Hunt moves around a lot. Two days before I saw him, he had been in Baltimore to watch the preseason clash between the Colts and his Chiefs, and then he had gone on to Boston the next day for the final of the United States Professional Tennis Championship at Longwood. The day after I saw him, he was in Tulsa for a luncheon talk en route to the Hunt family ranch in Wyoming. That morning, I returned, by prearrangement, to the twenty-ninth floor of the First National Bank Building.

Whenever a visitor talks with Hunt, he is apt to be distracted by the memorabilia in his eclectically decorated office. The piece that made the sharpest impression on me was a golden bowl mounted on a globe ornamented with a pair of crossed tennis racquets. This was the Kramer Cup, put up by the professional players in the early nineteen-sixties and named for Jack Kramer. It was intended to be a sort of professional equivalent of the Davis Cup. The third, and last, Kramer Cup match was held in 1963—Australia won it for the third straight year. After that, the competition was abandoned and no one thought about the trophy again. Last year, Rosewall was cleaning out his garage in suburban Sydney when he came across the cup, and, not knowing what to do with it, he shipped it to W.C.T. headquarters. It has been a long time since any object connected with sport sent my imagination churning the way the Kramer Cup did—nothing could symbolize more dramatically the ambitious hopes that professional tennis has periodi- cally entertained and their Ozymandian mortality. Under Hunt, of course, the pro game has the best chance it has ever had to establish the permanence that has always eluded it, not only because he has the financial resources to see it through hard times but also because, as his record makes clear, he is a stayer. Besides, my guess is that he is far more devoted to the welfare of tennis than a good many of the wheel- horses of the "amateur" associations, who, after all, are the men who for years were responsible for the hypocrisy of "shamateurism," with one hand pointing pious fingers at the professional promoters who would sully their game, and with the other hand paying off the amateur stars under the table. In any event, there is no doubt there will always be professional tennis outside the domain of the I.L.T.F., and what we are all hoping is that the I.L.T.F. realizes how fortunate it is in having a man of Hunt's quality to deal with, and that it will delay no longer in sitting down with him to work out an equitable solution to their joint prob- lems. The last thing the game needs at the moment is a drawn-out war of attrition. Besides, after three years of incessant bickering about cor- porate fees, sanctions, synchronized scheduling, and the rest of it, ev- erybody is heartily sick of the business of tennis and longs to get back to the tennis of tennis.

THE EMERGENCE OF CHRIS EVERT

(1971)

*We had heard about her—how cool she was and how well she played
—but we still didn't know how good Chris Evert was until, at sixteen,
she went all the way to the semifinals in her first appearance at Forest
Hills. (I would think that what most of us particularly remember are
the two daring placements she hit in her second-round match against
Mary Ann Eisel when Miss Eisel held triple-match point.) Chris has
gone on to enjoy a remarkably successful career, but nothing she has
ever done has been more dramatic than her performance in 1971—
especially her play in the twelfth game of the second set in that second-
round match.*

The 1971 United States Championships will not go down as one of the
most glittering in the annals of American tennis. Quite the reverse, if
anything. They will be remembered for one thing, though—the debut
of Chris Evert. On the second day of the tournament, Miss Evert, a
slender sixteen-year-old Floridian, who had emerged the week before
as the heroine of the American victory over Great Britain in the Wight-

man Cup match, brought Forest Hills to life by beating Edda Buding, an experienced German player, 6–1, 6–0 in the first round. She had first come to public attention just about a year before, when she defeated both Françoise Durr and Margaret Court in a tournament at Charlotte. This past winter, when she invaded the big time in the Virginia Slims Masters at St. Petersburg, she defeated Miss Durr once more and then won from Mrs. King when a leg injury forced the latter to retire after they had split the first two sets. Since everyone wanted to have a look at Miss Evert, her match against Miss Buding was played in the stadium, and the large crowd was entranced by her poise, her concentration, and her solid, consistent ground strokes—her two-handed backhand in particular. The daughter of James Evert, a teaching professional who runs a large tennis complex in Fort Lauderdale, she has a vivid court personality. In addition to being pretty—she wears her brownish-blond hair parted in the middle and tied back in the contemporary fashion—she has the awesome tight-lipped self-possession that one associates with Helen Wills. This quality was very much in evidence when, two days after her first-round victory, she met Mary Ann Eisel, a seasoned internationalist with a good serve, a fast volley, and, generally, the kind of game that can beat a baseliner like Miss Evert, who rarely comes to net. After winning the first set, 6–4, Miss Eisel broke Miss Evert's serve in the eleventh game of the second set and, at 6–5, was serving for the match. She moved quickly to 40–love—triple-match point. Here Miss Evert made a thrilling stand. She saved the first match point by taking a hard first serve and ripping a flat backhand down the line for a clean placement. She saved the second match point by moving in on a shortish second serve and whipping a forehand crosscourt for another outright winner. She got to deuce when Miss Eisel double-faulted, but she was still far from out of the woods, and had to fight off three more match points before she succeeded in pulling the game out. She went on to win the set, in the tie-breaker game, 7–6. The last set came easily, for by then Miss Eisel was thoroughly disheartened. Miss Evert left the court to a roaring ovation. She had captured the imagination of the spectators —and the millions watching over national television—as no other young American player had in years. From that moment on, she was the tournament. I cannot remember attending a major tennis event where there was so little conversation about the men players. Every so often, someone would turn to someone else and say, "Okker seems to be playing well" or "Ashe's serve looks better to me this year," but that was about it. In fact, the only player, male or female, that anyone talked about was Chris Evert, and soon people weren't even bothering to identify her by name. Two fans would meet and one would say, "Didn't she play well!" and the other would respond, "Marvellously. Who does she play next?"

Miss Evert's next opponent was Miss Durr. Like Miss Evert, she has a comparatively weak service, which is struck with an awkward, hammer-the-nail stroke, and she, too, relies principally on her sureness at the baseline. After Miss Durr had taken the first set, 6–2, Miss Evert, hitting out with more power, gained control of the exchanges and won the next two sets without undue trouble, 6–2 and 6–3. Miss Durr had played her "down the middle"—that is, she had purposely kept returning the ball down the center of the court, to give Miss Evert the minimum amount of angle on her drives—and her fourth-round opponent, Lesley Hunt, a young Australian, played her the same way. In what was very much a repetition of the Durr match, Miss Evert, after another slow start, outsteadied her, 4–6, 6–2, 6–3. Now she was in the semifinals, up against Mrs. King, a three-time winner at Wimbledon and for the past decade the best American woman player. A baseliner like Miss Evert, who has the ability to keep hitting the ball over the net—and, moreover, to keep hitting it a good length—is tough to beat; indeed, it takes absolutely first-class tennis to do it. When Mrs. King is in top form, she is eminently capable of first-class tennis: she has a strong serve and the finesse to chip and dink her returns of service, to throw off an opponent's timing; her ground strokes are sound; and up front she is far and away the best volleyer in women's tennis. Her weakness is her temperament. She is apt to get up too high for certain matches, and if things go wrong early she finds it difficult to dismiss her choler and her chagrin and get back to business. There was little doubt that if Mrs. King could produce her best all-court game she would beat her young challenger. On the other hand, if she allowed herself to become emotionally distracted, anything could happen. It was years since a women's match at Forest Hills had created such a stir.

Mrs. King and Miss Evert met on a warm, sticky Friday afternoon before a tense, expectant crowd that almost completely filled the horseshoe stadium. Miss Evert, serving first, dropped the first three points but then won the next five to pull the game out. She did not seem nervous. Mrs. King did. Her first service game went somewhat similarly —she lost the first two points and then took the next four. Each held service in the next two games—deuced games marked by extended baseline rallies. In the fifth and sixth games, each again held service, but it was significant that Mrs. King took hers at love; coming to net far more often than she had at the outset, she won two points on very pretty volleys and the other two when Miss Evert, feeling the pressure, hit two forehands well out of court. Mrs. King was in full flight now. She won the next three games handily to take the set, 6–3, and, after sweeping the first three games of the second set, ran it out, 6–2. In truth, considering the high pitch of anticipation, the match was something of a letdown. Though Miss Evert was not at her best, she did not play badly. It was simply that Mrs. King played outstanding tennis. She did everything right. She served very well, keeping the ball deep and putting lots of spin on it. She prevented Miss Evert from finding her best rhythm by constantly varying the spin on her ground strokes—slicing one return and topspinning the next, and so on. She threw in a number of deft drop shots. In the forecourt, she got to everything and volleyed or smashed it away decisively. I have never seen her play a better match—certainly not in this country.

To return to Miss Evert. Throughout the tournament, the older hands at Forest Hills asked each other regularly how they thought she compared with Maureen Connolly. The comparison was irresistible, because the late Miss Connolly was a confirmed baseliner, like Miss Evert, and was sixteen when she came out of California in the summer of 1951 and carried off the first of her three consecutive national titles. To these she added three consecutive Wimbledon titles, and there is no knowing the record she might have compiled if her accident had not forced her to retire from competition when she was only twenty. For myself, I would say that Miss Connolly at sixteen was a somewhat more advanced player than Miss Evert: her serve, though hardly a feature of her game, was better, and she hit the ball harder and with more control off both sides. For that matter, it is by no means a certainty that Miss Evert will develop into an authentic champion. To begin with, there are many departments of her game that must be improved, and, furthermore, what any young athlete of exceptional promise goes on to achieve or fails to achieve depends on his character—how much of himself he is willing to expend to reach his goal. Only time will tell whether Miss Evert will become our next great woman player or whether that distinction will fall to, say, Marita Redondo, the gifted fifteen-year-old Californian who took a set from Miss Evert in this year's national Girls' Championship—or, possibly, to Miss Evert's sister Jeanne, now thirteen, who is the current national Girls Fourteen-and-Under champion, and who looks as if she might grow up into a bigger and stronger player. Regardless of what happens in later years, however, the 1971 championships will always be remembered as Chris Evert's tournament, just as the 1951 championships are remembered for Maureen Connolly's victory at sixteen, the 1923 championships for Helen Wills' victory at seventeen, and the 1904 championships for the victory of the sixteen-year-old Californian May Sutton, our first great woman player.

THE SUMMER OF 1972:
KRAMER, LAVER AND EMERSON,
NEWCOMBE, EVERT, HOPMAN

(1972)

This chapter consists mainly of five set pieces: a glimpse of Jack Kramer at John Gardiner's Tennis Ranch in Carmel Valley, California; Rod Laver and his old Queensland buddy Roy Emerson running a camp for adults close to the Presidential Range in New Hampshire; John Newcombe, perhaps the best player in the world at that time, at his tennis ranch for boys and girls just north of San Antonio, Texas; Jimmy Evert at the public courts he operates in Fort Lauderdale, Florida, working out with his four oldest children: Drew, Chris, Jeanne, and John; and Harry Hopman and Hy Zausner, the latter the founder of the school, happily sorting things out at the Port Washington Tennis Academy, on Long Island. What I hoped to achieve was an impressionistic picture of the tremendous tennis activity that had become a staple of the American summer.

Like no other sport, tennis seems to be forever in a state of flux and rearrangement. A dozen years ago, its general structure was so utterly different from what it is today that when you look back it is hard to recognize the old neighborhood. For example, back in 1960 our Davis

Cup team, which has held the Cup for these last four seasons without much trouble, was beaten in the penultimate round by, of all under-developed tennis nations, Italy. As if this weren't bad enough, Jack Kramer, who had been running professional tennis since 1952, then signed our two best young amateurs, Barry MacKay and Butch Buch-holz, even though they hadn't done anything to warrant their being courted—they hadn't even been able to beat the Italians. This made Kramer Public Enemy No. 1 in the eyes of most of the officials of the United States Lawn Tennis Association. Well, today Kramer is one of the U.S.L.T.A.'s fair-haired boys, as he has been ever since 1970, when he organized the Grand Prix tournament circuit, the tennis establish-ment's answer to the W.C.T. circuit. A sectional delegate from southern California, he is a member of the U.S.L.T.A.'s Executive Committee and, yes, a member of the Davis Cup Committee. To move back to 1960 again, if there was at that time any one foreigner whom every red-blooded American tennis fan hated above all others it was Harry Hop-man, the perennial nonplaying captain of the Australian Davis Cup team. After Hopman, who had captained the team in 1938 and 1939, returned to do so in 1950, he was so successful in developing faceless teen-agers into brilliant replacements for heroes who had turned pro-fessional that it was a rare occasion when we were able to interrupt the parade of Australian victories in Cup play. When Hopman finally stepped down, at the close of the 1969 season, he left behind one of the most astounding records of captaincy in the entire history of sports: during his twenty-two seasons, his teams won the Davis Cup sixteen times. Where, you ask, is this scourge of American tennis today? An-other hundred-and-eighty-degree turn. Hopman has become a perma-nent resident of the United States, and, as the head of the faculty at the Port Washington Tennis Academy, on Long Island, he is now teaching young Americans how to win. It is all so different. Rod Laver, Roy Emerson, and John Newcombe, three of Hopman's old boys, have also settled in our country: Laver in Corona del Mar, south of Los Angeles; Emerson next door to him in Newport Beach; and Newcombe in New Braunfels, deep in Texas.

Speaking of the Australians who have transplanted themselves to this country, at this juncture I think an outright digression is justified. There is no question that the finest match of the year was the Rosewall-Laver final in the W.C.T. Championship, played indoors at the hot, stuffy Moody Coliseum, in Dallas, on May 14th. In fact, many people who know their tennis well rate this match, which fortunately was televised in its entirety, as the finest they have ever seen. Rosewall was the eventual winner, 4–6, 6–0, 6–3, 6–7, 7–6. During the last half hour of the match, which ran three hours and thirty-five minutes, Rosewall, who at thirty-seven is nearly four years older than Laver, appeared to be on the verge of collapse, but he managed to keep going, and in the (twelve-point) tie-breaker game he summoned a final gasp of inspiration when he was trailing five points to three and swept the next four points. That afternoon, *both* players were in top form—which doesn't happen often in tennis—and, with neither having quite enough power to put the ball away or upset the other's timing, they went at it like two master fencers, attacking and parrying superbly, each bringing out the best in the other. You never saw so many beautifully played points! Here, for example, is how the second point in the tenth game of the fourth set went:

Rosewall served to Laver's forehand; Laver played a shallow drive down the middle, which Rosewall punched crosscourt and deep; Laver—remember he is a lefty—scurried over for it and sent up a high backhand lob, which Rosewall let bounce and then smashed somewhat tentatively back to Laver's backhand; Laver, moving fast to the ball, whipped it to Rosewall's forehand; Rosewall chopped it back, but when he tried to follow in to net behind the shot Laver caught him just past the service line with a blistering topspin drive; Rosewall brought off a great backhand volley, but Laver moved in on the short ball and cracked a forehand down the line; Rosewall somehow got to it, and returned it with a lunging forehand volley; then he darted back to the center of the court in time to half-volley Laver's next thrust, looping the ball just over the net; coming up fast, Laver shovelled a little shot down Rosewall's right sideline; Rosewall, having some time, for a change, resorted to the lob, on which he had perfect touch this day, and he hit a beauty deep to Laver's backhand corner; Laver answered the lob with a lob; Rosewall watched the ball bounce high near his right sideline, and then, with the utmost deliberation, smashed an overhead straight down the line for a placement. Whew! N.B.C., thank goodness, has the match on tape. They should show it to us once every year.

It is a fascinating place, the new, rich, complex, expanding world of tennis, and perhaps the best way to suggest its dimensions and its flavor is to present some of its aspects in a series of short scenes.

The place is John Gardiner's Tennis Ranch, in Carmel Valley, California. The time is mid-June, and the 1972 United States Open (Golf) Championship is taking place sixteen miles away at Pebble Beach. In the early evening, Jack Kramer is seated in a wrought-iron chair on the terrace discussing the day's play with his father and his son. Kramer has come up from Los Angeles, where he lives, to watch the Open. He is a very capable golfer—he plays to a 7 handicap—and, more than that, he has had a major investment in the game since 1952, when he became a silent partner in the Los Serranos Golf Club, a semi-public course in Chino. Nine years later, he bought out his two partners. Today, Los Serranos has thirty-six holes, and the Southern California Golf Association thinks enough of the two courses to have selected them as the site of the regional qualifying rounds for this year's state amateur championship.

Kramer is now fifty-one, but you never would guess it. His face is unlined, his hair has hardly a speck of gray in it, his eyes are clear, he has one chin, his stomach is flat, and, all in all, he looks only ten years or so older than he did in 1947, when, after winning Wimbledon and defending successfully at Forest Hills, he turned professional. Kramer's indecently youthful appearance is attributable, up to a point, to his penchant for keeping in shape, but it is clear to anyone observing him on the terrace chatting with his father and his son that inheritance also plays a strong part. David Kramer, his father, is a trim, brown-haired man of seventy-four who could easily pass for fifty-four. He is a retired engineer for the Union Pacific, who got into railroading in Las Vegas at the age of eleven, when he was hired to wake up the engineers, firemen, and switchmen. John Kramer, Jr., the second of Jack's sons (he has five), is a tall, slim, bespectacled young man who is starting his senior year at Cal Poly, in Pomona. He is twenty-two, but, the Kramers being what they are, he doesn't look a day over twenty-one.

He is an interesting fellow, Jack Kramer—a man of great charm and multiple talents. For example, few people who made their name in sports have later shown an aptitude for business comparable to his. Indeed, it used to be said of Kramer that his only failing as a business-man was that he was entirely too good a businessman. Be that as it may, with so much happening in tennis it was bound to be just a matter of time before a man with Kramer's entrepreneurial experience would be back in the thick of things. (He retired as the czar of pro tennis in 1962.) For months, two rumors about him had been going the rounds: one, that a sect within the U.S.L.T.A. was eager to back him for president of that organization; and, two, that, with a professional tennis players' association again in the throes of creation, he was the leading candidate for the top post. That evening at the tennis ranch, Kramer was mainly concerned with Jack Nicklaus' method of striking the ball, but last month, on the first Friday at Forest Hills, he made his move. He agreed to become chairman and chief executive of the new Association of Tennis Professionals.

The place is the Mount Washington Hotel, a long, rambling building that went up in Bretton Woods, New Hampshire, in 1902, when the marathon veranda was in vogue. In the distance, across a wooded valley, the Presidential Range—Mt. Washington (6,288 feet), with a supporting cast that includes Mt. John Adams, Mt. Jefferson, Mt. Madison, Mt. Monroe, Mt. John Quincy Adams, and a recent added starter, Mt. Eisenhower. Directly in front of the hotel, a small stream—the Ammonoosuc—and ten tennis courts. It is the second week in July, and a group of thirty or so adults attending the second Rod Laver Tennis Week have gathered at a central court at nine-thirty on a bright-blue morning. Laver is there along with Emerson, his old friend and doubles partner, and Sean Sloane, a young man who is the tennis coach at Williams College and the hotel's director of tennis. "Good morning, ladies and gentlemen," Sloane says to the group, which runs the gamut from beginners to accomplished club players. "The stroke we'll be working on this morning is the volley. Rod Laver will be conducting the clinic today, and, without further ado, I'll turn things over to Rod."

Laver brushes some wisps of marmalade-colored hair off his forehead and steps forward, racquet in hand. "The volley requires only a short backswing and no follow-through at all. You should feel like you're hitting the ball way out in front. As the ball comes toward you, you cross your front foot over toward it, and at the same time your foot comes down you're hitting the ball. On the volley, always figure on being side-on to the net. If you can't move your feet fast enough to get into that position, at least pivot the top of your trunk." Speaking slowly and taking ample time to demonstrate his points, Laver talks for ten minutes on various aspects of volleying. The students then move onto the courts, and Laver, Emerson, Sloane, and four young men and a young woman from Sloane's Williams tennis teams circulate among them, rallying with them and, as they do so, calling out corrections and stopping to illustrate the players' errors and to push them into proper position—the whole arduous process of instruction.

As a general thing, when stars of the first magnitude lend their names to some promotion in the world of entertainment or sports, the most they do is to make a token appearance on the opening day or night, waving a genial hand to their admirers and then vanishing. Frequently, they don't even do that much. I mention this because Laver and Emerson are such remarkable exceptions. At Bretton Woods, they are on the courts teaching each morning from nine-thirty to twelve-thirty and each afternoon from two-thirty to five-thirty. I really cannot remember ever before seeing two athletes of the top international class give as much of themselves to what might be described as transient pupils—a new group arrived at Bretton Woods each Sunday and left on the following Saturday. (At three hundred dollars for room, meals, and instruction, this is one of the bargains of our time.) Emerson and Laver could not be less alike in makeup. Laver, a man of retiring disposition, never has much to say. When he is teaching, he relies mainly on short, crisp injunctions: "Watch that ball. Stay level." "Don't open up too quickly." "Keep that wrist firm when you hit that volley." Emerson, a flamboyant extrovert, who seems to like everyone, is a born teacher. As he moves around the court, his mouth set in a wide jack-o'-lantern grin beneath his longish nose and his sleek black hair, he releases a stream of colorful exhortations: "Move. You could've got there and still had a rest." "Get that elbow up on your serve. Tighten that bolt." "My grandmother could have made that shot with a frying pan." The two men, who are both from Queensland, have the same kind of background. Emerson grew up on a dairy ranch in a village in the outback called Blackbutt, and Laver, whose father raised cattle, grew up in the small town of Rockhampton, three hundred and twenty-five miles up the coast from Brisbane. They first met at a tournament in Brisbane in 1953, when Laver was fifteen and Emerson a year and a half older, and they are devoted to each other.

As most Americans are only too well aware, the domination the Australians have exercised over our players, and others, in the postwar era has depended at least as much on superior physical conditioning as on superior tennis ability. They simply outwork us. Accordingly, I was not really surprised when, at the end of his long day of teaching, Laver, who was getting ready to rejoin the tournament circuit (Emerson would be remaining at Bretton Woods all summer), stayed on the court for a special form of tuneup that the Australians call a Workout. Facing Emerson and Sloane, who were up at net slapping shot after shot back at him, Laver ranged along the baseline for forty minutes, practicing all his ground strokes, running for everything, never resting. He then practiced serving for fifteen minutes. After that, he and Emerson played nine holes of golf. They did it in under an hour, jogging to and from their electric cart between shots. After dinner, Laver relaxed with his wife and young son, but Emerson, as usual, had energy to burn, and, starting at ten-thirty, he put on an hour-long floor show in the hotel lounge. He told a few jokes and, in a very presentable baritone, rambled through a motley selection of songs that included "Twilight Time," "Rollin' on the River," "Hava Nageela," and, necessarily, "Tie Me Kangaroo Down, Sport" and "Waltzing Matilda." Then he was ready to call it a day.

The T-Bar-M Tennis Ranch is situated four miles from the wooden bandstand in downtown New Braunfels, a German settlement thirty miles northeast of San Antonio. This is the Texas hill country—gently rolling land dotted with live oaks and cedars and with outcroppings of orange-brown rock. In early August, when the second (and last) two-week session of John Newcombe's Tennis Camp convenes at the ranch, nearly every morning a heavy layer of low-lying clouds covers the wide sky, but by ten o'clock the sun has burned them away and is pouring down barbarously. The temperature, which seldom dips below eighty-five during the day, often gets up into the middle nineties, and while you can usually rely on a breeze from the southeast to help things out, it never really expels the resident humidity. However, the hundred-odd campers—boys and girls between the ages of eight and sixteen—seem oblivious of the heat and stickiness. At six o'clock in the evening, after four hours on the courts in the morning, working on the mechanics of the game—how to move the ball, how to hit the ball, where to hit the ball—and three hours in the afternoon, playing singles and doubles, they appear incredibly fresh when they assemble for the Circuit Run, the final event of the day, under a massive peaked roof that covers four "indoor" courts. The explanation for this, as Newcombe sees it, is that his camp attracts the hard-core tennis players—kids who take the game seriously and never get enough of it. Most of them have come to the camp (which, incidentally, costs three hundred and fifty dollars for the two-week session) because they have set their hearts on becoming good enough to make their school team. Most of them already hit the ball very, very impressively.

The amount of teaching that Newcombe himself does varies from day to day, depending on the other demands on his time, but he is always on hand for the Circuit Run—the name he uses for a composite of thirty minutes of exercises, which both the girls and the boys do, and a cross-country run, which is meant for the boys but is open to the girls. From Rockhampton to Perth, no Australian is higher on the importance of keeping fit than Newcombe, a broad-shouldered, lithe six-footer from Sydney, who started to exercise systematically in gymnasiums at the age of eleven. Standing between the nets in the narrow lane separating two courts, equidistant from all the campers, who are divided into four groups to add the zest of team competition ("Wimbledon," "France," "Australia," and the "United States"), he leads them through such staples as straddle jumps, deep breathing, trunk twists, and knee bends, plus such Down Under specialties as running in place very fast with the knees up high, springing high in the air with the feet together, sprinting in place in a crouched position, and bringing the knees up to the chest while jumping. Each exercise is followed by twenty seconds or so of jogging in place to keep the action continuous. At the conclusion of the last exercise, Newcombe excuses the girls and, calling out, "Are you ready, boys?," takes off at a good fast trot down the side of a hill, up the side of another hill, along a lengthy ridge punctuated with live oaks, and then, reversing his route, back to the courts under the big peaked roof. The campers, strung out behind him in a long white line, stay with his pace fairly well, and, surprisingly, at the finish of the run—a good mile and a quarter—only a few of them are breathing hard. (There was a rock dance that night after dinner, and they took that comfortably in stride, too.)

An intelligent, well-rounded man of twenty-eight, who is the son of a dentist, Newcombe currently spends six months of the year on the tournament tour, two months in Australia, and the remaining four at the tennis ranch, where he and his wife and two young children live in a contemporary-style house. He is associated in the T-Bar-M with Clarence Mabry, who has been the tennis coach at Trinity University, in San Antonio, since 1956, and whose 1972 team won the National Intercollegiate Championship. Five years ago, when Mabry needed a new site for the summer tennis camp he had run since the nineteen-fifties, he formed a syndicate to buy the T-Bar-M, a hundred-and-fifteen-acre dude ranch that had seen better days. The following year, Newcombe happened to be looking for a base of operations, and he and Mabry, who had known each other for some time, worked out their present arrangement. They have made a number of improvements on the property— it now has twenty-four tennis courts and an air-conditioned dormitory for the summer campers—and they recently acquired an adjoining parcel of a hundred acres, on which they plan to build condominiums grouped around additional courts. During the autumn, winter, and spring (you can play outdoor tennis in that part of Texas the year round), the T-Bar-M caters mainly to adult guests, but, of course, it is busiest in the summer months, when the kids pour in for the two two-week sessions of Newcombe's camp, three one-week sessions of Newcombe's camp, three one-week sessions of Mabry's Texas Tennis Camp, and a series of week-long camps run by various tennis organizations that rent the ranch's facilities. "This past June, Clarence and I saw we had one week open this summer," Newcombe told me during my visit. " 'Why don't we have a Tony Roche Tennis Camp that week?' I said. Tony, you know, is my doubles partner and one of my oldest friends, and he's always at the ranch when he isn't playing tournaments. Within three weeks, the Tony Roche Tennis Camp was completely sold out. That's a sign of the times, isn't it?"

The Tennis Supervisor for the city of Fort Lauderdale is Jimmy Evert, a strong-featured, graying, solidly built man of forty-nine, who has held that post for twenty-four years but has recently become better known even in his own bailiwick as the father of Chris Evert. During the summer months, Evert regularly arrives at his office, in the Holiday Park Tennis Center, at eight-thirty in the morning and leaves at seven-thirty. Among other things, he checks on the maintenance of twenty clay courts, runs tournaments, works with a staff of three teaching pros, and teaches three hours daily himself. All this is usually out of the way by six o'clock, and then he is free to spend an hour or so working with his children: Drew, a tall, husky young man of nineteen, who entered Auburn this fall on a tennis scholarship; Chris, now approaching eighteen, who won her first national women's title, the United States Clay Courts Championship, this summer; Jeanne, a pleasant, outgoing girl of fourteen, who at thirteen was the national Girls Fourteen-and-Under champion, and who astonished everyone last winter by defeating Rosemary Casals, one of the top women professionals, in an open tournament at Fort Lauderdale; and John, eleven, who is ranked fourth in Florida in the twelve-and-under division but who could well move up to first this year, since the three boys ahead of him will have turned thirteen. The fifth and youngest child, Clare, now four, will doubtless be swinging into action before long, for Evert likes to start his kids off when they are five and a half or six.

On this particular day in mid-August, Evert has departed slightly from routine: a local doctor has had to cancel his four-thirty lesson, so at that hour Evert has taken eleven-year-old John out to Court 10 to see how he is hitting the ball. A good-looking towhead, John is just getting back into action after breaking a small bone in his right hand four weeks before when he fell on the court while practicing. There certainly seems to be no vestige of the injury—not from the way John is busting the ball across the net. Like his sisters, he uses a two-handed backhand, but there is one minor difference: he takes his left hand off the racquet the instant after impact. He hits the ball equally hard off both sides, but the most remarkable thing about him, as it is about all the Everts, is the length he gets: eight out of every ten shots land between the service line and the baseline. His father, wearing a floppy white hat with a wide brim, moves along the opposite baseline droning a steady patter of instruction: "You don't have to hit it hard, boy. Just step into it." "Keep moving those feet." "Nice, firm wrist on that shot, kid. You didn't whip it over." A half hour of this and then a breather. It is a hot, heavy afternoon, with hardly a lick of air stirring the palm trees in Holiday Park—a large municipal park, in which the tennis complex is just one of many sports and entertainment facilities.

A little after five, Chris and Jeanne, followed within a few minutes by Drew, arrive at Court 10. The Everts seldom assemble like this, but this afternoon a photographer for the Boca Raton *News* has come down to take some group shots as well as some individual ones. (The children's mother, Mrs. Colette Evert, plays tennis, but not in competitions.) This over, back to business. Evert, standing on one side of the net with Drew, rallies with Chris while Drew rallies with Jeanne, and then the other way round. When Evert is called to the office, Drew plays some one-on-two with the girls; returning, Evert coaches Jeanne first, then Chris, on their overhead and volley. Both girls then work on their serve, each hitting three baskets of fifty balls. By then, it is nearly seven, and Evert signals that this practice session—the third workout of the day for both girls—is over. During the summer, he likes them to get in four hours of practice daily, but he is by no means a slave driver. He makes it clear to his children that each of them is free to work just as hard as he or she chooses. In return, he tries to match each one's degree of dedication. Since one of the most difficult things in tennis is to teach one's own kids how to play the game, Evert's success would seem to argue that he is an exceptionally good instructor.

Evert has been in tennis since he was eleven, when he became a ball boy for George O'Connell, the professional at the Chicago Town and Tennis Club. He was nationally ranked third as a junior, went to Notre Dame on a tennis scholarship, played at Forest Hills five times as an amateur, and turned pro in 1948, when he learned of the opening in Fort Lauderdale. He looks back with special affection on the summer of 1947. "At the close of the school year, our college team went on a trip on which we played a tournament a week," he told me. "I still remember the itinerary: Chicago, Tulsa, L.A., Salt Lake City, Tacoma, Seattle, Vancouver, Milwaukee, and then east to Forest Hills. In Vancouver, I won the biggest title of my career, the Canadian Championship. But it was the whole atmosphere of the trip—the great people you met. I always hoped my kids would take to tennis, so that they'd have a chance to enjoy the same wonderful experiences the game opened up for me."

Late August, two days before the start of Forest Hills, and one of those mornings when you first detect a faint whiff of autumn in the air, or like to think you do. Harry Hopman, driving down a side road in Port Washington, about twenty miles from Manhattan, swings onto the blacktop parking lot before the clustered buildings and the fourteen courts that form the campus of the Port Washington Tennis Academy. Hopman got back to the Academy only yesterday, after spending six weeks in Amherst running the Harry Hopman Tennis Camp plus another four weeks there co-running the Harry Hopman–Nick Bollettieri Tennis Camp. At sixty-six, he looks the same as ever: same pale-blue eyes, same shining pinkish skin, same sandy hair. Same youthful figure, too, which is no more than one expects of the man who practically invented the concept of training hard for tennis. As he walks through the crowded lounge of the Academy's main building, a middle-aged man compliments him on his trimness. "I got up to a hundred and fifty pounds last winter and I had to do something about it," Hopman replies, with a pleased smile. "Up in Amherst, I lost the first four pounds doing sit-ups. And then I missed so many meals my belt went from thirty-four to thirty-one. When I weighed myself yesterday, the scales ticked over at one thirty-six."

Hopman makes his way to an indoor court, where his associate, Hy Zausner, the founder of the Academy, is beginning the onerous chore of testing five hundred and fifty of a total of seven hundred junior players—eighteen and under—enrolled for the 1971–72 season, in order to determine what class they belong in: Intermediate, Advanced, or one of the five different levels into which the top class, the Junior Championship Program, is divided. (The remaining hundred and fifty juniors are Beginners and don't need to be looked at.) Hopman and Zausner confer briefly, Zausner turns the job of testing over to one of the Academy's professionals, and he and Hopman retire to a relatively quiet office to discuss their plans for the upcoming term. A white-haired, bespectacled New Yorker with a quiet step and a soft voice, Zausner is about the same age as Hopman, but they are so completely different in background and personality that the tennis set in Port Washington likes to refer to them as the Odd Couple. Zausner is as remarkable in his way as Hopman. After graduating from Brooklyn Law School, he went into his father's business, Zausner Foods—one of the country's major manufacturers of cream cheeses and puddings—but he left after a year to start his own cheese-importing company, which he named Flora Danica, because most of the cheeses it handles come from Denmark. Today, not only is Flora Danica the leading importer of cheeses in the United States but its brand of Danish blue is carried by every major grocery-store chain in the country and outsells all its competitors. Somehow or other, Zausner manages to run this global business from his home, in Sands Point, with the aid of only a secretary. (In actuality, he runs it from his office at the Academy.) He got into tennis at the age of fifty-nine when his oldest son, watching him play handball on his private court, suggested that he switch to some less strenuous diversion, like golf. Zausner switched to tennis, and, flinging himself into the game, set up the Academy—two courts and a patchy little clubhouse to begin with. From the start, the raison d'être of the Academy has been to get boys and girls pointed in a healthful direction, or, as Zausner puts it, "We're out to get the kids hooked on tennis." At the Academy, a nonprofit institution, seventy-five per cent of the total court time is set aside for junior players. The tuition is extremely low, and there are a hundred scholarships for promising and needy youngsters. In order to attract and keep top-quality instructors, Zausner guarantees his pros a minimum salary of eighteen thousand dollars a year, and the industrious ones can earn close to double that amount. Hopman, of course, supervises the teaching staff as well as the curriculum. The present composition of the staff reflects his international orientation, being made up of three Americans, three Australians, two Chileans, one Peruvian, one Mexican, one Indian, one Nigerian, and one Rumanian.

When Hopman came to this country, in 1970, he was overwhelmed with offers. The reason he elected to go to the Academy was that he wanted to work with young players and Zausner's junior program appealed strongly to him. This revealed a side of Hopman most Americans had never suspected existed. For us, he had always been the old fox, the cold old fox. We had seen him principally in those infrequent years when the Australians came over to try and wrest back the Davis Cup, and, with that on his mind, he had had little to say and no time for anybody but his team. Over the past two years, he has shown himself to possess unexpected humor, warmth, and spontaneity—this complicated man, the son of a Sydney schoolmaster, who first came to attention as a doubles specialist on the Australian Davis Cup teams in the late nineteen-twenties, who in 1932 moved to Melbourne, where he made his tennis headquarters at the famous Kooyong Club, and who did all his tennis coaching as an amateur while supporting himself by writing sports for the Melbourne *Herald* and, much later on, by working as a stockbroker.

The best way to grasp the essential Hopman, of course, is to listen to him talk. Here he is at the end of a long day at the Academy, roving around on one of his favorite subjects, physical fitness: "I became a devotee of roadwork when I was just a young fellow. Then, after the war, in helping young Australian players, I became convinced that one of the most useful forms of running is a series of hundred-and-fifty-yard sprints—fifteen yards jogging, a thirty-yard burst at top speed, another fifteen yards of jogging, another burst, and so on. I always tried to find a hotel for my teams that would put us close to some good place for running. In London, we used to stop at the Kensington Palace Hotel, right across the road from Kensington Park. There were several flat stretches there where the boys could do those sprints, and when you wanted to go for a long run you were right next to Hyde Park. . . . Our fitness program really started with Frank Sedgman. He was a tall, skinny lad, and I sent him to a gymnasium to build himself up. In twenty months, he put on twenty pounds. I was also coaching him at Kooyong, and when he won the Australian Championship in 1949 and 1950, that made me look like I knew what I was doing, and I was given the captaincy of our Cup team again. . . . Relaxation is one of my pet themes. During a match, when the players changed courts every second game, I'd take the racquet out of my player's hand as he came by and I'd say to him something like 'Just breathe deeply.' Maybe he was already breathing deeply, having just been in a fierce rally, but if you tell him to do something it takes his mind off the game for a moment and lets him relax."

CUPA DAVIS

⸺⬤⸺

(1972)

It was the frenzied atmosphere at the Davis Cup match at Bucharest that one remembers most of all—the spectators shouting so wildly for the Rumanian players that the actual tennis seemed to matter little to them; the local linesmen viewing it as a patriotic duty to call any Rumanian shot close to the lines "in" and any American shot close to the lines "out"; the whole Challenge Round, in truth, almost a travesty. Under the strange pressure at Progresul, the American team could easily have lost, but Nastase folded against Smith in their singles on the first day, inexplicably; Erik van Dillen, so long a chronic disappointment, justified his entire career with his inspired play in the doubles; and Smith on the third day played a courageous fifth set against Tiriac to win the deciding point. But it was all hard work at Bucharest.

The Progresul Sports Club, the scene of the final-round match of the 1972 Davis Cup competition—Rumania versus the United States—is situated about two miles from University Square, a broad expanse in the center of Bucharest bordered not only by the fine classical-revival build-

ings of the University of Bucharest but also by the new Hotel Inter-
Continental Bucharest, a twenty-four-story pile of masonry in the shape
of a super Fontainebleau Hotel. To get to the Progresul Sports Club
from the square, you cross Boulevard Balcescu and take a right down
Boulevard Gheorge Gheorghiu-Dej, a wide avenue thick with red-and-
white streetcars and buses, and lined, as most of the city's streets are,
with linden and chestnut trees. You follow the boulevard past the
equestrian statue of Michael the Brave (1558–1601) and the feet-on-the-
ground statue of a more modern hero, Spiru C. Haret, a mathematician
and former Minister of Education; past the imposing Central House of
the Army; on past bookshops, cafés, camera shops, half a dozen movie
houses, an assortment of municipal buildings, and the lovely Cismigiu
Park, with salvia, begonias, asters, and dahlias bordering its long vistas;
and, finally, on past a stretch of ochre and gray apartment houses, five
or six stories high, to Opera Square and the new opera house, completed in 1953. There you turn left onto a narrow residential street called
Costache Negri, and a quarter of a mile ahead, its main entrance flanked
by tall eucalyptus trees, lies the Progresul Sports Club, an impressive
complex consisting of three soccer fields, two basketball courts, a field-
hockey field, a volleyball court, and eight clay tennis courts. What is
called the stadium court—it is set apart from the others—is surrounded
by stands that have recently been enlarged to hold six thousand spectators. On the afternoons of October 13th, 14th, and 15th, when the Davis
Cup final took place there, every seat was filled, the aisles were clogged,
and the entranceways were bursting with standees. For weeks, Bucharest had been talking about nothing but the big match, and no wonder.
Not only was it the most important athletic engagement with the West
in Rumanian history but, more than that, it was quite probably the most
significant East-West sports confrontation ever held behind the Iron
Curtain, far surpassing, because of the immense prestige of the Davis
Cup, the previous encounters in track and field and in ice hockey.
Throughout the match, the air at Progresul was heavy with tension. Just
about the only people in the area who kept their cool were the city
street-sweepers—middle-aged and elderly women clad in orange
smocks, who quietly continued to sweep the autumn leaves off the
nearby streets with brooms made of twigs bound together.

The Davis Cup, inaugurated in 1900, ranks as one of the oldest
attempts to further friendships between countries through sports.
Though it is hard to believe, Australia and the United States have so
dominated play in recent decades that the meeting in Bucharest this
October marked the first time in thirty-five years that a Davis Cup
final had been staged in Europe. This year brought another change.

From its inception through 1971, the format of the competition called for the nation that held the Cup to stand off to one side the following season while the hopeful contenders battled it out for the honor of meeting the defender in the Challenge Round—which, by the way, was always played in the defender's country. However, in a very generous move, the United States, the victor in the Challenge Round from 1968 on, agreed to a plan whereby, beginning in 1972, the defending nation would have to enter the elimination rounds, just like everybody else, the idea being that this might add a helpful pinch of spice to the old stew. It did. This year, after defeating Jamaica, Mexico, and Chile without much trouble, the American team, up against Spain in the semifinal round, in Barcelona, just got in by the skin of its teeth—three points to two. In the other semifinal, Rumania, which had made its way past Switzerland, Iran, Italy, and the Soviet Union, eliminated Australia, 4–1, in Bucharest. Since we had played our semifinal *away* from home and the Rumanians had played theirs *at* home, some of our tennis parliamentarians contended that under the hazily worded statutes of the revised Davis Cup format we were entitled to hold the final in our country. This provoked a terrific howl from Rumania, and with good reason, too. As the Rumanian spokesmen pointed out, in 1969 their team had come to the States and played the Challenge Round in Cleveland—played it, moreover, on a very fast asphaltic-composition surface of a kind that neither of the Rumanians had ever played on until two weeks before the match. Rumanians, like all Continental Europeans, are clay-court specialists. We won 5–0 that year. In 1971, when Rumania again qualified for the Challenge Round, we took them to Charlotte, North Carolina. This time, we did relent a trifle, playing the match on clay, though on a much harder and faster type of clay than is common in Europe, where, if one can believe the stories one hears, there is usually a very thick layer of spongy clay and soft sand between the surface and the first evidence of the crushed-rock base, or whatever porous material is used for a base. In any event, Charlotte produced a much closer match; we scraped through, 3–2. This autumn, the prospect of being maneuvered by legal chicanery into playing yet another final in the United States particularly enraged the veteran two-man Rumanian team of Ion Tiriac and Ilie Nastase. It was Rumania's turn to hold the final, they asserted. They said they wouldn't play if the match was not held in Rumania, and they said it as if they meant it. The United States Lawn Tennis Association thought the matter over carefully and at length decided that, O.K., Bucharest it would be. Things then began to happen fast. Two weeks before the opening day of the final,

Dennis Ralston, the captain of the American team, flew his charges to Paris, so that they would have ample time to shake off the effects of jet lag and get used to European clay. Ten days or so before the match, he took them on to Bucharest, so that they could get the feel of the deep red clay at Progresul. By that time, the windows of dozens of stores in Bucharest were filled with photographs of the ranking national heroes, Nastase and Tiriac.

Friday, the first day of the Finala of the Cupa Davis (the Rumanian language, surprisingly, has a Latin base), brought a cloudless blue sky and weather so balmy that the male spectators soon discarded their jackets. The way the draw had worked out, in the opening singles, scheduled to start at eleven o'clock, Nastase, the current United States Open Champion and the Rumanian No. 1, would be facing Stan Smith, the current Wimbledon Champion and the American No. 1; in the second singles, it would be Tiriac against Tom Gorman, the latter having been selected over Harold Solomon, who had played the second singles for us against Chile and Spain. (In the Davis Cup, as every tennis fan knows from the time he is old enough to distinguish between "rough" and "smooth," the doubles match takes place on the second day, and on the third day there are the two concluding singles, the players switching opponents.) Before the draw had been made, the betting had favored Rumania, but the feeling in Bucharest after the draw was that America's chances had been considerably enhanced, since Nastase would probably have preferred to meet Gorman first, and not Smith. During the last eighteen months, Smith, a tall (six-four), blond twenty-five-year-old Californian, has gained a good deal of maturity. As he demonstrated in defeating Nastase at Wimbledon in a final that could have gone either way, he stands up very well under pressure—and there is no greater pressure in tennis than representing one's country in the Davis Cup. A victory by Smith over Nastase in the opening match could be pivotal, because, in the final analysis, Rumania's chances depended largely on Nastase's being in such brilliant form that he would take both his singles and combine with Tiriac to take the doubles. However, with Nastase nothing is ever certain. The son of a Bucharest bank teller, he is an emotional, mercurial young man of twenty-six. On some days he is capable of the most inspired kind of whirling, imaginative shotmaking and on others he performs with a weird listlessness, his thoughts apparently kilometres away from tennis.

The Progresul Sports Club was all decked out for the big day. Up above, along the east, south, and west sides of the stadium, the flags of fifty-odd nations fluttered in the breeze. On the north side, a line of Rumanian flags—handsome blue, yellow, and red tricolors—waved above a large rendering of the national coat of arms, a busy design that features a red star above a multirayed sun, some green forests and pinkish mountains, and an oil derrick, all framed by encircling sheaves of wheat. There were a few commercial notes: at the foot of the stands, banners advertised Martini, Marlboro, and the Assicurazione Ausonia, an insurance company, while the cloths draped over the cold-drink facilities provided for the players bore the trademark of S. Pellegrino mineral water. Perched in the umpire's chair, we had an official of the Rumanian Tennis Federation. Calling the lines, we had Rumanian linesmen—a final quashing of the persistent rumor that the U.S.L.T.A. had insisted on neutral linesmen to guard against overly patriotic decisions, which, under the stress of Davis Cup pressure, have been known to happen not only in Rumania but in most European countries. Completing the cast, a referee—Enrique Morea, a tall, dignified veteran internationalist from Argentina—was seated at mid-court, next to the umpire's elevated chair. In the mid-nineteen-sixties, in an effort to keep things under control, the Davis Cup nations ordained that in Cup play—provided both teams agreed to it—there should be a referee from a neutral nation who would have the power to overrule or confirm a decision by the umpire or a linesman. On with the match.

Nastase, it was soon evident, was in a nervous mood. A lean young man with long black hair and the look of a bony Joe Namath, he was not covering court with his customary speed, and there was no sharpness to his strokes. Smith broke his serve in the sixth game, but three games later, when Smith was serving for the set, Nastase suddenly snapped to life and broke him back with a succession of crisp attacking shots. The stands erupted in appreciation, chanting "Na-sta-se!" in unison after each winning thrust. When Nastase then held service to tie the set at 5–5, the chanting became louder, backed by heavy rhythmic clapping. Both men were now playing beautiful tennis. In the thirteenth game, Nastase saved two set points, to the loudest chanting yet. In the seventeenth game, he broke Smith's service. Delirious chanting. And then, serving for the set, Nastase, inexplicably, seemed to lose his concentration. He let three games drift away with unforced errors and presented the set to Smith, 11–9. In effect, he presented him with the match, for once Smith was safely past the first set he really opened up. He served with explosive power, he blasted Nastase's serve for outright winners, and he ranged swiftly around the forecourt, hitting one biting volley after another. While the clay at Progresul turned out to be a bit faster than we had been led to expect, I have never seen a man hit his shots on clay with the pace that Smith maintained in winning the next two sets, 6–2 and 6–3. He played exactly as if he were playing on grass —fast grass.

Progresul cannot offer you strawberries with Devonshire cream, as Wimbledon does, but it had made excellent preparations for the gala occasion. In the twenty-minute interval before the start of the second singles, the tennis crowd moved around the grounds buying cold meats and pickles, sausages, midget frankfurters, beer, and soda pop, and there were two garden cafés where fancier food and drink was obtainable. At a number of souvenir shops, crowds lined up to buy racquet covers, tablecloths, lighters, drinking glasses, shoulder bags, T-shirts, silk scarves, and chocolate bars, all imprinted with the glamorous legend "Cupa Davis, Bucuresti '72." Whatever else they were doing, they were all discussing Nastase's disappointing showing. The explanations covered a wide range of views. (a) The pressure of the Davis Cup had again been too much for him. The year before, at Charlotte, he had played a remarkably similar opening match against Smith. After dropping the first five games, he had rallied to sweep the next five, and had then collapsed totally. (b) Nastase, many Rumanians felt, could not get "up" for the match, because it did not mean enough to him. In their opinion, he had become too Westernized over the last four years and wasn't spending enough time at home. (c) Fred Perry, the great English player, and other veteran observers felt that the Rumanian Tennis Federation should have ordered Nastase back to Bucharest immediately after his victory at Forest Hills in mid-September. That way, he would have had time for a good rest before preparing himself for the Cup match. Instead, Nastase had stayed on in the United States for two more tournaments, and was physically and psychologically run-down when he finally arrived home. That was the player we had seen.

The Gorman-Tiriac singles started out as if it would be short work for the American, a burly, pleasant all-round athlete from Seattle University (Class of 1968), who has been a semifinalist both at Wimbledon and at Forest Hills. In winning the first set, 6–4, and the second, 6–2, Gorman led off each time by breaking Tiriac's opening service. In the third set, impatient to wrap it up, he began hurrying his shots, and before he realized it he had lost the set, 4–6, and had let Tiriac back in the match. That is always a dangerous thing to do, even though Tiriac's talent for tennis has conspicuous limitations. A big, ponderous, hunch-shouldered man of thirty-three, he is very slow afoot. While he has an adequate spin service, his overhead is erratic, and his ground strokes are ordinary, his backhand especially—an ungainly inside-out push on which he either slices the ball or pulls it at the last instant with a quick twist of the wrist. As John Newcombe, the Australian star, has put it, "You always feel you should walk right through Tiriac, but he's much tougher to beat than you think." One reason is that Tiriac is a very experienced competitor; he has played top-level Rugby and basketball, and he was a member of Rumania's Olympic ice-hockey team in 1964. In addition to all this, he is a tenacious fighter and, depending on how you look at it, one of the most resourceful or one of the most disgraceful gamesmen in all sport. He has the look of a "heavy," all right. His hair is a mass of Brillo that droops in a sort of Transylvanian Prince Valiant style. Beneath beetle brows, his eyes slant downward, giving him a mien both dolorous and forbidding. The rest of his face is overpowered by a thick black Fu Manchu mustache. Tiriac comes from Brasov, north-west of Bucharest, where his father was a clerk in the mayor's office. He himself, one hears from time to time, is a member of the secret police. Anyway, he speaks eight languages and is straight out of Eric Ambler.

In the opening singles, Morea, the neutral referee, had been called on to make only a couple of decisions, but he had his hands full throughout the Tiriac-Gorman match. Early in the first set, to cite one example of the Rumanian's bagful of tactical ploys, Tiriac sat down on a linesman's platform behind the baseline after a first serve by Gorman which Tiriac thought was out had not been called out. At the request of the Rumanian captain, Stefan Georgescu, Morea walked out and inspected the area under discussion. (On a clay court you can see the mark a ball makes, but there is no certainty that the mark you are looking at is the one made by the shot in question.) Morea, bending low, his hand on his chin, ultimately ordered the point to be replayed. It should be brought out emphatically, though, that Morea proved to be a hard man to intimidate; throughout the meeting at Bucharest there were many, many occasions when he coolly overruled the Rumanian linesmen's calls and refused to yield to the protests of Tiriac, Nastase, and Georgescu and to the clamor of the partisan crowd. In the Tiriac-Gorman match, this was not an easy thing to do, for by the fourth set, with Gorman beginning to fade and Tiriac coming on, the gallery was roaring out its chant of "Ti-ri-ac!" with a fervor that would put the Notre Dame cheering section to shame. During that set, which eventually went to Tiriac, 6–3, he had pulled out all the stops. For example, to break Gorman's rhythm when the American was serving he would stand with his eyes fixed on the ground; when he at length looked up and Gorman prepared to start his service motion, Tiriac would look down at the ground again. He also acted as if he were running the match. I particularly remember one point on which, after a linesman had made a questionable call of "out" on a drive by Gorman, Tiriac bestowed on him a lordly nod of confirmation. Still, to give the devil his due, Tiriac clearly outplayed Gorman in the fourth set. The young American was holding his poise admirably in the wild atmosphere, but his concentration was shot now, and so was his confidence.

As the fifth set got under way, I looked around at the spectators at Progresul. The majority struck me as essentially friendly, good-natured people, delighted to be present at such an exciting event. However, as the set wore on and the prospects for a victory by Tiriac grew, the extremists in the stands really turned it on. Previously, they had been applauding each error by Gorman. Now they applauded whenever he failed to get his first serve in, and, in an effort to distract him further, they started to cough when he was about to toss the ball up on his second serve. This rather surprised me, and so did one other display of bad manners by the extremists. Whenever the small enclave of American rooters—no more than a hundred were on hand—cheered Gorman on, these super-Rumanians expressed their resentment splenetically, almost as if to say, "Either you cheer for our man or you don't cheer at all." In any event, down on the court it was Tiriac all the way now. Stalling, protesting, grimacing, baiting, he ran out the set at 6–2 to cap a thoroughly remarkable comeback. Pandemonium. He was instantly mobbed. Someone threw a gigantic white towel over his head, and, covered like a tent, the victorious gladiator left the arena to booming shouts of "Ti-ri-ac! Ti-ri-ac! Ti-ri-ac!"

With the score locked at 1–1, the doubles assumed increased importance. It was played on a warm Saturday afternoon beneath a mottled gray sky, and familiar melodies from "My Fair Lady" floated out over the stadium's loudspeaker system as the two pairs warmed up. (The day before, we had been treated to everything from French ballads to sweet rock.) The Davis Cup was being televised nationally, and before entering the stadium I spent a few minutes watching the warmup over a TV set in one of the garden cafés. The Rumanians' picture is a little sharper than ours, and there is nothing wrong with their camerawork.

The general feeling in Bucharest—and elsewhere, no doubt—was that the United States would be darned lucky to win the doubles. Our team of Stan Smith and Erik van Dillen, a slim twenty-one-year-old Californian, had performed more than creditably this year in reaching the final at Wimbledon. Nevertheless, the two had been playing together for only sixteen months, whereas the solid, sophisticated partnership of Tiriac and Nastase went all the way back to 1966. Also, who could forget that in the Cup match at Charlotte last year Nastase and

Tiriac had destroyed Smith and van Dillen in straight sets? After that debacle, there had been a movement in some quarters to find a less flighty partner for Smith, but in the end nothing had been done about it.

The doubles turned out to be no contest. From the outset, Nastase and Tiriac, as expected, went after van Dillen, who, as it happened, served the first game. They broke him, at fifteen, but not because of any errors on his part. Tiriac served the second game. Knowing Nastase's propensity for "poaching," van Dillen and Smith played two returns of service straight down the line, right through the area that Nastase had vacated; after that, Nastase was a lot less adventurous at net. In the third game, with Smith serving, the Rumanians went after young van Dillen again, firing bullet after bullet at him. With his fast racquet, he stood up equally under the fusillade. In fact, he finished off one exchange with a sharp crosscourt volley and finished off two others with brilliantly angled smashes. Midway through the first set, Nastase, who had started out playing rather well, lost his touch, drastically and irredeemably. The Americans then rattled off eleven straight games. It was all over in sixty-eight minutes: 6–2, 6–0, 6–3. Smith had done some wonderful things, but I am tempted to say that van Dillen was the best man on the court. Ralston was ecstatic. "Erik always plays some streaks of great tennis," he said. "Today, he played great tennis throughout the whole match."

It turned cold on Sunday, with the sun a small oyster-colored spot in a slate sky. In the first match of the day, it was Smith versus Tiriac. Smith's job was clear: it was up to him to win the third, and clinching, point, so that it wouldn't matter if Nastase suddenly regained his form against Gorman in the remaining singles match. Tiriac's job was no less clear: up against one of the three best players in the world, he had to beat him by whatever means he could devise. Looking back at their five-set battle—and what a battle it was!—I find myself torn between admiration for Tiriac's fighting spirit and disdain for his ruthless contempt for fair play. (Forget about sportsmanship!) Be that as it may, he played the match of his life. To begin with, he had an intelligent game plan, which he persevered with: he kept feeding Smith slow, deep, high-bouncing balls to rob him of his usual pace and upset his timing. Smith, after losing the first set, took the next two largely because he got his big, pulverizing serve working. (The correction he made was to toss the ball higher.) By the fourth set, just when it seemed as if Smith had worn down the last sinew of resistance in his weary, perspiring opponent, Tiriac somehow roused himself for one more effort. Setting up openings with his slow stuff and exploiting them with some devastating ground strokes, he regained control of the play. How that had the galleries roaring! (After each point that Tiriac won, Morea permitted the gallery to chant "Ti-ri-ac! Ti-ri-ac!" for ten or twelve seconds, or until the two players were almost ready to begin the next point. Then he would tap the leg of the umpire's chair, the signal for the umpire to call out *"Liniste va rog,"* which means "Silence please." Instantly, there would be silence.) Maintaining his momentum, Tiriac went on to win the fourth set from an obviously worried Smith.

And then there came another abrupt turnabout. Smith began the deciding set with an ace. From that point on, he forced himself to hit out on every stroke, and he pushed himself to move faster and keep moving. He played an almost perfect set and blew Tiriac off the court —an amazing achievement under the circumstances. The match had taken two hours and fifty minutes. The scores were 4–6, 6–2, 6–4, 2–6, 6–0. There is no point in describing in detail Tiriac's antics or the inexcusable performance by the corps of linesmen. Suffice it to say that Captain Ralston was successful in having a linesman removed after the man had made three flagrantly incorrect calls against Smith in the fifth game of the second set. This stabilized the situation a bit, but not completely. I am thinking specifically of a point on which Smith returned a serve by Tiriac for a winner, whereupon the official calling the service line spoke up and said that he had called the *serve* out. Tiriac then played a second service.

By the way, though it was now irrelevant, since Smith's victory had assured the United States' retention of the Cup, Nastase beat Gorman, in four sets. Gorman had made the mistake of watching the Smith-Tiriac duel on TV, and was emotionally overcharged before his own match had even begun.

Bucharest is a lovely city at night, and an evocative one. Across a broad square, the moon lights up an exquisite Byzantine church, and your thoughts go back to the era when Rumania was Dacia, an outpost of the Roman Empire. As you move down a narrow back street, an automobile skids maniacally close to you, and you are reminded of the Vienna of "The Third Man." (For the Rumanian élite, I would guess, the West begins at Vienna, and their capital city is, as it always has been, Paris.) As I walked around the city with friends the night after the final, there were many things to think about. Funny things. Like the way that Dwight F. Davis, Jr., the son of the donor of the Cup, perpetuated the grand old American tradition of the high-flying fluff by telling the spectators during the closing ceremony at Progresul that he was delighted to be in Budapest. And complicated things. Like the gracious speech delivered at the closing ceremony by Tiriac, that walking dichotomy, who spoke only of Nastase—with whom, it is said, he no longer gets along—and asked his countrymen not to forget, in their disappointment, that Rumania would never have reached the final except for the heroic feats of Nastase against Italy, Russia, and Australia. And thoughts about the future. The ethics of sport may not be the most important thing in the world, but the final at Progresul, for all its color and thrills, was a travesty of a kind that no game can afford. Some tennis people have suggested that, beginning as soon as possible, all Davis Cup matches, from the round of sixteen on, be held at *one* venue, with the conduct of the matches entirely in the hands of neutral officials. That seems right on the mark to me.

THE FIRST HUNDRED YEARS

(1973)

In June 1973, at about the time that the early rounds of Wimbledon were being played, I visited two of the locations associated with Major Walter Clopton Wingfield, the man who invented tennis a hundred years before. The trip to Wingfield Castle, in Suffolk, did not go as smoothly as I might have wished, but the trip to Nantclwyd, in northern Wales, was all, and more, than one could have hoped for. Major Wingfield was an exceptional man, and thanks to the research of George E. Alexander, the tennis historian from Boise, we know far more about him than we did a quarter of a century ago. We even know, for example, that later he founded the Cordon Bleu school of cooking.

Major Walter Clopton Wingfield, the man who invented tennis, must surely rank among the most colorful and controversial figures in the history of sport. A cavalry officer in Victorian England, Wingfield was a scion of an ancient and prominent family whose ancestral seat, a castle in Suffolk near the Norfolk border, is said to have been erected in 1362, though there are those who contend that it antedated the coming of

William the Conqueror. A good many of the Major's forebears had distinguished themselves as soldiers and diplomats. For example, Sir Richard Wingfield was Marshal of Calais in 1511, and later, as the Ambassador to the Court of France, was present at the Field of the Cloth of Gold. Beginning in 1521, Sir Robert Wingfield served as Ambassador to the Court of Charles V. In the middle of the sixteenth century, Sir Humphrey Wingfield put in a stint as Speaker of the House of Commons, and Anthony Wingfield, a kind of maverick, was a reader in Greek to Queen Elizabeth I. However, by the early eighteen-sixties, when Major Wingfield returned home from China, where he had commanded a cavalry troop, the family had long since lost most of its eminence and wealth. Wingfield Castle, no longer inhabited, was fast becoming a ruin, the outline of its towers obliterated by a rank growth of vines, the drawbridge across its moat rusted and broken. Major Wingfield, who was assigned after his China command to the Montgomery Yeomanry, a Welsh outfit, had enough money to get by on, but a few extra pounds would not have hurt, and he began to ponder how he might go about acquiring them. A tall, athletic young-middle-aged man with a handsome face framed by a full beard, he got around a good deal socially, and one of the things he noticed about the Britain he had returned to was how mad everyone was for sport. Organized cricket, soccer, Rugby, and rowing had become enormously more popular, but the rise of team sports wasn't the particular development that caught the Major's shrewd eye. What did was a new facet of the cult of games —the games that ladies and gentlemen played together on weekends on the wide, well-kept lawns of the fashionable country houses. Croquet, the oldest of these games, remained the leader, but it was obvious that many of its practitioners, including the females, were finding it too tepid. A good many of them had already switched to badminton, originally called Poona, that was imported from India in the early eighteen-seventies by some British Army officers and renamed after the country seat of the Duke of Beaufort, where the first important demonstration of the game had taken place. The trouble with badminton was that it required an absolutely breezeless day; otherwise there was no controlling the shuttlecock. Wingfield was certain that the national passion for sport would keep on growing, and it struck him that a small fortune, along with a substantial renown any man would be pleased to have, awaited the person who could devise a really fascinating lawn game. He began to think along those lines himself.

Wingfield had the background for it. In his youth, he had played the various forms of handball and just about all the racquet games. (According to Edward C. Potter, Jr., in his book "Kings of the Court,"

there had been a court-tennis court in Wingfield Castle. Moreover, as
Potter brought out, among the people who had supposedly made use
of it was Charles d'Orléans, a grandson of the King of France, who had
been captured at Agincourt by the English and consigned to Wingfield
Castle during part of his long captivity.) In any event, in 1873, after
considerable deliberation, the Major came up with a game that combined certain features of these earlier games—the net came from badminton, the ball from Eton fives (a form of handball), the method of
scoring from hard racquets, and so on. (Until special racquets were
manufactured, the player was free to use the racquet from his favorite
game.) Wingfield called his amalgam Sphairistiké, or Lawn Tennis—
"Sphairistiké" because he had heard that there was an ancient Greek
game of that name, and "Lawn Tennis" because it seemed a natural
spinoff from "court tennis," and thus suggested a game that was both
old and aristocratic. (As Potter has pointed out, "Wingfield had little
idea how Sphairistiké was played but . . . he could be sure that even
antiquarians had forgotten its rules.") Another advantage gained by
calling his game Sphairistiké was that it emphasized its originality, and
this, Wingfield felt, would greatly increase his chances of obtaining a
patent for it. That was crucial—a patent. Once he had it, he would be
able to manufacture and sell sets of his game and, he hoped, reap a small
fortune. His concern about gaining a patent also prompted several of
the new wrinkles he had introduced into his game, such as decreeing
that the court not be rectangular but shaped somewhat like an hourglass—thirty feet wide across the baselines and only twenty-four feet
wide at the net. In December 1873, Wingfield tried out the game with
a group of young people who were members of a houseparty at Nantclwyd Hall, the country estate, in Denbighshire, Wales, of the family of
a good friend of his, Thomas Naylor-Leyland. Apparently, the game was
a big success. There is no record of what the weather was like at Nantclwyd Hall during that stretch, but even if it had been freezing cold,
the Major would have been undaunted, for he maintained that there
was no reason Sphairistiké could not be played as pleasurably on ice as
on grass.

On February 23, 1874, Major Wingfield was awarded a preliminary patent for his game, and the patent was confirmed five months
later. The moment he received word in February that the patent office
had registered his application for "A New and Improved Portable Court
for Playing the Ancient Game of Tennis" (in his presentation the Major
had heavily emphasized that tennis in its earlier forms had always been
an indoor amusement), he arranged for sets to be manufactured and for
the Messrs. French & Company, of 46 Churton Street, Pimlico, to act

as his exclusive sales agent. A set cost five guineas—a fairly substantial amount in those days. Encased in a wooden box thirty-six inches by twelve by six and bearing the label "Sphairistiké, or Lawn Tennis" on the cover, a set contained poles, pegs, a main net a little over four and a half feet high, two small side nets (they adjoined the main net like wings), a mallet, a brush, a bag of balls, and four tennis racquets, made by Jefferies & Mallings, which were a sort of cross between the conventional hard-racquets racquet and the conventional court-tennis racquet. Wingfield left it up to his clients to supply their own colored cord, tape, or paint for lining the court, but he did throw in a slim pamphlet called "The Book of the Game," in which he set down the dimensions of the court and provided instructions for installing one in five minutes. The pamphlet also included a brief, if fuzzy, account of the game's history, along with an explanation of its scoring system and the rules of play. On the page facing the title page ("The Major's Game of Lawn Tennis, dedicated to the party assembled at Nantclwyd in December, 1873, by W.C.W.") were two interesting paragraphs. The one at the top went as follows:

> This game has been tefted practically at feveral Country Houfes during the paft few months, and has been found fo full of intereft and fo great a succefs, that it has been decided to bring it before the Public, being protected by Her Majesty's Royal Letters Patent.

There then appeared a facsimile of the royal coat of arms and, beneath it, a paragraph headed "Useful Hints":

> Hit your ball gently, and look well before ftriking, fo as to place it in the corner moft remote from your adverfary. A great deal of fide can be imparted to the ball by the proper touch, which, together with a nice appreciation of ftrength, adds much to the delicacy and fcience of the game.

The rest of the pamphlet similarly used the romantic, archaic "f" instead of the modern "s." The Major, Madison Avenue incarnate, never could stop selling.

Lawn tennis caught on instantly. In a matter of months, with the Major pushing it vigorously and using his influential friends with characteristic chutzpah, it became *the* social game, driving croquet and badminton from the velvet lawns of the stately homes of England and the rest of Britain, and also establishing itself with the better military garrisons around the world. With the boxed sets selling so rapidly, the Major brought out a second edition of his game before the year was over, refining some of the rules, modifying some of the equipment (the side nets, for example, were dispensed with), and also raising the price of a set to six guineas. Before many more months had passed, a third edition became necessary. At this time, bowing to mounting pressure, he gave up the name Sphairistiké. Thenceforward, the game would be known simply as lawn tennis. To Wingfield's deep gratification, the game had quickly gained many enthusiastic converts among the nobility. During the first year it was on the market, sets were bought by the Prince of Wales, the Crown Princess of Prussia, and Prince Louis of Hesse; by eight dukes, including the Duke of Edinburgh and the Duke of Devonshire; by fourteen marquises, including the Marquis of Landsdowne and the Marquis of Exeter; by forty-nine earls, including the Earl of Cadogan, the Earl of Leicester, and the Earl of Salisbury; and by eight viscounts, including Viscount Halifax and Viscount Bangor.

For all its dazzling success, however, Wingfield's invention did not bring him the fortune he dreamed of, or anything like it. With the third edition, sales of the sets began to fall off drastically. One reason was that many of the people whom Wingfield had viewed as potential customers thought it foolish to lay out six guineas for the Major's equipment when they could make—or had already assembled—their own. Indeed, as a large number of them pointed out in irate letters to *The Field,* the leading periodical dealing with outdoor life, hard-racquet or court-tennis devotees in various sections of Britain had thought up and had been playing games very similar to the Major's long before he entered the picture. The dimensions of these other courts were somewhat different, of course, and so were many of the rules of play, but, essentially, these games were the same game as lawn tennis. Besides castigating Wingfield for his presumption in presenting his brainchild as a wholly original creation, the letter writers made it clear that they considered their own versions of tennis far superior to his. Other troubles lay ahead for Wingfield. For persons who did not have a spreading lawn of their own, an obvious site for a tennis court was the grounds of the local cricket club. By late 1874, the Marylebone Cricket Club, the governing body of the national game, was becoming a trifle worried over the inroads the fashionable new game was making. The fact that tennis players had appropriated the white shirt and white flannels of the cricketer as their own outfit was of no great importance, but lawn tennis had the look about it of a game that could cut deeply into cricket's vast popularity, and that *was* serious. The prudent course, the M.C.C. decided, was to step in and take over lawn tennis before the

game became too big. The top men at the M.C.C. also had a few
suggestions that they thought would make lawn tennis a much better
game, such as lowering the net and adopting the method of scoring used
in court tennis. On several occasions in 1875, a committee from the
M.C.C. met with Wingfield to talk things over, but in the stormy sessions that inevitably resulted Wingfield stubbornly held his ground.
Shortly after this, heavy pressure was exerted on him by another sports
organization—the All England Croquet Club, which had been founded
in 1868 in Wimbledon, on the southwestern edge of London. Commer-
cially, croquet had fallen far short of the club's hopes for it, so in the
mid-seventies the A.E.C.C. had, as an experiment, laid out a tennis
court in one corner of the club property. As it turned out, the court was
filled with players from morning to night. Obviously, the way to make
money was to plunge into lawn tennis in a big way. Very much in the
manner of the M.C.C., the A.E.C.C. was soon challenging Wingfield's
right, patent or no patent, to run lawn tennis singlehanded, particularly
since the game had already developed an alarming number of variations and seemed to be developing more. At length, late in 1875, his
obstinacy worn down by months of slow sales and fast talk, Wingfield
suddenly agreed to accept all the changes proposed by an M.C.C. committee, insisting only that the game be played on a court shaped like
an hourglass. This peace treaty, however, turned out to be next to
meaningless, because in 1877 control of the game was captured by the
All England Croquet and Lawn Tennis Club—note the change of name
—which, under the leadership of three members who were both veteran administrators and ambitious ballgame intellectuals, announced
not only that it would be holding a national lawn tennis championship
in July but that the event would be played on a rectangular court, under
a new set of rules worked out by the club's high-powered troika. The
M.C.C., after a session with the A.E. & L.T.C., gave in on every point.

Twenty-two men entered the first Wimbledon—the first lawn
tennis championship put on by the All England Club, in its bailiwick in
that suburb. The winner was Spencer Gore, an old racquets player from
Harrow. He was succeeded by P. F. Hadow, another old Harrovian, and
then by the Reverend J. T. Hartley, who had been a court-tennis champion at Oxford. In 1881 the first great tennis player arrived on the scene
—Willie Renshaw. He won the singles at Wimbledon seven times and
with his twin brother Ernest carried off the doubles seven times.

As for Major Wingfield, he lived on until 1912, the last thirty-
five years in almost total oblivion as far as tennis was concerned.
(Wimbledon, after appropriating control of the game, had simply
shunted the Major to one side.) When he finally died, at the age of
seventy-eight, the obituary in the London *Times* dwelt on his mili-

tary career, his ties with the famous old Suffolk family, some pamphlets he wrote late in life ("Bicycle Gymkhana" and "Musical Rides"), and a term he served as justice of the peace in Montgomeryshire. There was not a word about his being the inventor of the thriving international game of lawn tennis.

This spring, when I was in England during the second week of Wimbledon, I took a couple of days off from the tournament in order to visit two locales that had played a vital part in the fascinating saga of Walter Clopton Wingfield: Wingfield Castle and Nantclwyd Hall. Through the assistance of Ann Allison, of the British Information Services in New York City, I had learned that Wingfield Castle was still in existence. Just what condition it was in, Miss Allison had not been able to tell me, and her information about the village of Wingfield was limited, too. All things considered, she felt that perhaps the best procedure for me, if I was serious about visiting the castle and the village in this the centennial year of lawn tennis, was to get in touch with the Reverend W. G. Muir, of Wingfield. I wrote to him immediately. Through Miss Allison's good services, I also got in touch with Nantclwyd Hall. At her suggestion, I wrote to the clerk of the Rural District Council in Ruthin, which is the village nearest to Nantclwyd. The clerk of the council passed my letter on to Major B. G. Rhodes, the representative of the trustees of the Nantclwyd Settlement, which administers the Nantclwyd estate, and Major Rhodes sent me a long, friendly letter in which he said that he had cleared the matter with the trustees of the Nantclwyd Settlement, and that it would be a pleasure to welcome a lawn tennis pilgrim to the grounds on which Major Wingfield introduced his game to the world in 1873. "Although the original lawn-tennis court is not still in use, it is clearly identifiable," Major Rhodes wrote. He also explained that "Nantclwyd Hall . . . has been and remains the home of the Naylor-Leyland family since 1840," and that Major Wingfield's friend Thomas Naylor-Leyland was "the great-great-grandfather of the present baronet, Sir Vivyan Naylor-Leyland, who now lives in Nassau."

I decided to undertake the expedition to Wingfield first, because it was the more chancy of the two: I had received no answer from the Reverend Mr. Muir, and I would be descending on the village cold. To get to Wingfield, I took a train from London to Colchester, in Essex, and there hired a taxi to take me the remaining forty-odd miles. As we began our drive northeast across the deep green dales of Essex and Suffolk on a typical English summer's day, the dark-gray clouds in the wide sky occasionally pierced by bolts of brilliant sunshine, I noticed in talking with my driver, a cheerful middle-aged man, that he spoke with a slight European accent, and I asked him about it. He told me that his name was Tony, and that he was born in Italy and had been living in England since the war. "I was captured by the British at Benghazi," he added, breaking into a radiant smile. "Happiest day of my life!" It took us about an hour to get to Wingfield, which lies in an out-of-the-way part of East Anglia, about thirty miles by road from Bury St. Edmunds, about twenty-five from Lowestoft, and about twenty-five also from the local metropolis, Norwich. The area around Wingfield grows good wheat, oats, and barley, and also has a reputation for raising good pigs. The village now has a population of two hundred and twenty-nine, and just about all the farmhouses and other buildings are set along a narrow, winding paved road, which another narrow, winding paved road meets at a right angle. Wingfield's handsome old stone church lies two hundred yards down the second road. The side door to the church was open, and, entering, I asked the only person in sight, a well-dressed elderly lady, where I might find the Reverend Mr. Muir. I learned that he had left the village almost two years before and that his successor was currently on holiday. I then asked her about Wingfield Castle, fearful that I would learn that it had slipped into the moat and disappeared from sight. Here the news seemed definitely better. Not only was the castle standing but it had been meticulously restored by its present owner and resident, Baron Ash. That put a whole new complexion on things. The next step, obviously, was to speak with Baron Ash, if this was possible, and, at the lady's suggestion, I went into a small, bleak pub almost directly across the street from the church to see if I could reach him by telephone. I learned from the barmaid, who bore little resemblance in looks or manner to the enchanting breed that has been a staple of English films since the first camera handle was turned, that the pub had no phone but that I would find a phone box at the corner. "You won't get to see the Baron, I can promise you that," she added, with a rough little laugh. "I don't care what your business is. The Baron's not seeing anyone these days." And with this she broke into that unpleasant laugh again.

To my surprise and relief, there was a Norwich Area directory in the phone box. Not only that, but a number was listed for G. Baron Ash. (I should interject before proceeding any further that although everyone in Wingfield spoke of G. Baron Ash as either Baron Ash or the Baron, as if he were a nobleman, the way his name was listed in the phone book stirred some doubt in my mind on this point. Weeks later, on my return to New York, I learned that my doubt was warranted. Ash, evidently an extremely rich man, was considered important enough to be included in the British *Who's Who,* but he was by no means a peer of the realm. His first name was Graham, and Baron was simply his middle name. It could as easily have been Earl.) Be that as it may, Tony dialled the number for Wingfield Castle, and as he did, I studied the signpost at the intersection: Syleham 1 1/2, Eye 7, Diss 9—to the west; Weybread 3 1/2, Harleston 5 1/4—to the northeast; Stradbroke 2 3/4, Laxfield 7 3/4—to the southeast. We really were out in the middle of nowhere! Then the number Tony had dialled began ringing, and he handed me the phone. A deep-pitched, edgy voice at the other end said, "Yes?"

I asked to speak to Baron Ash.

"This is Baron Ash," came the reply. "Who are you and what do you want?" All this in a most peremptory tone.

I explained that 1973 marked the hundredth anniversary of the invention of lawn tennis by Major Wingfield, and asked if it might be possible to visit Wingfield Castle.

"No, you can't," Baron Ash answered, his voice rising to a roar. "That's absolutely out of the question. I have a right to my privacy. I'm eighty-three years old. Don't you think that at that age I have a right to my privacy?"

I said I certainly did.

"The last thing I want is publicity," he went on, dropping his voice to a more conversational pitch and speaking with less petulance. "Nevertheless, people are always bothering me. They drive right into the driveway, as if the castle were their home and not mine. It's a constant annoyance. It's twenty-five years since I bought the castle. I've loved rebuilding it. It's been my baby. But I'm not going to stand quietly by and let people I don't know invite themselves into my private grounds. This year, it's been far worse than ever before. People every day."

I said I wouldn't have guessed that the centenary of the birth of lawn tennis would lead so many people to seek out Wingfield Castle.

"Good heavens, man, tennis has nothing to do with it!" the Baron roared. "It's those blasted Wingfields. They're a very prolific family, spread all over, and they keep coming round to inspect the ancestral castle. Constant interruptions. This morning, there were five automobiles filled with people parked in front of my breakfast room while I was eating my breakfast."

I was properly sympathetic. I went on to say that I had heard that the Baron had done a superb job of restoring the castle. Then I said, "All I want to do is to take a very quick look around."

"Don't you understand me?" Baron Ash boomed out. "I don't

want to be disturbed by you or anyone!" And with that he crashed the phone down into its cradle.

Wingfield Castle, I had learned from the lady in the church, lies only a short distance past the intersection, on the road to Syleham, and is fairly visible from the road, even though it is set back a couple of hundred yards and is partly hidden by a screen of tall trees planted along the front of the estate and along most of the rest of its perimeter. As Tony and I were driving over to get the catch-as-catch-can glimpse we would now have to settle for, we passed the village post office, and I decided to drop in for a moment. It took up less than half of a rather slapdash, faded white wooden structure, in which the postmaster, a man named Matthias, also ran a jumbled odds-and-ends shop. A tall, thin middle-aged fellow, Matthias proved to be outgoing and highly articulate, and he seemed to enjoy filling me in on Baron Ash. (It was always Baron Ash or the Baron.) To the best of Matthias' recollection, when the Baron came to Wingfield it was from Buckinghamshire or some place in that general vicinity, where he had a palatial country home. The Baron, he had heard, was related to the Marlborough family. The trouble was that, being a real showplace, his home attracted tourists by the busload, and one day, his patience exhausted, he decided to get away from it all. He turned that estate over to the National Trust and bought Wingfield Castle, which had the advantage of being well off the usual tourist routes. The castle was then in terrible shape, but the Baron calmly went about fixing it up, from its drawbridge to its twin towers, pouring a small fortune into the project until, in the postmaster's phrase, "the edifice was as neat as a pin." Matthias went on, "When he came here to Wingfield, the Baron had a staff of twenty-seven people looking after him—valets, maids, cooks, gardeners, and all the rest, you know. Now he's down to a staff of three. Most people of his class have had to do that in recent years. When he arrived here, he drove a Rolls-Royce. Now he's down to a Rover and an Austin. He pays the man from the local garage five pounds when he wants them washed. That's a generous sum, but the Baron is a very generous man. I remember how a couple of years ago I mentioned to him one day when we were having a bit of a chat that a woman who had taught in the village school was retiring after many years of faithful service. The Baron didn't know her, but he sent her a check for a hundred and fifty pounds."

The Baron Ash he was describing, I interposed, certainly didn't resemble the crusty character I had talked to on the telephone.

"Yes, he has changed," Matthias agreed. "When he first came to Wingfield, he was friendly with the people in the village. He attended the village functions, like the church fairs, quite regularly. When he went out for a stroll in the evening—he's an old bachelor—he had a cordial word for all of us. Then, I'm afraid, the local hooligans began to act up. Once, I remember, when he was away on a trip, they mucked up the cherry trees he had planted on his lawn. Baron Ash had been very proud of those trees. There were other incidents like that, and he gradually withdrew from the life of the village. I can picture him saying to himself, 'Well, if that's the way they want it!' or, you know, words to that effect. At heart, I think, he's a kind and friendly man. When the dustmen come round, he often has them in for a whiskey or two. Another example comes to my mind. A couple of years ago, I sold the last of a batch of postal cards of the castle which I stocked here at the store, so I asked the Baron for permission to take another photo and have another batch of cards printed up. The Baron explained as how he wanted no more cards of the castle to be distributed, but then, after turning me down, he sent me, through his butler, a five-pound note to make up for the money I would have made through the sale of the cards. He's a good chap, the Baron. I think him being a bachelor and in his eighties is what makes him grumpy, you know. You would never guess his age by looking at him. He's a tall, slim, straight-backed chap who still rides a bicycle. He loves the castle. I hear that in one of the banqueting halls in the towers there's an oak table large enough for forty people to eat at! Then, there's a saloon in one of the towers where three or four hundred people can dance! That's what I hear."

In spite of his evident affection for Baron Ash, Matthias was exceedingly helpful when I asked him the best way I could get a good look at Wingfield Castle. His instructions were to continue along the road, past the driveway to the castle and the protective screen of trees, until I reached an open field. That was common land, and if I walked in a ways from the road a close, unobstructed view of the castle would present itself. I followed his instructions to the letter, tiptoeing warily past a couple of Holsteins grazing in the open field, and, when I had walked in about a hundred yards, suddenly there were no more trees on the right to block my view, and, seventy-five yards away, there was the castle, looming up as clear as a postcard. The water in the wide moat sparkled, as did the refurbished bridge leading over the moat to the front entrance and the massive twin towers framing it. (The draw-bridge, at the rear of the castle, was out of my line of sight.) It was as magnificent a castle as I have ever seen. Near the base, the walls were of old gray, white, and black stone, but as they rose the stone gradually gave way to brownish brick, then to dull-red brick, and, finally, to a dark-red brick that reminded me of the brick in some of the older colleges at Cambridge University, like Jesus. The crenellated central towers were of this deep-red brick. From where I stood, I could see only a small piece of the castle grounds. Not a soul was in view, but I could hear the clatter of a couple of power mowers, which were probably trimming the lawns along the driveway.

As I stood gazing at Wingfield Castle, an odd mélange of thoughts surged through my mind. If the Baron was so continually pestered by unwanted visitors, why didn't he simply shut the gates to the driveway? That would have solved his problem neatly and completely. For another thing, I really wished I had been able to visit the castle. I would have particularly liked to find out whether any traces remained of the court-tennis court described in Potter's book. This led me to the thought that overrode all the others—Baron Ash's apparent ignorance that one of the Wingfields had invented lawn tennis a hundred years before, and his total lack of interest in the matter. When I got back to New York and looked up Graham Baron Ash in *Who's Who*, his attitude became a little less enigmatic. His entry was one of the shortest and tightest in the volume. Ash, it said, was born in 1889, was educated at Radley, and served in the Royal Air Force in both World Wars. From 1938 to 1939, he was High Sheriff of Warwickshire. Under "Recreations" he had listed only one—shooting. Under "Clubs" he had also listed only one—the Royal Automobile. That was it. It was ironic, considering how passionately Major Wingfield had longed for fame as well as for money, that the family castle had fallen into the hands of a shy, introspective old man who had no taste for publicity and promotion, and only wanted to be left alone.

The expedition to Nantclwyd Hall went much more smoothly. It began with a comfortable railroad trip of just under three hours from London to Chester, the old Roman city that today serves as a sort of gateway to northern Wales, and it ended with a taxi trip of around twenty-five miles. I was lucky in that the driver I happened to draw at the Chester railroad station was a soft-spoken, companionable young man who had spent some time in Wales and could understand the directions we were given in Ruthin when we asked the way to Nantclwyd. To me, the words were unintelligible.

The drive to Nantclwyd was a scenic one. I hadn't been in Wales in almost twenty years, and I had forgotten how lovely the rural sections are—the distinctive way the hills, colored a dozen shades of green, sweep softly down to the small valleys, and the beauty of the trees that dot the hillsides and the valleys. About four miles south of Ruthin, we came upon the entrance to Nantclwyd Hall. A dirt road took us under a stone archway, past a herd of Holsteins, past a large bronze statue of a boar, and over a small bridge. *Nant* in Welsh means a brook or gorge or ravine, and the stream that runs through this valley is the Clwyd—pronounced "clude." Ahead lay the hall, a handsome three-story, ten-bedroom, multi-chimneyed nine-teenth-century gentleman's country residence built of handmade brick, some of it a deep red. It had been remodelled several times— most recently in 1958, by Sir Clough Williams-Ellis, a specialist in the Italianate style, who, among other things, refinished the back of the house in orange-brown plaster. All told, the property owned by the Naylor-Leyland family covers four thousand rolling, fertile acres. On the right, as the visitor approaches Nantclwyd Hall, a hill of moderate size, clustered with oaks and sycamores, descends to a well-mowed lawn, which sets off the house on all sides. To the left, or east, a hun-dred yards or so from the house, is a small lake, with a number of swans on it. Closer to the house on the left—the moment you spot it, you know that this is where the first lawn tennis court must have been situated, and you are right—is a broad lower lawn, separated from the upper lawn by a sharp five- or six-foot bank. When you walk over this sward, you discover that it is not half as smooth as it looks from a distance. This helps to explain why Major Wingfield's tennis-playing friends at Nantclwyd Hall pinned the nickname of Bumpers on him: no one else was half as agile when it came to adjusting to the erratic bounces the ball took on the bumpy court.

This last piece of information—as a matter of fact, practically everything I wanted to know about Nantclwyd Hall and the Naylor-Leyland family—was supplied to me by Major Rhodes, who acts as a sort of manager of the estate and has an office in a ground-floor cor-ner of the hall. (For the most part, the hall is closed these days, but a section of it is kept open so that friends of the family who are passing through the area can be put up.) A neat, solidly built man of unusual courtesy and affability, Major Rhodes is utterly unlike most of the retired British Army officers I have run into—particularly the stuffy, imperious types who for many years now have latched on as secretaries at many British golf clubs and have come to constitute one of the game's chief hazards in that land. The Major's helpfulness confirmed the impression I had got from his letter, which had been three pages long and packed with information that he felt might help me to understand what lawn tennis was like at the start. He had even gone to the trouble of drawing a diagram of the original hourglass-shaped court and noting its dimensions. As we talked, in a sitting room near his office, he provided me with copies of four old photographs of Nantclwyd Hall and the part of the grounds where the tennis court had stood. Then he brought out a fairly large bronze plaque, only recently arrived, which the present baronet, Sir Vivyan Naylor-Leyland (Eton, Oxford, the Grenadier Guards), had had prepared, with instructions for it to be affixed to the steep bank to the east of the hall. The inscription read as follows:

> Opposite this plaque and a few feet away is the center of the first and original lawn tennis court. Here at Nantclwyd the Naylor-Leylands and their friend Major Wingfield invented and played the game in 1873. Then named Sphairistiké. This plaque is placed here in 1973 centenary year. At the suggestion of Sir Vivyan Naylor-Leyland, baronet. By the trustees of the Nantclwyd Settlement.

Major Rhodes and I then walked around to the front of the house, down the bank, and onto the lawn where the first court had been situated. As I was inspecting the historic turf, trying not very successfully to transport myself back a century, Major Rhodes said, in his genial way, "You can see how bumpy it is! We could put it in much better shape, of course, but it really isn't worth the trouble. As I mentioned, friends of the Naylor-Leylands will occasionally drop by to spend a night at the hall, but that's about it. Nantclwyd is too remote, I would gather, to draw people who are interested in tennis. Even in this centenary year, we've had only one visit from what you might call a tennis group: a television company sent down a crew to photograph the court, and a bearded actor dressed in period costume impersonated Major Wingfield."

I looked across the lawn to the small lake, edged here and there with clusters of tall, graceful trees. A few swans floated on the water. The afternoon sun made everything glisten. Major Rhodes must have read my mind, for he said, "I was just thinking that if, for any reason, at some time in the future anyone should want to get the lawn into playing shape and put up on it a replica of the 1873 court, what an ideal setting this would be for a shrine to the game."

After we had returned to the back of the hall, the Major led the way past some flower beds, which had been left rather shaggy, and on to a low building, covered with grapevines, in which there was a small swimming pool. Just beyond it, Sir Vivyan had later built a small outdoor pool, bordered by yews. A short distance beyond this second pool, most unexpectedly, I caught sight of a rough-finished, pitch-black asphalt tennis court, date of birth unrecorded. It was set off by darkish brick walls eleven feet high. I cannot remember ever coming across a gloomier court, but I was delighted to see it. It was heartening to know that at the place where lawn tennis was first played a love of the game had existed decades later.

Major Rhodes made me a good cup of tea, and then it was time to return to Chester and catch the train back to London and Wimbledon.

MRS. KING VERSUS MR. RIGGS

(1973)

The source is the "Guinness Book of World Records." Listed under "Tennis" is an entry called "Greatest Crowd," which goes like this: "The greatest crowd at a tennis match was the 30,472 who came to the Astrodome in Houston, Texas, on September 20, 1973, to watch Billie Jean King beat Bobby Riggs, over 25 years her senior, in straight sets in the so-called 'Tennis Match of the Century.'" It wasn't much of a contest. Riggs was in poor form, and Mrs. King, in just the right mood, played an almost perfect match.

Billie Jean King's spectacular triumph at Wimbledon, where she was at the top of her game in defeating Chris Evert in straight sets (6–0, 7–5), was just the thing needed to get the machinery for an autumn meeting between her and Bobby Riggs started again. The previous May, after he had defeated Margaret Smith Court with no trouble at all in their nationally televised match on Mother's Day, there had been a lot of talk to the effect that he should next play Mrs. King to prove that his victory was no fluke, but nothing had been pinned down. Now, on her return from Wimbledon, there was spirited bidding among the television networks for the rights to a King-Riggs confrontation, and in mid-August the American Broadcasting Company announced that it would be televising the match in prime time on the night of Thursday, September 20th, from the Astrodome, in Houston, for a purse of a hundred thousand dollars—winner take all. Within a matter of weeks, the two participants had been deluged with all kinds of commercial tie-ins, and it became clear that the *loser* would pull in at least a hundred thousand dollars from these subsidiary gleanings and that the winner's total haul would far surpass two hundred thousand.

All this constituted an astounding coup for Robert Larimore Riggs, considering that, at fifty-five, he was twenty-five or thirty years past his prime time as a tennis player. In 1939, he had won Wimbledon; in 1939 and 1941, Forest Hills; in 1946, 1947, and 1949, the United States Professional Championship. As a professional, he had held a decided edge in his many meetings with the great Don Budge, but somehow Riggs' exceptional talents—the dependability of his strokes, the shrewdness of his tactics—were underestimated, even when he reigned as champion, possibly because he had such a large supply of whatever is the opposite of charisma. He was too short: five-seven and a half. He had a pesty, chesty personality. (He became much more likable in later years.) Above all, he was a gambler—an honest, self-avowed hustler but a hustler nonetheless. This was one of the chief reasons he was continually in hot water with the United States Lawn Tennis Association during his amateur years. It was typical of Riggs that just before the 1939 Wimbledon tournament began he got down a bet of a hundred pounds at 3–1 odds that he would win the singles, and talked the bookmaker into letting the money ride, in the event that he took the singles, on the doubles at 6–1, and then on the mixed doubles at 12–1. He won all three titles and £21,600, or a hundred and eight thousand dollars. From his early years, Riggs, the fifth, and youngest, son of a Los Angeles minister of the Church of Christ, had to have some "action" going in order to enjoy his tennis thoroughly. Since his acuteness as a bettor soon got around, he was forced to invent all sorts of zany, offbeat wagers to lure the pigeons to his roost. There is a wonderful story—no doubt embellished over the years—of how, during his amateur days, he was pitted in an early round of one of the big Eastern tournaments against a run-of-the-mill player who would normally have been lucky to get more than two games in a set from Riggs. When their match had been in progress about an hour, some friends of Riggs' walked over from the clubhouse to see how close he was to wrapping it up. They were astonished to find that the second set had only just got under way. Indeed, it took Riggs well over two hours to subdue his much inferior opponent. This was hard to believe to start with, but what made it all the more enigmatic was that the scores were 6–0, 6–0, 6–0. When his friends demanded an explanation, Riggs said, with a little smile, "I had a bet going that I could beat that bum love, love, and love without coming in past the service line. That's why it took so long." According to locker-room lore, Riggs in time became a compulsive gambler; that is, if he lost a string of bets he had to keep on betting until he was cleaned out or finally broke his losing streak. For example, the story goes that in the summer of 1948, after losing a dozen or so bets running, he ran into Bob Falkenburg. Wimbledon champion that year, Falkenburg was not an outstanding all-round player, but at that time he unquestionably had the most powerful serve in the world. Riggs, in his desperation to win a bet, proposed to Falkenburg that they play a match for five hundred dollars. It would be for one set, and he was prepared to give Falkenburg a sizable handicap—five games and his serve. Somewhat stunned by this proposition, Falkenburg didn't answer immediately, and, interpreting his silence as a sign of possible lack of interest, Riggs quickly added, "Also, I'll wear an overcoat." Falkenburg took the bet. Riggs, flopping around the hot court in a heavy camel's-hair job, took the set 7–5. He was healthy again.

Riggs' penchant for hustling—first at tennis and later at golf, where he became a 3-handicap player and a deadly putter under pressure—helped to break up his two marriages. Last winter, after he had been out of the spotlight as long as Alida Valli and Steve Van Buren, he became news again. At that time, having become immersed in the booming new senior (forty-five and over) tennis circuit, he grew annoyed by the demands that Mrs. King and the other women stars were making for a larger share of the prize money at Wimbledon, Forest Hills, and the other traditional championships. He genuinely felt that the women simply didn't deserve more money—they didn't even play as good tennis as the best seniors did. To drive home his point, he declared that a man like himself, with one foot in the grave, could still beat the top women players. This led him to formally challenge Mrs. King to a match; he would put up five thousand dollars—winner take all. Mrs. King turned him down, but Mrs. Court, whom he approached next, accepted his challenge. Riggs instantly launched a fantastic promotion campaign—among other things, billing himself in this age of women's lib as the country's No. 1 male-chauvinist pig—and he eventually stirred up such interest in the match that the Columbia Broadcasting System decided to televise it. It was held at the San Diego Country Estates, in an atmosphere that recalled the bizarre bygone era when heavyweight fights for the world championship were held in small, remote towns of the old West (Corbett vs. Fitzsimmons at Carson City, Nevada, in 1897; Jeffries vs. Johnson at Reno, Nevada, in 1910; Dempsey vs. Gibbons at Shelby, Montana, in 1923). Work had been started only a few months before on the San Diego Country Estates, a resort development in the arid Cuyamaca Mountains, fifty miles northeast of San Diego, and close by Wildcat Canyon. The players, press, and officials were put up at the clubhouse of the San Vicente Golf Club, which is a part of the project. (Though the clubhouse was completed, only a few of the holes were, which is par for the course these days.) For the big match, the management put in a cement court and erected bleachers for thirty-five hundred spectators. During the first game—as early as that—it became evident that Mrs. Court, who throughout her career has been subject to strange *crises des nerfs,* was not herself at all. Riggs, for his part, was as relaxed as if he were in his own living room. He walked through the two sets, 6–2, 6–1, with an almost errorless display of controlled, soft-ball tennis. He had trained hard for the match and was in perfect trim. Under the direction of Rheo Blair, a Hollywood nutritionist, he had reduced from a hundred and sixty pounds to a hundred and forty-four in eight weeks. He had followed a strict diet of protein and dairy foods, and had built himself up by taking four hundred and fifteen pills a day, containing liver extract, germ oil, vitamins, and predigested proteins. Blair is no man for halfway measures. The night before the match, he came down to the San Diego Country Estates and personally prepared Riggs' dinner—a baked potato and an avocado salad.

Because of the considerable interest in the Riggs-King match, which was to be held eleven days after the conclusion of Forest Hills, a good deal of extra attention was paid to Mrs. King's progress from the first day of those championships. In winning her first two matches, she played quite well, but both on and off the court she looked a bit wan and seemed to have less verve than she had at Wimbledon. Some Riggs partisans, who regard him as the most gifted psycher since Rasputin, claimed that Mrs. King was already feeling the strain of her coming evening in the Astrodome, but most people attributed her lack of animation to the heat. The day before the start of the championships, a fearsome heat wave, which was to last nine days, hit the New York area, and, with the temperature constantly in the nineties and the humidity intense, the field at Forest Hills found the going enervating. In the third round, Mrs. King came up against Julie Heldman, an experienced internationalist, who can play good, intelligent tennis on her day but who more often than not finds it difficult to maintain her patience and her concentration. (For some inexplicable reason, this match was scheduled not for the stadium court or the grandstand court but for the clubhouse court, which is distractingly noisy and also has such scabrous grass that old Bumpers Wingfield himself would have found it hard to cope with the bounces. Mrs. King and Miss Heldman did not like this court assignment at all.) For a while, their match went much as one might have expected. Mrs. King, in fair enough form, won the first set, 6–3, and went to a 4–1 lead in the second. Then the pattern of play gradually changed. Mrs. King began to move more and more slowly to the ball, and Miss Heldman, encouraged by a series of passing shots, began to hit the ball more forcefully, especially with her forehand. She swept the next five games, to take the set, 6–4. After she had gone out in front 3–1 in the third, and deciding, set, she asked Mrs. King, who by then had slowed down to a walk, how she was feeling. Mrs. King replied that she felt as if she were going to faint but said she wished to continue. When they were changing courts after the next game (Miss Heldman had won it, to lead 4–1), Miss Heldman, ready to begin play, asked the umpire if the minute's rest allowed was up. Mrs. King then said, "Well, if you want it so much, you can have it," and told the umpire she would have to retire from the match. Dr. Daniel Manfredi, the tournament's chief physician, who examined Mrs. King, announced later that it was a good thing she had stopped play when she did, or she might well have collapsed in the ninety-six-degree heat. He explained that Mrs. King, who had been suffering from a cold, had been taking penicillin, and that the combined effect of the drug and the tremendous heat had brought on chills and nausea.

With Mrs. King's unfortunate early departure, the women's singles lost a good deal of their interest, naturally. The winner at Forest Hills was Margaret Court, who defeated Chris Evert in the semis and Evonne Goolagong in the final.

Preceded by ten days of incessant hoopla and drumbeating, the day of the second Battle of the Sexes, September 20th, at length rolled round. That evening, more than thirty thousand people, the largest crowd ever to watch a tennis match, piled into the Astrodome to see how well Mrs. King would do against Riggs. (She went in a 5–2 underdog.) Along with this, about fifty million Americans, supplemented by the citizens of fifteen foreign countries, eventually watched the telecast. Something— maybe just the knowledge that they would be making sports history in a big way—beguiled the promoters into providing the match with an atmosphere that was part circus, part Hollywood première, part television giveaway show, and all bad taste. Escorted by a troupe of male attendants waving hot-pink, fuchsia, and white plumes, Mrs. King made her entrance carried high on a litter, like an Ethiopian potentate of old. Riggs, clad in a gold-and-maroon warmup jacket with a commercial message for a candy bar—Sugar Daddy—inscribed on it, was wheeled in by some showgirls as he reclined in a chariot. For the life of me, this resembled nothing so much as the late Bobby Clark, with his painted-on glasses, making *his* entrance in a Broadway musical. To add to the rampant maladroitness, the anchorman for the telecast was Howard Cosell, complete with dinner jacket and a conspicuously thin understanding of tennis. To make sure that the woman-vs.-man theme of the promotion was not forgotten, Cosell was assisted by Rosemary Casals, Mrs. King's longtime friend and doubles partner, and, to balance things, Eugene Scott, a former Davis Cup player. From the outset, there was nothing tentative—to use Miss Casals' favorite word—about her remarks but, rather, an unvarying belligerence. Scott had comparatively little to say; as a man who had picked Riggs to win easily, there just wasn't much for him to comment on. As everyone knows, Mrs. King defeated Riggs very soundly in straight sets, 6–4, 6–3, 6–3. To Miss Casals' credit, she had predicted the score right on the nose.

The first mild shock of the match came in the sixth game of the first set when Riggs, who had just broken Mrs. King's service to go into the lead, was immediately broken back. This is precisely what doesn't happen in a typical Riggs match, and it reinforced a feeling many viewers had had from the start that he was in much less sharp physical shape than he had been against Mrs. Court. Too much partying, probably. At any rate, after that break-back, Mrs. King was never in trouble of any sort the rest of the evening.

A second mild shock was provided by the way in which Riggs lost the first set. With games 4–5, he was serving. The score went to 30–all. On the next point, a critical one, he threw up a lob to Mrs. King's backhand side—a good tactical play. It was a little short, though, and Mrs. King put it away with a sensational leaping backhand volley. (Miss Casals was also right in reminding us early on that Mrs. King plays the backhand volley as well as anyone in the game.) Then, on set point for Mrs. King, Riggs, the fabled nerveless hustler, double-faulted.

After that, I don't think anyone was surprised that Mrs. King won, but they were by the ease with which she did it. Despite the hard occasion, she kept her nerves well in check. She was the superior player in just about every respect. She served better on the fast acrylic-fibre surface. (Riggs could not get his first serve in all night.) With her fine anticipation and her speed afoot, she ran down most of his chips and dinks and other junk, frequently ending these exchanges with passing shots for clean winners. His famed lob, which was not working well, gave her no trouble, and, by my count, she missed only one overhead smash in the three sets. And, finally, and most emphatically, she beat him cold in the forecourt, outmaneuvering him and playing better shots.

This brings us to the real enigma of the match. What was Riggs, the master strategist, the Einstein of the *en-tous-cas,* doing playing serve-and-volley all night? That is Mrs. King's game, not his, and he doesn't play it well. To put it another way, why didn't Riggs spend more of his time back at the baseline, where he thrives, patiently playing *his* game, and feeding Mrs. King his best junk, the stuff that has been winning for him for years? And why, with all his tennis acumen, did he keep playing Mrs. King's stalwart backhand? I have no idea. Perhaps Mrs. King was so much the superior player that night that nothing Riggs tried would have prolonged the match appreciably. Anyway, the South Sea Bubble of 1973 has burst—with the difference from the original that everyone has got rich. I'm sorry that Major Wingfield couldn't have been around to see his game played in the Astrodome and, possibly, to slide in for a few well-paying commercials himself.

ASHE REACHES MATURITY

●

(1975)

When Arthur Ashe first began to attract national attention in 1963, it seemed that in time nothing would be beyond his achieving. His game continued to improve and he won an increasing share of the prize money after he became a professional, but in the early 1970s many observers felt that he had not fulfilled the promise he showed as a hard-hitting young man with a barely visible serve and a whiplash crosscourt backhand. Ashe kept working to become a more flexible player who would be able to probe the weaknesses of his opponents and keep them better in check. His big chance came in 1975 when he made his way to the final at Wimbledon for the first time and met the formidable defending champion, James Scott Connors.

Hazel Hotchkiss Wightman, the donor of the Wightman Cup (which women's tennis teams from Great Britain and the United States play for annually) and the winner of forty-four national tennis titles (including the United States Women's Singles Championship in 1909, 1910, 1911, and 1919), died in early December last year, two weeks before her eighty-eighth birthday. It was typical of her that she remained physically active in tennis through the last summer of her life despite an ailing left leg that forced her to use a cane. I was hardly surprised when I learned from a friend that Mrs. Wightman, who loved to teach young players, appeared one day at a small tennis camp twenty miles south of Chestnut Hill, Massachusetts, where she had her home, and coached a cross-section of the campers, standing on the baseline and rallying with them, her cane in her left hand and her racquet in her right as she sent back a succession of forehand shots. During one exchange, a ball was hit to her left side. Instead of letting it go, she lifted up her cane, so that she could move quickly into position, and after chopping a crisp backhand over the net exclaimed, "Oh, I'm not supposed to do that!" This picture—a most appropriate one of this exceptional woman—remains implanted in my mind.

In the last few years, however, I have found myself thinking frequently of Mrs. Wightman for reasons quite apart from her hardiness and longevity. As much as any tennis player I know of, she epitomized the ethic that an athlete can be fiercely competitive and at the same time, through instinct and character, perform with authentic sportsmanship. As a young girl entering her late teens in California, her home state, at the start of the century and attempting to find her way in tennis, Mrs. Wightman—then Hazel Hotchkiss—did not have an easy time of it. She came from Berkeley, in the central part of the state, and as her game improved and the orbit of her tournament play widened she ran smack into the prides of southern California—the famous Sutton sisters, from Pasadena. There were five Suttons in all. May, the youngest, was far and away the best. A sturdily built girl with a crushing forehand drive, limitless stamina, and the pugnacity of a bulldog, she abhorred the thought of losing and was not above consciously putting her opponents off if she felt that it would make victory surer. Having cleaned up all competition on the West Coast, in 1904, at the age of seventeen, she went East to the Philadelphia Cricket Club for the United States Championships and carried off the women's singles title with the loss of only three games in two sets. She didn't enter the Nationals again during her peak years, but in 1905 she undertook the long trip to England and became the first American, man or woman, to capture a Wimbledon championship. When she returned there the next year to defend her title, she was defeated in the challenge round by Dorothea Douglass, but the following year she turned the tables on Miss Douglass (who had become Mrs. Lambert Chambers). After that, Miss Sutton never went back to Wimbledon. In her first meeting with Hazel Hotchkiss, in California, she overpowered her. Miss Hotchkiss, who was a year older than May, was a compact young woman barely five feet tall. She had good control of her ground strokes, but the best of them couldn't begin to compare with May's awesome forehand. The only departments of Hazel's game that were superior to May's were her volley and her overhead, but getting to net against May was a very difficult thing. Early in 1910, the year after Hazel won *her* first United States Women's Singles Championship—thanks in good measure to May's absence—she at length succeeded in taking a set from May, which was something that no American woman except the other Suttons had ever done. Later that year, in the Ojai Valley tournament, she actually defeated her. The score was 2–6, 6–4, 6–0, and May did not like it at all. She marched off the court without congratulating the winner, and Hazel had to run around the net and intercept her, so that there could at least be a token handshake. By this time, Hazel had discovered that she could get to the net against May if she did it in two moves. First, after hitting a deep forehand or backhand, she moved from the baseline to the service line. This is a position where few players can live, but Hazel, a virtuoso at volleying, could handle May's returns at midcourt with a volley or half volley, after which she moved the rest of the way to net and put the ball away with an angled smash or volley.

Later that year, the two young Californians had a tremendous battle in the Pacific Coast Championship at Del Monte—"the Newport of the West." May won the first set, 7–5, but Hazel fought back and took the second, 6–4. Then May did a startling thing. Instead of returning to the court after the brief rest period for the deciding set, she told the umpire that she would like a cup of tea. During the twenty minutes it took for the tea to arrive and May to drink it, she stretched out in a wicker chair and regally took her ease. This outrageous stalling—it should never have been permitted—worked: she won the third set, 6–4. Following this extraordinary incident, the Hazel-May confrontations took on, for their supporters, the cold, strained grimness of an open feud, each side trying to outneedle and outshout the other. May was the winner in most of these matches, but one she didn't win was her first meeting with Hazel on grass, in 1911 at Niagara-on-the-Lake, in Ontario. May had whipped through the first set without dropping a game and was leading 5–1 in the second when Hazel began to hit the ball harder and better. As her play improved, May's fell off a little, and Hazel won six straight games to rescue the set, 7–5. She kept going, and ran off six more games in a row for the third set and the match. The point that should be brought out is that during this extended rivalry Hazel Hotchkiss, though disturbed by May Sutton's chronic bellicosity and appalled by the rowdy partisanship of the galleries, kept control of herself and played up to her ability. The understanding she gained of how to compete under intense pressure helped to make her a most effective teacher of young players with tournament ambitions, but what made her such an invaluable influence on them was her conviction—undoubtedly heightened by its absence in May's makeup—that good sportsmanship is crucial to the true enjoyment of tennis and other games.

In marked contrast, during the past several seasons certain men in the top stratum of the game have made followers of tennis only too well aware of how hollow the whole concept of sports becomes when players, especially of championship class, are guilty of bad and sometimes outlandish manners. The two chief offenders—this is not exactly in the nature of a scoop—have been Ilie Nastase, of Rumania, and Jimmy Connors, the twenty-three-year-old whiz kid from Belleville, Illinois. Nastase makes it a practice to argue with the umpire, to fuss about and take inordinate time getting into position to receive service, to provoke small tempests that allow him to stall, and so on—anything to throw his opponent off stride and break his concentration. Connors is an even more regrettable case, since the young American, a left-hander with a two-handed backhand, has demonstrated over the last two years that he is very likely not only the best player in the world today but perhaps the finest tennis talent that has emerged in this country since Pancho Gonzales, a quarter of a century ago. He is amazingly quick in getting to the ball, and he whacks his shots, both his ground strokes and his volleys, harder than anyone else in recent history—even harder than Lew Hoad, the Australian strong boy, did in the mid-nineteen-fifties. One has to go all the way back to Ellsworth Vines, in the early nineteen-thirties, to find Connors' equal in sheer ferocity of hitting. Unfortunately, Connors has marred his achievements by his behavior on the court. He is addicted to ploys of arrant gamesmanship, such as blowing on his racquet hand for long, annoying seconds when he is getting ready to serve and, also, bouncing the ball a distracting number of times just before starting his service motion. Often after he has made a brilliant shot, he turns his back on his opponent with a calculated flourish to rub it in. He has on many occasions topped off his general rudeness by using foul language that can be heard in the stands and by indulging in vulgar gestures, sometimes in response to taunts from spectators but at other times without any apparent provocation. Until late this summer, when he settled down a little, Connors did not seem to be unduly bothered by the knowledge that his court manners offended nearly all sports fans, and in particular the very people who best appreciated his uncommon skills.

It was as much his controversial personality as his dynamic tennis during the preceding twelve months that made the 1975 Wimbledon final, in which he was unexpectedly defeated by Arthur Ashe, one of the most fascinating and dramatic matches in tennis history. Before examining it in some detail, I feel a few general observations might well be made. Weeks after Wimbledon, tennis buffs were still talking about the match, and it is hard to remember another in the last decade that has been analyzed so carefully or discussed so frequently over so long a period. Certainly one reason the Wimbledon final aroused such attention is that, as the tennis world has long been aware, there is no love lost between Connors and Ashe. Last year, Connors filed an anti-trust suit, asking thirty-one million dollars in damages, against the officers of the Association of Tennis Professionals, the players' trade union, which Ashe was instrumental in forming, and which he currently serves as president. Then, in answer to a three-million-dollar libel suit filed against Connors and his flamboyant manager, Bill Riordan, by Jack Kramer, the executive director of the A.T.P., Connors and Riordan filed a counter-claim for ten million dollars against the A.T.P. officers. One of the bases of this complaint was a letter that Ashe had written to some members of the A.T.P. in which he called Connors "seemingly unpatriotic" for repeatedly turning down invitations to play on the United States Davis Cup team. Whereas Connors is as contentious as May Sutton was, and lets it all hang out, Ashe, like Mrs. Wightman, adheres to the principles of sportsmanship, regardless of the circumstances. "I'd be embarrassed if I had the temperament of Ilie Nastase," Ashe said this spring when he was interviewed by Edwin Newman on the television program "Speaking Freely." "I don't think Nastase could play tennis if he had my emotional makeup," he added. "Unless Nastase can emote, he can't play."

Ashe began to learn to control his feelings when he was very young. Born in Richmond, Virginia, in 1943, the son of a remarkable man who started out as a chauffeur, became a special police officer for the city's Department of Parks and Recreation, and later, while continuing to hold that job, organized his own custodial and landscaping businesses, Arthur played his first tennis at seven, on the courts at the Brook Field playground. This was one of the playgrounds his father supervised, and the family's house was situated on the property, close by the pool and the courts. By the age of ten, Arthur was the most promising of the young black players in the Richmond area. This earned him a number of summertime stays in Lynchburg with Dr. Robert W. Johnson, a black general practitioner and tennis enthusiast, who had set out to help the best prospects he could discover, with the aim of developing players able to hold their own against all comers in the tournaments put on by the United States Lawn Tennis Association. Dr. Johnson taught his protégés not only advanced tennis but good manners. "He figured that in the segregated South at the time—early fifties—if any of the tournament directors could figure out any excuse for kicking us black kids out, they would do it," Ashe explained when he appeared with Newman. "So Dr. Johnson had to selectively go through the screening process and pick only the kids who could take the mental pressure of not exploding on the court, as well as measuring up to the winning and losing. So we were taught, for instance, first of all, when you walk onto the court you have to be impeccable in your appearance. Your shorts and your shoes . . . When we got on the court during the junior days, we didn't have linesmen. You had an umpire, and that's all. You called your own lines and he helped. Every close call would go to your opponent, so that they could never say you cheated. When you changed sides, to change ends of the court, if your opponent happened to be serving next, you were to pick up every ball—the balls on your side—and hand them to your opponent. In fact, you were to be the most courteous guy—you know, faultless person—one could find. And this went on for eight or ten years."

While he was under the aegis of Dr. Johnson, Ashe won the United States Indoor Junior Championship in 1960 and 1961 as well as the United States Interscholastic Championship in 1961—the first black male to capture a national tennis title. (Althea Gibson had won the United States Women's Championship in 1957 and 1958, and also the women's championship at Wimbledon those two years.) When Ashe was old enough to go out on his own, he could conceivably have rebelled against this intensive drilling in deportment, but he had done his own thinking on the subject and reached the conclusion that the traditionalists were right—how you played the game *was* more important than whether you won or lost. As a result, because of the big difference in the two men's approaches, the Ashe-Connors final had not only the gravity of a grudge match but more than a touch of the hyped-up atmosphere of a jousting duel in a Walter Scott novel, with one of the combatants portrayed as the last word in chivalry and the other as villainy incarnate.

Connors was the odds-on favorite, offered at 3–20 in William Hill's bookmaking tent on the Wimbledon grounds. It was understandable. In 1974, he had established himself as the No. 1 player in the world by winning Wimbledon, the United States Open at Forest Hills, the Australian Open, the South African Open, and just about everything else he entered. On New Year's Day, 1975, his parade was halted when he lost to John Newcombe after a prodigious battle in the final of the Australian Open. Then Connors, a medium-sized athlete (five-ten, one-fifty) who is all whipcord, began marching again. In two challenge matches at Las Vegas, produced for national television, he defeated Rod Laver in February and Newcombe in April in very convincing fashion —he never looked like losing. During the cold-weather season, appearing for the most part on the rather weak Independent Players Association indoor circuit, which Riordan directs, he swept through one event after another, and, in fact, went unbeaten until he flew to Europe to play in some grass-court tournaments in preparation for Wimbledon, which starts the last week in June. At Chichester, he lost in the semifinals to a comparative unknown, Bernie Mitton, of South Africa, and at Nottingham he lost in the quarter-finals to Roscoe Tanner, a rising young player from Tennessee. On both these occasions, though, Connors was concerned primarily with getting his game tuned up for Wimbledon and not with winning these relatively unimportant tournaments. He had apparently paced himself perfectly. At Wimbledon, he did not drop a set in defeating John Lloyd, Vijay Amritraj, Mark Cox, Phil Dent, Raul Ramirez, and Tanner en route to the final. He was especially impressive against Tanner, who made the mistake of trying to outpower him. Connors, who probably has the best return of service in the game, simply waded into Tanner's cannonballs and blasted them back even faster than they had come over the net. Many old tennis hands say that they have never seen anyone else hit a tennis ball as hard as Connors did that day.

Ashe, in getting himself ready for the final, studied the films of Connors' matches against Ramirez and Tanner. "The Tanner match showed me how not to play Connors, and the Ramirez match showed me how to play him," Ashe said when I talked with him eighteen days after the Wimbledon final, at the annual Washington *Star* tournament. We were sitting in a trailer near the courts, where some of the players rested and relaxed between matches. "Ramirez has wonderful mobility and lots of shots, but he needed more firepower when he was in charge of the rallies. What he lacks is the ability to shift into high gear and blaze down the highway." Ashe's strategy called for him to cut loose when the situation warranted with his blistering ground strokes (his backhand is one of the fastest, and finest, in the world) and to make appropriate use of his wicked service (particularly a wide-swinging serve to Connors' two-handed backhand in the deuce court), but the root of his strategy was to give Connors as little pace as possible. He meant to feed him a steady diet of chips and dinks, keeping his shots low, changing their speed, and playing many of them down the middle to deny Connors the maximum crosscourt angles. He also meant to lob him a good deal. In defeating Bjorn Borg, the gifted nineteen-year-old Swedish player, in the World Championship of Tennis final at Dallas in mid-May and again at Wimbledon, Ashe had mixed in a much higher percentage of soft, short, angled strokes than he usually does, and it had worked out well. He had never employed these tactics against Connors, however, having concentrated mainly on playing him down the middle and attacking his second serve. They had met three times before, and Connors had won all three matches: 6–3, 4–6, 6–4, 3–6, 6–2 in the final of the 1973 United States Professional Championship; 6–4, 7–6, 6–3 in the final of the 1973 South African Open; and 7–6, 6–1, 6–3 in the final of the 1974 South African Open. Despite the fact that Connors was such a heavy favorite, Ashe went into the Wimbledon final in an exceedingly confident mood. He had played good and steady tennis during the first six months of the year, winning four W.C.T. tour tournaments—in Barcelona, Rotterdam, Munich, and Stockholm—in addition to the grass-court tournament at Beckenham, outside London, and he had also carried off a big event, the World Championship of Tennis. This helped immensely, as did the soundness of his tennis at Wimbledon, where he defeated Borg in four sets in the quarters and the renascent Tony Roche in five sets in the semis. What helped most of all was his conviction that the revised game plan he had formulated for Connors would be effective.

It was. Ashe beat Connors 6–1, 6–1, 5–7, 6–4. The score accurately reflected Ashe's superiority. It is probably safe to say that even the most devoted of Ashe's admirers had not dreamed he could ever dominate Connors that thoroughly. In the first set, Ashe broke Connors' service three times, handcuffing him with an adroit assortment of slow stuff. The second set came as easily. Sticking closely to his game plan, Ashe made few errors—in his mind, this was the first priority—and Connors, flustered by his inability to do what he wanted to do, continued to play far below his standard. For example, he hit a great many shots low into the net. Ashe was doing everything superbly. He was getting his first serve in consistently, and there was tremendous action on his key serve, the one he was hitting wide—and short—to Connors' backhand. He had almost infallible touch on his lobs. His volleying, usually the least dependable part of his game, was solid all the way. As tall and slender as a stalk of corn—he is six-one and weighs a hundred and fifty pounds—Ashe often fails to get down to the ball on his volleys, but on this day he was seeing the ball early and had plenty of time to move into position. The situation changed in the third set, however. Down a service break, Connors broke Ashe's serve in the sixth and twelfth games to take the set, 7–5. He had finally untracked himself and was now whipping the clean placements that one expected from him across the court and down the line. In the face of this surge, Ashe's play lost some of its authority. In the fourth set, Connors continued to come on. He won the first three games, breaking Ashe's serve in the second. Command of the match definitely seemed to have swung. Ashe nevertheless maintained the astonishing poise that had distinguished his play from the outset, and, staying patiently with his game plan, he regained the upper hand. In the fifth game, he won Connors' serve, setting up his points with care and imagination. In the ninth game, he won Connors' serve still another time, losing only one point. Now, at 5–4, he was serving for set, match, and championship. Often when players reach this stage in a match, their very nearness to their goal undoes them and they find a way to lose. Ashe, interestingly, had taken the precaution before going on the court to plan how he would serve the last game if he was out in front, feeling that it might help to allay anxiety if he had already made this decision. In this pivotal game, he really blazed down the highway, starting and finishing with two sharply hooking serves that Connors was barely able to get his racquet on. Ashe was the Wimbledon champion, and, for all his practiced cool, he could not prevent himself from punching the air with his fist to underline his joy.

There is no question that Ashe's conquest of Connors constituted the top performance of his career. The most fascinating aspect of it, of course, was that it was wrought by a type of tennis utterly uncharacteristic of Ashe. The younger Ashe whom we had watched mature—upsetting Roy Emerson at Forest Hills in 1965, at the age of twenty-two; reaching the final against Emerson in the Australian Championship in 1966, the year he graduated from the University of California at Los Angeles; reaching the semifinals at Wimbledon in 1968 and, later that year, the first year of open tennis, defeating Tom Okker, of the Netherlands, in the final at Forest Hills—had regularly hit the ball with such velocity that the gallery had difficulty following it. This made him an exciting player to watch, but his penchant for belting *every* shot made his matches oddly dull at the same time: most of the points were over before they had really got started—if Ashe didn't put the ball away with an immediate placement, he slashed it into the net or out of court. His failure to develop a fully orchestrated game, with subtlety and finesse supplementing his power, made him a great disappointment to many veteran observers who had judged him to have the talent to become perhaps as complete a player as earlier champions like Bill Tilden, Don Budge, and Pancho Gonzales. As the nineteen-seventies began, the general feeling in tennis circles was that Ashe would probably not fulfill his vast potential. For one thing, his match-playing ability was not at all on a par with his shotmaking ability. At times, he looked unbeatable, but all too often he lost matches he should have won, the most notable example being the Forest Hills final in 1972. Up against Nastase, he was ahead two sets to one and leading 4–3 in the fourth with his serve coming up. All he needed to do in order to win was to hold his serve twice. But he suddenly lost his concentration, and with it the fourth set, 4–6, and then the fifth, 3–6. He came to be regarded as a player who let his opportunities slip away. During the first seven months of 1973, for example, he reached the final of eight tournaments but won only one. By mid-1973, when the tennis boom had really exploded internationally, Ashe was thirty and was whirling around the world, involved with the W.C.T. circuit the first five months of the year and pursuing his own exotic schedule the rest of the time. When one watched him in action in person or caught him on television, it was evident that he was working diligently to introduce greater flexibility and sophistication into his tennis, and was making encouraging progress: his play had become more disciplined, and he was now much better at maneuvering his opponents. For all this, it came as a mild surprise when Ashe won those six tournaments in the first six months this year to move into a position just below Connors on the professional ladder, and it came as a stupendous surprise when he beat the unbeatable Connors at Wimbledon by throwing off his timing with that potpourri of chips, dinks, chops, underspin lobs, changeups, and spins.

Before the match, I doubt whether many people would have thought that this was the correct strategy to use against Connors or that, if it was, Ashe possessed the skill to execute it. Ashe understands this skepticism very well. "I think a good analogy would be the Muhammad Ali–George Foreman fight," he said when we talked. "Against a knockout puncher like Foreman, who would have expected Ali to adopt a strategy that called for him to lean back against the ropes and let Foreman keep coming at him until he punched himself out? Until the fight was over, you couldn't be sure the strategy *would* work. You know, right up to the last round, Foreman might have caught Ali with a big punch and knocked him out, and then everyone would have said that Ali's strategy had been dead wrong." Ashe paused for a moment. "I know that after I won the first two sets I wasn't gloating to myself, 'Gee, I'm playing well!' Rather, I was saying, 'My, Connors is playing badly!' I was wondering why he hadn't changed his game when he saw how I was playing him, and I was thinking that he'd probably start clicking at any moment—which he did in the third set. After I lost that set, I asked myself, 'Do I change my tactics now?' I decided not to. The basis for this was that I felt I could have won the third set. From then on, I worked mainly on avoiding errors and getting my first serve in, and I won the important games because Connors started making mistakes again. I suppose that is what surprised me most—the number of errors Connors made."

As has been appreciated for quite some time, Ashe is not only a marvellous tennis player but a man of unusual intelligence, articulateness, and width of vista. He knows his own mind clearly, and it is his credo that he has the right to lead his own life and establish his own priorities. This hasn't been easy, for no other athlete today has as much pressure put on him as Ashe does to appear at numberless functions and involve himself in all kinds of programs and causes. Aside from Muhammad Ali, he is undoubtedly the outstanding black athlete participating in an individual sport, and since people relate much more naturally to him than to Ali, what he does and says has enormous influence. His recent book, "Arthur Ashe: Portrait in Motion," which he wrote in collaboration with Frank Deford, offers a splendid picture of this singular young man and the complex world he lives in. It is made up of entries in a journal he kept for a year, from the weeks preceding Wimbledon in 1973 through Wimbledon in 1974. Over that period, he travelled a hundred and sixty-five thousand miles on the hundred and twenty-nine airplane trips he made to five continents to play tennis. Besides covering the events in his professional and personal life during that year, the entries present an amalgam of his thoughts on many subjects: the game of tennis, his colleagues as players and as individuals, his father, his boyhood, the best hotels and restaurants he has hit on his travels, his experiences as the first black male to play in the South African Open and his profound observations about that country, his friends, old Davis Cup traumas (e.g., Ecuador 3, United States 2), his long-range ambitions, what it is to be black, and why Connors is so good. There is an awful lot to be learned from this book.

From the opening pages, one is conscious that "Arthur Ashe: Portrait in Motion" is an altogether different kind of undertaking from the dozens of vapid, superficial books about star athletes that are churned out every year. Here, for example, is a short excerpt from the first entry, written in London on June 11, 1973:

> And then, at last, today was also the day that my Grandmother Cunningham died. . . .
>
> I had a moment's hesitation about whether I should spend the money just to fly over and right back for the funeral, but there was really no

decision to make. Big Mama was one of my heroines. I must go.

She was my mother's mother, and she raised ten children, almost single-handedly. The oldest of them was only seventeen when my grandfather died. You hear so much about matriarchal black families —well, Big Mama was a black matriarch but only because she had to be and because she was good at it. She kept the family together, all the while working full-time in the kitchen at a white public school. She was a strong, dear, fine woman. I'll go home.

And here is the brief second entry, written the following day:

I ran this morning in Hyde Park; I've run in some of the great parks of the world. I was up by the Inn on the Park, where Howard Hughes lives on the top floor. They say. Then this afternoon, Kathy and I visited a few museums. We started at the Lefevre Gallery, which was showing a collection by Edward Burns. Then we went on to the Tate Gallery and finally to Harrods, where I got carried away and bought a Rembrandt etching. It's entitled *The White Negress,* and it set me back some money. But I'm damned excited. There are only eight of this particular etching in the whole world; after they were run off, they destroyed the plate. So, I own an original Rembrandt, and I'll probably do a lot of bragging.

The book keeps building all the way. There are countless other passages in it that I would like to quote, but I will limit myself to two. The first is an analysis of Connors' game after their first meeting, in Boston in July of 1973:

I didn't underestimate Connors going into this, but I came out with an even greater respect for his ability. You seldom encounter anyone who can hit ground strokes as deep as he did as consistently as he did. He was pressing me all the time, and for someone who is as immature as Connors is, he is surprisingly court-smart. I think a lot of that comes from Pancho Segura, who has helped coach Jimmy for several years. . . .

While he has no intellectual pretensions whatsoever, he does have a sharp court mind, a sort of spatial sixth sense that some guys have that tells you: if I hit such-and-such a shot from this spot in such-and-such a way, the odds are x that the ball will be returned to such-and-such. Segura probably heightened that awareness, but it is not the sort of thinking that can be drummed into someone; Connors must possess the instinct. As a consequence, and since he moves well, Connors always seemed perfectly placed and in just the right form to hit back any shot of mine.

And, finally, here is a portion of Ashe's entry for November 29th, written on the plane taking him from Johannesburg to New York:

> We learned today that nonwhites will be permitted to compete on the Sugar Circuit. The situation isn't perfect. The players must be affiliated with SALTA, the approved white tennis organization, to have their entry considered, and also, the Sugar Circuit is a relatively high class of play. If the South African Open is pro ball, then the Sugar Circuit is the equivalent of major college, and you can't succeed in bigtime college athletics any more than you can in the pros unless you can compete freely at all lower levels of play. But there may be some advantages to starting out at the top. You get more publicity. And maybe you learn faster out of embarrassment. When Dr. Johnson finally got his black players admitted to the interscholastics, it took three years before one of his boys so much as won a game. But they got the chance—and hardly a decade later I won the title.
>
> I've decided to set up a foundation for the nonwhite South African players. Those who show promise will get money for equipment and coaching. Also, all the used rackets and clothes and any other tennis paraphernalia that I have left over will go to black South African players. I've already been criticized by a black American newspaper-woman for making this decision and for not providing for the tennis players of Harlem first. Funny how people like to make up your mind for you.

When Ashe is in this country, he generally spends some time at an apartment he has in New York and at one he has at the Doral Country Club, in Miami, but he is obviously happiest when he is on the professional tennis tour, wherever it happens to be pitching its tent that week, and is surrounded by his friends and rivals. The tour is currently the nearest thing he has to a home—"not so much a physical place as an environment," in his view. On his travels, he takes along as many as sixty-five tapes of music he likes and a large supply of books. His mother taught him to read when he was four, and he has been close to books ever since. He has read all of Hermann Hesse's novels and reread most of them. "Hesse's philosophy really fits tennis players," he says. "I think that's because it's so individual, so first-personal and introspective. It has a sense of aloneness about it." He has read and reread Robert Ardrey's three major books, and he is an admirer of the work of William Styron, John Updike, and James Michener. He also likes to chase down facts in the World Book Encyclopedia: "When you look something up, most of the time it leads you to several related subjects that are loaded with interest." His taste in music ranges from Brahms' Violin Concerto to

George Harrison and Stevie Wonder and tapes he makes himself of the soul music played on WBLS, a black FM station in New York. "The stuff from WBLS sounds terrific when I'm in Europe—the incongruity of it all makes you feel so comfortable," he told me. "Another thing. I love Beethoven's Ninth. It's rather corny to say that, because nearly everyone loves it. Anyhow, there's nothing I enjoy more than to get up on a Sunday morning in some hotel—say, the Westbury in London, or the Hong Kong Hilton, or the Négresco in Nice—order breakfast from room service, and then put on the Ninth Symphony and let it fill the room." On such a Sunday morning, Ashe is likely to be wearing a T-shirt with "World Citizen" across the front—an item he sent for after he saw it advertised in the *Saturday Review*. He does think in global terms. I remember well how during our talk in the players' trailer at the Washington *Star* tournament he paused at one moment and surveyed the long, narrow room. "Let me see how many different countries the fellows sitting around here come from," he said. "I make it seven. This is just a small sampling of all the touring players, of course. The point is we all get along pretty darn well. It would be nice, wouldn't it, if the world were like this."

THE EVER MORE
COMPLEX WORLD OF TENNIS

(1976)

Tennis has long been called, and with reason, the Balkans of sport: Just when it looks as if the various power blocs and ambitious promoters have reached an understanding, the entente breaks down. During the prosperous years that followed the arrival of open tennis, new organizations, such as World Team Tennis, for example, wanted a piece of the action. When W.T.T. succeeded by signing a number of the top stars to big contracts, this meant that the European spring features (like the Italian and French Opens) in which they usually appeared were deprived of much of their lustre. The players with reputations naturally profited from this demand for their services. At the same time the standard of their tennis naturally suffered if they tried to take on too much. The only real winners were the individuals whose sense of proportion balanced out with their sense of economics.

It was not until after the First World War that tennis became the global game we know today. For example, all the Wimbledon champions, men and women alike, came from English-speaking countries—Britain, Ireland, the United States, Australia, and New Zealand. While the tennis world of the twenties was made up of far more international fields, there were only a few minor modifications in the annual tournament schedule that had prevailed for decades. In the winter and early spring, the players occasionally competed indoors on wood, mainly in and around Paris, but for the most part they congregated on the Riviera, coming up against each other at Menton, Nice, Cannes, Monte Carlo, and the other oases on the Côte d'Azur. In May, the caravan moved on to the premier clay-court event, the French Championships, founded in 1891, and then it was time to head for England and tune up for Wimbledon and tennis on grass by entering one or two of the scattering of ancient grass-court tourneys, like Beckenham and Queens. When Wimbledon was over, most of the European players returned to the Continent for the lesser championships; meanwhile, the Americans came home for our national clay-court championships, after which they began the week-by-week crawl up the East Coast before heading for Forest Hills and the national singles championships. At intervals during the year, Davis Cup preliminary rounds, leading to the Challenge Round, were held, and at the end of December, after what was usually a restful autumn, the old year concluded and the new year began with the Australian Championships, established in 1905 and regarded as the fourth major championship, the others being Wimbledon, the American, and the French. The dramatic arrival of the United States and France in the twenties as first-class tennis powers did alter the style of play and the general flavor of the game to an appreciable degree, but, for all that, the tempo within the microcosm of tennis remained stately and unhurried. The stars rarely took part in more than twelve or fifteen events in an average year, resting and practicing and learning during the open weeks. Since the players were not chronically over-tennised, as they now are, and so had the mental and physical reserves to rise to the big occasions, small wonder that there were so many memorable matches.

I mention all this because the tennis scene is so different today. Throughout the year, there is scarcely a week in which a big event is not scheduled, and some weeks there are three or four events of stature being played on as many continents. It might be instructive to note, briefly, the extent of the activities and domains of the leading entrepreneurs—World Championship Tennis, Virginia Slims, the Commercial Union Grand Prix, and World Team Tennis. All of them, one way or another, came into being because of the enormous expansion of professional tennis in the last decade and the commercial opportunities that this made available, particularly when television became more and more interested. World Championship Tennis, the organization that Lamar Hunt, of Dallas, has headed since 1968, the year in which open tennis actually arrived, was connected this past season with twenty-seven tournaments played in twelve countries between the second week in January and the first week in May. Fifty-seven players took part in one or more of these tournaments, most of which offered a purse of sixty thousand dollars. At the same time that the men were competing on the W.C.T. circuit, the women were playing the Slims circuit, which was founded by the women professionals in 1970: eleven tournaments, all in the United States, and each worth seventy-five thousand dollars in prize money. As soon as W.C.T.'s allotted segment of the year—the first four and a half months—was finished, in stepped World Team Tennis and the Commercial Union Grand Prix. World Team Tennis, which Larry King, Billie Jean's husband, helped to start and continues to guide, is alive and well in its third year, and is even showing signs of growth, despite the almost unanimous prediction of the experts that it would never make it. It is at present composed of teams (with rosters of six or seven players) representing ten cities or localities, from coast to coast. Each team engages in forty-four matches between early May and mid-August, with a three-week hiatus for Wimbledon. Interestingly, it is the women who have made W.T.T. go. Whereas Ilie Nastase and Rod Laver were the only men ranked in the top ten in the world who contracted to play in the league this past year, all the outstanding women players were in its fold, including the top five: Chris Evert, Evonne Goolagong, Martina Navratilova, Billie Jean King, and Virginia Wade. It was the women who were the drawing cards, Evert and Goolagong especially. This was Evert's first year in W.T.T., and when she decided to sign with the Phoenix team, for which her best friend, Kristien Kemmer Shaw, plays, it practically guaranteed the survival of the league. (Evert had had reservations about joining W.T.T., with its punishing schedule and constant travel, but after Navratilova signed with Cleveland last autumn she really had no choice: if she had stayed out, she would have had no opportunity to play against the best women players, except at Wimbledon, over a stretch of three and a half months, and her game would have suffered.) Finally, there is the Grand Prix, now in its seventh season. This year, it is made up of forty-eight tournaments held in twenty-two countries from the middle of May to the end of November. At the close of the year, a bonus pool—it will be close to a million dollars—will be parcelled out in graduated amounts among the thirty-five leading point scorers in singles and the twenty leading doubles players. Last year, Guillermo Vilas, of Argentina, who led the

Grand Prix singles players, won the top prize in the pool—a hundred thousand dollars.

In addition to all the competitions coordinated by the Grand Prix, W.T.T., Virginia Slims, and W.C.T., any reputable tennis player who may have a few idle moments can find a little action on several minor circuits and in a number of independent tournaments of a fairly high class. It is safe to say that nowadays a very small number of the men and women on or near the top level play fewer than twenty-five tournaments a year, and several play close to forty. With the towering prize money now available, it is easy to understand why most players find it so difficult to take time off periodically from the grind for a spot of rest and relaxation. Who knows when the Golconda will run out? On the other hand, there is little question that the almost continuous tournament pressure accounts in large part for the failure of many talented young players to realize their promise, and also for the astonishing lack of consistency in the performances of both the young players and the veterans in what used to be the most form-abiding of sports.

This season, a striking illustration of how gruelling modern tennis, with its crammed schedule, can be was provided by Chris Evert. This was ironic, inasmuch as she is one of the few players who are intelligent enough to make it a practice to escape regularly from the competitive maelstrom and to take a breather for a week or two. Evert's commitments, however, caught up with her in July. On Friday the second, she played the Wimbledon women's singles final, defeating Goolagong. On Saturday the third, she teamed with Navratilova to win the Wimbledon women's doubles final. On Sunday the fourth, she flew back to New York. Customarily, Evert gives herself a week or two after arriving home to recuperate from the strain of the Wimbledon fortnight. This year, however, having joined W.T.T., which starts the second half of its season directly after Wimbledon, she didn't have the time to spare. On Monday the fifth, she flew to Cleveland, where Phoenix was playing, and won her singles from Navratilova. On Tuesday the sixth, Phoenix met Boston in Boston, and Evert won her singles from Kerry Melville Reid. On Wednesday the seventh, a day off, Phoenix travelled to Pittsburgh, where, the following night, she lost her singles to Goolagong. On Friday the ninth, on to Indianapolis, where she defeated Mona Guerrant, of the Indiana team. No rest for the weary. The next day, she had to fly out to Oakland for the W.T.T. All-Star Game, in which she was again defeated by Goolagong. During the two weeks after the All-Star Game, she played on eight nights, and then this killing pace caught up with her. She came down with a virus and was confined to bed for several days, missing three matches before she was ready to play again. However, there is no need to get all worked up about Chris Evert's problems. Last year, this sturdy, sensible young lady, pacing herself well, earned $412,977 in prize money alone, which is more than many of us make in two years, or even three.

Over the last twelve months, such an abundance of interesting and provocative developments have taken place in tournament tennis that it would be a sizable task just to list them all. Perhaps the best solution would be to set down, as briefly as possible, eight aspects of the international scene that seem to have especial significance.

ITEM: Granted that too much attention has already been lavished on Ilie Nastase, the enigmatic Rumanian, I'm afraid there is no avoiding comment on his achievements and aberrations previous to the recent United States Open Championships at Forest Hills. (We will get to these later.) After a mediocre season, in which his once wide repertoire of strokes had lost their gleam and sting, he suddenly began to play exceedingly well again late in 1975. In late November and early December, in the Kungliga Tennishallen, in Stockholm, packed houses of thirty-seven thousand fans watched the Grand Prix Masters, hoping to witness the eventual triumph of nineteen-year-old Bjorn Borg, the national idol of Sweden. On the first night, Nastase almost wrecked the tournament by going into a stalling routine so outrageous that his opponent, Arthur Ashe, for all his stoicism, could stomach it no longer and left the court in disgust. It took a lot of high-level confabulation by the officers of the International Lawn Tennis Federation before everything was straightened out. Anyhow, in the final, Nastase administered a shocking defeat to Borg, losing only five games in sweeping three straight sets. Nastase continued to play first-class tennis in 1976. He twice defeated Jimmy Connors, generally regarded as the best player in the world, during the indoor season, and at Wimbledon, after Connors had been upset in the quarter-finals, Nastase was a heavy favorite to win the title. He did not. In the final, Borg, an altogether different player from the one Nastase had trounced in Stockholm in December, beat him decisively. All in all, however, Nastase enjoyed such a renaissance this year that one might think he would have been only too happy to dispense with his familiar olio of unsportsmanlike acts—rude personal slurs and swearing, delaying play and abusing officials, and so on. Not on your life. As shrewd as a ward heeler, he appreciates his power as a box-office attraction and the consequent timorousness of the tennis hierarchy about penalizing him for his behavior, lest such a move hurt the ticket sales at upcoming tournaments. This past March, an official finally took the type of action against Nastase that was long overdue.

The official was Charles Hare, a former British Davis Cup player, who was serving as the referee at the American Airlines tournament in Palm Springs. In the quarter-final match between Nastase and Roscoe Tanner —Tanner was in front all the way and was leading 6–3, 2–1, and 40–0 when the end came—Hare defaulted Nastase when he left the court and stretched out in a box with his feet hoisted over the railing. Previously, after warnings by Hare, Nastase had made a mocking gesture at him and had sworn at him. Why Nastase feels compelled to cheapen everything he touches is beyond understanding, but I think it must be clear by now that, for a man with his earning power, little wrist slaps like fines of a few thousand dollars or short suspensions mean nothing at all. (After his performance at Palm Springs, the International Professional Tennis Council, incomprehensibly, did not so much as reprimand him.) Tennis has rules, and whenever Nastase breaks them he should immediately be defaulted. If he insists on breaking the rules regularly, he should be suspended—for six months or a year, depending on the circumstances. It is as simple as that. Ilie Nastase is an extremely talented athlete, but the success of tennis tournaments assuredly does not depend on whether or not he is appearing.

ITEM: In Stockholm, just before Christmas, Borg more than made up for his disappointing showing against Nastase in the Grand Prix Masters two weeks earlier by leading the Swedish Davis Cup team to a 3–2 victory over Czechoslovakia in the Challenge Round. Borg had a hand in all three points that Sweden won. In his first singles, he overwhelmed Jiri Hrebec, 6–1, 6–3, 6–0. He teamed with Ove Bengtson to defeat Vladimir Zednik and Jan Kodes in the doubles, 6–4, 6–4, 6–4, and then nailed down the victory with a great performance against the redoubtable Kodes, 6–4, 6–2, 6–2. Sweden thus became the first European country in over forty years to win the Davis Cup, and only the seventh country to win it since the competition was inaugurated, in 1900. The others have been the United States, Great Britain (or the British Isles, as it was called in the early days), Australasia (Australia and New Zealand in combination), France, Australia, and South Africa, which in 1974 won the cup from India by default.

ITEM: Lately, we have developed a penchant for bungling our early-round Cup matches against Latin-American nations. In 1974, we were eliminated, 4–1, by Colombia, in Bogotá, and in 1975 by Mexico, 3–2, in Palm Springs. We kept this streak going last December. Mexico ousted us, 3–2, when Raul Ramirez, who seems to come up with inspired tennis in the Davis Cup, outclassed Jimmy Connors in the deciding singles, 2–6, 6–3, 6–3, 6–4. The match at Mexico City marked Connors' long-awaited début in Davis Cup play, and the confident way

Ramirez handled him in the clutch disclosed certain vulnerabilities in Connors' game and temperament which we had not been quite so clearly aware of before.

ITEM: Why are so many young athletes who could pursue success-ful careers in other sports leaning more to tennis than they used to? Well, look at it this way: On February 28th, in a nationally televised "Challenge Match" played in Las Vegas, Connors met the Spaniard Manuel Orantes, who had defeated him in the final of the 1975 United States Open Championship, at Forest Hills. It was no contest. It took Connors about an hour and twenty minutes to whip through Orantes, who seemed quite unprepared physically and mentally. The score was 6–2, 6–1, 6–0. For this brief workout, Connors, one hears in the Rialto, received around half a million dollars and Orantes around a quarter of a million. Orantes is a decent, worthy young man, and when one at-tempts to figure out why he did not train more assiduously for this match and pour more heart and effort into it, one can only conclude that he was unable to adjust to the dizzying prospect of making such an unreal amount of money for just showing up. Money can bewilder as well as corrupt.

ITEM: The best tennis of the year was probably played by Chris Evert and Evonne Goolagong. Indeed, a good case can be made that the standard of their play in all but two of their seven meetings this year was as high as has ever been attained over a sustained period in women's tennis, for the fact is that Suzanne Lenglen and Helen Wills Moody, during their long but separated reigns, seldom came up against opponents whose skills approached their own, and the same situation existed during the shorter reigns of Alice Marble and Maureen Con-nolly, the two other women players whom many old tennis enthusiasts rate among the top four talents. When players of relatively equal profi-ciency meet in an individual sport, such as tennis, it is a rare occasion when both manage to produce their best stuff, but this year Goolagong and Evert did it frequently. In fact, each kept forcing the other to raise the pitch of her game, and in the many long and beautifully played points during their duels both were often compelled to improvise shots they had never attempted before and to devise spontaneous new tactics in response to unexpected patterns of attack. Goolagong, a classically graceful athlete from the wheat country of New South Wales, has been known since her arrival on the international scene, in 1971, chiefly for her speed of foot, her naturally fluent backhand, and her wandering concentration. In 1975, just before Wimbledon, she married Roger Cawley, an English metals broker. She has been so conspicuously happy in this marriage that many court-side psychologists flatly predicted that her famed "walkabouts"—the passages in her matches when her mind drifted away from her tennis—would be increasingly frequent and prolonged. They couldn't have been more wrong. This year, for the first time, Goolagong got down to work in every match and displayed a wholly new determination to win.

The formidable appeal that both Goolagong and Evert possess derives not only from their ability to play such fine assertive tennis but also from their innate sportsmanship—an uncommon commodity these days. They are not close friends, but ever since they first came to know each other, in Dallas in 1972, they have had an instinctive mutual liking and respect. They are considerate of all their opponents, but Evert is especially careful not to rob Goolagong of the glory of a deserved victory, and Goolagong has the same concern in regard to Evert. While Evonne's qualities are properly appreciated by the tennis crowds, I am not at all sure that Chris' are, because her court manner is so disciplined. From the moment she walks on the court for a match, she is all business and concentration—that is the way she was taught to approach a match. She has no convenient smiles for the spectators in the stands. She is completely wrapped up in the task at hand. Though she is not as poker-faced as Helen Wills Moody was, she shows little emotion on court. Every now and then after losing a point she feels she should have won, Chris will frown a little and twist her shoulders around quickly as she walks toward the baseline, but that is about the extent of her histrionics. She is an unfailingly courteous and gracious competitor, but because she devotes her attention exclusively to playing tennis and remains so cool and unsweaty (hence her appellation the Ice Maiden) galleries have a tendency to overlook these attributes. It is not surprising that she has never really caught on with Wimbledon's famous "mums," the middle-aged women who turn out faithfully each afternoon of the tournament, year after year. The mums' ideal is a different type of girl: a nice, good-natured, well-mannered, sort of floppy English girl (like Christine Truman), a smiling girl who plays good tennis but comes across primarily as a jolly good sport—in short, a girl whom you could take home to Mum and who would pitch right in and help her make the cucumber-and-watercress sandwiches for tea.

ITEM: During the past few seasons, there has been a definite effort among the organizations that promote tennis in a big way to move up a notch in importance and gain acceptance on about the same level as the traditional major tournaments. The three that have most zealously sought this enhanced status are the United States Professional Indoor Championships, the Grand Prix Masters (an eight-man tournament that wraps up the long Grand Prix season), and the World Championship Tennis Finals (which is also made up of an eight-man field and similarly brings the W.C.T. season to a climax). The people behind each of these events feel that the efficient way it is conducted, the calibre of its field, and the sizable prize money it distributes should entitle it to as much prestige as, say, the French Open.

Having long been impressed by Lamar Hunt—the low-pressure, dignified manner in which he brought W.C.T. along has undeniably had important repercussions all through professional tennis—I thought it might be a good idea this past May to go down to Dallas for the W.C.T. Finals and see if they had the ambience of a major sports occasion. I'm afraid that, for me, they didn't. The tennis was dreary. This was inevitable, for the players were having to belt the slow, heavy "Australian" ball, which is manufactured in the United States, on an extremely slow and heavy Supreme plastic court. In just about every match, as a result, each player camped on the baseline waiting until his opponent hit a short ball; then he came up and played a forcing stroke. On many points, thirty or forty cautious topspin shots were exchanged before one of the players ventured into the forecourt to see what he could do with a slightly mis-hit return. During one rally in the final, in which Vilas faced Borg, the ball crossed the net no fewer than eighty-five times before Vilas sliced a loose backhand eighteen inches into the alley. As Don Budge, the great champion of the nineteen-thirties, commented after the match, "I should think they would get bored having to hit so many balls to win a point. It would be easier to make a deep shot, go to the net, and get the point over with." Anyhow, in their battle of attrition Vilas was defeated (1–6, 6–1, 7–5, 6–1) by Borg, who, incidentally, had lost in the final the two previous years.

ITEM: Given Jimmy Connors' extraordinary talent, how does one account for his disappointing record during the first eight months of the year? I am thinking particularly of his two defeats on grass by Roscoe Tanner—first at Beckenham, in a warmup tournament for Wimbledon, and then his decisive loss (6–4, 6–2, 8–6) in the Wimbledon quarter-finals. One possible explanation is this: When Connors, essentially a power hitter, finds himself behind in a match, because he is a bit off form that day or because his opponent is employing tactics he had not anticipated, he appears to think that the one way to regain the upper hand is to rev up his own game—serve harder, get to the ball faster, whack that forehand, knock the cover off the ball with his backhand, and so on. It doesn't always work, because by overhitting everything he often throws his timing off, and when that happens his confidence begins to ebb. One wonders why Connors, after spending so many years in competitive tennis, hasn't developed a second, different game, which he can resort to on these occasions. When things have not been working well, most champions have been able to change from their usual style of play to another style, which enables them to slow down an opponent and quite often makes it possible for them to find a way to beat him. Tilden, who without a doubt had a greater diversity of defensive and offensive maneuvers in his repertoire than anyone else in tennis history, used to preach that the key to winning a match is to break up your opponent's game. Connors hasn't learned this yet, but no doubt he will in time.

ITEM: This past year saw Bjorn Borg fulfill his immense promise when, in early July, a month after his twentieth birthday, he won Wimbledon. When he was nine, his father, Rune Borg, who was a clothing salesman in Södertalje, near Stockholm, won a tennis racquet as a prize in a table-tennis tournament. He gave the racquet to his son, who became captivated by tennis and thought of almost nothing else. In 1972, at fifteen, he made his début as a member of the Swedish Davis Cup team and defeated Onny Parun, the solid internationalist from New Zealand, in five sets after dropping the first two. Two years later, he won both the Italian and the French Championships and also the United States Professional Championship, and in 1975 he successfully defended his French and U.S. pro titles. By that time, he had grown into a tall, slim, strong young man with long blond hair and Nordic light-blue eyes, and had required the protection of a police bodyguard to survive two turbulent Wimbledons during which he was repeatedly mobbed by armies of English schoolgirls. However, he had never played a really good Wimbledon and had played only one good Forest Hills—last summer, when he lost in the semifinals to Connors—and since many people felt that he had improved hardly at all between seventeen and nineteen, considerable controversy centered on him. One group felt that Borg's manager, Mark McCormack, an American who operates on a worldwide scale, overbooked him for exhibitions and tournaments, with the result that when the big events came around he was so worn down that he hadn't enough strength left to fight his way back into a match once he had fallen behind. Another group believed that what had held him back was the fact that he had been coached not by any of the well-known gurus but by Lennert Bergelin, a former star of the Swedish Davis Cup team, who serves as the team's nonplaying captain. A third group was frankly doubtful whether Borg actually had a champion's game. With his wonderful ability to retrieve just about anything, and his coolness under stress—his normal pulse rate is reported to be forty-five—he was a tough man to beat, but his shotmaking wasn't all that impressive. His serve was all right, but neither exceptionally fast nor exceptionally accurate. His ground strokes were the heart of his game. With his semi-Western grip, he whipped his forehand with heavy topspin, and he also relied on a two-handed backhand hit with heavy topspin. He could hurt you with these strokes, for he used the most tightly strung racquet of any player—it is strung with almost eighty pounds of tension, or about twenty pounds more than most tournament players use—and this gave him a good deal of pace. However, he lacked the approach shots to supplement his topspin drives, and rarely came in to net. When he did, he demonstrated himself to be a fairly able volleyer but not an outstanding one.

This June, a very fortunate thing happened to Borg. In the French Championship, he was eliminated in the quarter-finals by the smooth young Roman Adriano Panatta, who had just won the Italian Championship and went on to win the French as well. This gave Borg the better part of a week to rest up, and then, before Wimbledon, another full week, which he and Bergelin spent at the Cumberland Club, in North London. They devoted five hours each day to building up Borg's serve and volley—the type of game that usually wins on grass. They had never made that kind of preparation before, and it brought about a small miracle. At Wimbledon, Borg served much more powerfully over a protracted stretch than he ever had in the past. It appeared that he had altered his service motion so that he was hitting the ball more at the top of his arc—an extended arc—and his timing seemed discernibly better. In any event, his serve came streaking off his racquet, and since it was also beautifully controlled, even seasoned players like Marty Riessen, whom Borg met in the third round, couldn't handle it at all. With most of the experts concentrating on the progress of Connors and Nastase, Borg's round-by-round advance through a very rugged quarter of the draw did not attract the attention it might have until he reached the semifinals. There he defeated Tanner, Connors' conqueror, 6–4, 9–8, 6–4, serving as effectively as Tanner, who probably has the swiftest, heaviest serve among the players capable of winning championships. Borg was now in the final. He had not dropped a set, despite the fact that from the fourth round on he was handicapped by a pulled stomach muscle, incurred, unquestionably, by the increased effort he was putting into his serve, as well as by the strenuous pre-Wimbledon week when he had worked so diligently to develop that bigger serve. The rest of the tournament, he took cortisone injections before his matches to dull the pain, and occasionally during a match he applied an anesthetic spray to his stomach during the changeovers between games.

The final, Borg versus Nastase, loomed as a tremendous match, since Nastase also had not dropped a set during the championship. Like Borg, he had been serving superbly—as, in fact, he had during most of the 1976 season. Nastase is not a big, muscular man, but, with his wonderfully strong and flexible wrist, he was hitting his serves with great speed and putting the ball just where he wanted to. In the final, he got off fast. He broke Borg's serve in the second game, and in the fourth game, leading 3–0, he held break point three times. Borg, with his serve at last beginning to crackle, staved him off. Then and there, Borg took control of the match, which he ultimately won, 6–4, 6–2, 9–7. There is no doubt that his hard, skidding service had a great deal to do with his victory—he put in seventy-one of a hundred and eleven first serves, a very good percentage—but his all-round play was clearly superior to Nastase's. It was a magnificent achievement for Borg, this sudden bursting into full bloom at just the age when the talent of many youthful prodigies begins to fade, so that before you know it they start to slip back and become undistinguished members of the pack.

FOREST HILLS AND
THE FINAL BETWEEN
CONNORS AND BORG

(1976)

*Jimmy Connors was born in September 1952, and Bjorn Borg in June
1956. The difference in their ages largely explains why Connors had the
upper hand in the early meetings between these prodigies, such as his
7–5, 7–5, 7–5 victory in the semis at Forest Hills in 1975. The following
year Connors and Borg each made his way to the final at Forest Hills,
and a tremendous battle ensued. The deciding factor was the tie breaker
—it went to twenty points—that determined the winning and losing of
the third set. This was a wild and woolly tournament, and there have
been few matches west of Bucharest as bizarre as the collision in the
fourth round between Nastase and Tanner. Held at night beneath the
lights that had been set up the year before, it reached its climax a few
minutes before one o'clock in the morning.*

Last year, as you may remember, the United States Open Championships underwent a radical transformation. The old grass courts at the
West Side Tennis Club, in Forest Hills, which had deteriorated terribly
over the years, were dug up and replaced by courts made of Har-Tru,

a material manufactured from crushed greenstone, which resembles clay in texture and, like clay, produces a slower, higher bounce than grass. As a result, the serve-and-volley artists, who thrive on grass, were no longer the dominant force in the championships. In their stead, there came to the fore a whole different set of players, from all over the world, who had grown up on clay, *the* international surface, and were skilled in the specific strokes and tactics that clay encourages.

By Labor Day last year, when the field in the men's singles had been reduced to the last sixteen, there was no doubt that this was indeed a new and different U.S. Open. The players who were now commanding the matches were the skillful baseliners who could get the ball back over the net time after time with their reliable topspin forehand and sliced or topspin backhand. For the most part, they were content to wait for an error by their opponent, but every so often they would take advantage of a short return and move into the forecourt behind a forcing shot. (Since games and sets took more time on Har-Tru than on grass, in order to keep the tournament on schedule, the men's singles matches during the first three rounds were shortened from the traditional best of five sets to the best of three.) Foreign players with solid clay-court credentials but with only the skimpiest of reputations in this country suddenly popped into the spotlight. In the second round, for example, Balazs Taroczy, a slim Hungarian, ousted Tom Okker, of Holland, the sixth seed, in straight sets. In that same round, Hans Kary, of Austria, whom, to be frank, I had never heard of before, gave Jan Kodes, the Czechoslovakian star, a terrific battle and held one match point before he went down, 5–7, in the third set, a victim of Kodes' courage in the clutch and his own wavering belief in his ability to win —the old story. As I sat watching this struggle in which all the shades of torment and hopefulness passed across the faces of the two antagonists, whenever I studied the spectators tensely packed in the field-court stand I got the fanciful notion that all of them came from somewhere close to the route of the Danube and had been well acquainted from childhood with that special Mittel European experience—the clay-court match fought with all the bitter zeal of a boundary dispute.

This year, representatives from no fewer than thirty-one foreign countries—including three in Africa, eight in South America, and two in Asia—were on hand at Forest Hills. On September 1st, the opening day of the twelve-day tournament, I spent a modicum of time taking in the action on the stadium court and devoted most of the afternoon to wandering around the outside courts and immersing myself in the pungent international atmosphere. For example, after watching Corrado Barazzutti, of Italy, dispose of Paul Kronk, of Australia, in the grandstand court, I stayed there for the start of the match between Raul Ramirez, of Mexico, and Patrick Proisy, of France, then moved around the field courts and caught a little of such confrontations as Brian Fairlie, of New Zealand, versus Colin Dowdeswell, of Rhodesia; Balazs Taroczy, of Hungary, versus Steve Krulevitz, of the United States; and Vijay Amritraj, of India, versus Kim Warwick, of Australia. (There are no women's matches on the opening day.) As I moved from one grim, gritty gray-green court to another—Har-Tru delights the eye hardly more than Kipling's "great, grey-green, greasy Limpopo River"—I found myself reminded repeatedly of the unvarying characteristics of clay-court tennis at the championship level: the looping forehand with heavy topspin; the softly sliced backhand; the somewhat tentative first volley by players who have more confidence in winning from the base-line; the long, nerve-racking rallies from the baseline; the taut-faced older players pointing out ball marks on the court to show why they disagree with a linesman's call that has gone against them; and all the players, whether they are winning or losing, inwardly exhorting them-selves to be patient, patient, patient. The world of clay-court tennis never changes much. Neither, in a basic way, does Forest Hills—though, heaven knows, there has for decades been plenty of room for improvement in the staging of the championships.

There was one change, however: four light towers were erected, so that matches could be played at night on the stadium court. The illumination was excellent, but the evening crowds were not, averaging about six thousand people—considerably less than half of the stadium's capacity.

Shortly after the United States Tennis Association had appointed the veteran umpire Winslow (Mike) Blanchard the new tournament director and Charles Hare the new referee, the word went round that the U.S.T.A. was planning to give Forest Hills a thorough overhauling. A few long-needed changes *were* made, but the trouble was that these improvements scarcely made a dent in correcting the things that have chronically been so disappointing about Forest Hills: the inefficiency of the overall operation of the Open, the apparent unawareness of the people in authority of the many shortcomings, and, as a result, an atmosphere that is fundamentally lacking in distinction and in the flavor of championship tennis.

On Tuesday night—the seventh day of the tournament—one of the most dramatic matches ever played at Forest Hills took place. Nastase and Tanner, a strong young left-hander from Tennessee, met in the fourth round, watched by a gallery of 14,418 spectators—a record for the stadium. It was, in truth, more of a crowd than a gallery—the type of rowdy arena crowd that at a hockey game, say, derives its pleasure mainly from the fights on the ice and not from the skill of the players or the vigor of the game. A good proportion of the spectators had unquestionably been attracted by the reports of Nastase's bullying, intimidating conduct in his match with Hans Pohmann, of West Germany, in the second round, and some of them were out to give him a taste of his own medicine. Although Nastase was relatively well behaved during the Tanner match, this anti-Nastase bloc yelled at him whenever he protested a call, and generally tried to provoke him into one of his tantrums. When he was in the act of serving, for example, shouts of "Double fault!" and "Foot fault!" frequently cut through the air. On the other hand, at least fifty per cent of the spectators—or so it seemed to me—were as violently pro-Nastase, and they eagerly accepted the challenge of trying to drown out the more vocal of Tanner's supporters with cries of "Come on, Nastase!" and "Let's go, Ilie, let's go!" and the like. In this bizarre, belligerent atmosphere, more redolent of the Colosseum in Rome than of a tennis stadium, Tanner and Nastase proceeded to produce a thrilling match, filled with superbly played points. They divided the first four sets, Nastase winning the first, 7–5; Tanner the second, 7–6, after a tie breaker, and the third at 6–1; and Nastase the fourth, 7–6, after another tie breaker. Incidentally, for the second straight year the twelve-point tie breaker, and not the nine-point version, was used in the championships. If the first twelve points are split 6–6, the tie breaker continues until one of the players gains a two-point margin.

This extended match lasted three hours and fourteen minutes. At about a quarter to one in the morning, under a full moon riding high in a lightly clouded sky, the point that will undoubtedly make this match historic was played. In the fifth set, with the score 4–4 in games, Tanner was serving, only too conscious that if he failed to hold service it could well mean defeat. He saved one break point to get to deuce. He fought off two more break points, but moments later was faced with still another. A medium-length rally took place on this vital point. When Nastase followed a deep approach shot in to net, Tanner attempted to pass him with a forehand, but Nastase stepped into it and angled a forehand volley toward the right-hand sideline. Tanner was not able to reach the ball. He obviously thought that it had hit the line, for he kept on running and, without looking back, made his way to his chair at courtside to rest up during the short changeover pause. Had he looked back, he would have seen the linesman at his end of the court, Adrian Clark, signalling that Nastase's volley was out. Merle Irwin, the umpire, must also have missed the linesman's gesture. In any event, he failed to acknowledge it, and announced, "Game, Mr. Nastase. He leads, five games to four." As for Nastase, he had headed directly off the court after hitting his volley, as if there was no question that the point and the game were his. Tanner, for his part, after observing the linesman's protest that the ball was out, might well have gone along with him on such a crucial point—most players would have—but, as a man dedicated to the code of sportsmanship, he stood by his first position: he thought the ball had hit the line, and that was that.

Now a real callithump was under way, since the linesman stubbornly refused to go along with the umpire or the players. One could only guess at the gist of the linesman's argument, but more than likely he was asserting that it was not up to the players to call a ball in or out —that this was his prerogative and he meant to stick to his call. After an emphatic four-way exchange of viewpoints which lasted three or four minutes, the umpire decided to summon the referee to help straighten things out. Hare came bounding through the marquee onto the court. He talked first with Tanner and then with Nastase. Then he spoke with the umpire and had a brief discussion with the linesman. After that, he spoke with the umpire again and went bounding off the court. The umpire then addressed the aroused, bewildered spectators over the public-address system. "The ball was on the line," he stated. "The referee has instructed me to overrule the linesman."

Play was resumed. In the next game, Nastase held service after the score had gone to deuce. This gave him the set and the match, 7–5, 6–7, 1–6, 7–6, 6–4.

Shortly after the conclusion of the match, Hare was asked to explain how he had reached his decision. "I wanted to talk to the players," he declared. "Both of them very strongly said that the ball was good. Then I talked with the umpire, and he also said the ball was good. That made it three to one, and that's what I based my call on. I think three to one is a pretty good percentage." That is true, and quite a number of the people I talked with were of the opinion that Hare had made the right decision. Other people—and these included many old friends of Hare's—were not so sure he had. Their disagreement with his decision was based on the fact that the umpire had failed to follow the procedure established by the U.S.T.A. for handling such situations, and that the referee had ignored this. The rules do make it clear that it is the linesman who has the authority to decide whether a shot is in or out, and that "his decision shall be final" unless he indicates to the umpire that "he is unable to make a call on a shot that lands within his area of responsibility." If the umpire finds himself not in accord with a linesman's call, the protocol in this country goes like this: the umpire can ask the linesman whether he is sure of his call, and if the linesman says that he isn't, the umpire can make the call himself; if the linesman says that he *is* sure of his call, the umpire can ask him whether he will yield to the chair, thus implying that he feels the linesman's call to be wrong; if the linesman yields, the umpire can overrule his call; however, if the linesman doesn't yield, there are no provisions in the rules for the umpire to overrule him, nor can the referee (except in Davis Cup or Wightman Cup competition). Accordingly, Clark, the linesman, was understandably miffed when Irwin, the umpire, did not acknowledge his call in the first place and then did not observe the established procedure of asking him whether he was sure of his call or whether he would yield to the chair. For another thing, the persons who were displeased at how the dispute was handled were critical of the role assumed by Nastase and Tanner, inasmuch as it is not the players' right to call the shots. If it were, there would be no need for any officials on the court. While Tanner is to be warmly commended for his sportsman-ship—the game can use it—it was not up to him to rule whether Na-stase's volley had hit the line or been wide. If he differed with the call, he had a perfect right to make his opinion known to the umpire but should not have implied that his call was the significant one. One more thing: I have an idea that the highest code of sportsmanship in tennis is the one that the great Australian players of the Sedgman-Laver-Rosewall-Newcombe era followed in their matches. They played every call, whether or not they agreed with it, hoping that matters would even out in the long run, never making an issue of it if they didn't. There is a certain fragility implicit in the structure of tournament tennis —and of other sports as well—and the Australians apparently sensed this danger and preferred to make it a policy to concentrate purely and simply on playing tennis.

Quite a few informed tennis hands thought that Nastase might go all the way, but he didn't; he lost to Borg in straight sets in the semifinals. There was no fire at all in Nastase's play, and since his de-meanor on court during this match was exceptionally mild—in truth, almost polite—many of us were reminded that one reason Nastase goes into his act probably is that he usually plays better when he is angry than when he is pacific, and consequently thrives on inciting the wrath of the spectators and then showing them up. (Connors likes to antago-nize a gallery for much the same reason. He and Nastase also share a distorted view of their relationship with galleries. Mistaking cause and effect, they would have you believe that tennis fans are hostile because they are a pack of animals—completely bypassing the fact that their own conduct in previous matches, if not in that day's match, is what provoked the hostility.) In the other semifinal, Connors, who had been in top form throughout the tournament and had not dropped a set—though he came close to doing so in his contumacious quarter-final match with Kodes—speedily dispatched Vilas, 6–4, 6–2, 6–1. Evert and Goolagong had earlier won their semifinal matches, and so we had that rare situation in which the No. 1 and No. 2 seeded players in both the men's and the women's divisions—Connors and Borg, Evert and Goolagong—had reached the finals.

Evert, of course, was the favorite to win the women's final, for clay is her surface. En route to the final, she had simply devastated her opponents, losing a total of only nine games. Nevertheless, everyone at Forest Hills expected a tightly contested match and hoped for one that would be filled with the brilliant tennis that had marked many of the meetings between Goolagong and Evert this year. During the opening minutes, just such a match looked to be in the offing, for Goolagong, unbothered by a southwest wind that was swirling around the stadium, moved quickly into high gear, sweeping the first seven points and, in the process, holding her serve at love and setting up a break of Evert's serve. In the third game, Evert, increasing the pace of her ground strokes, broke Goolagong's serve, and after that, in retrospect, the match was over. Goolagong encountered all sorts of difficulties, but perhaps the main thing that went wrong was that she missed her first three overheads; her smash is usually one of her most reliable strokes, and these errors seemed to cut deeply into her confidence. (In the gusty wind, she might have been wiser to let the ball bounce on those shots.) From there on until the end of the match (Evert, 6–3, 6–0), Goolagong did few things right, and her forehand, her most suspect stroke, was particularly shaky. After a while, she was just pushing the ball back with it. Evert can do that to you on clay—destroy you. She started playing tennis, on clay, at her father's club, when she was six, and four years later she entered her first tournament, on clay. It is the perfect surface for her game, which is built on her hard hitting and dreadful accuracy from the baseline. Clay gives her just the extra time she needs to get her body into perfect position so that she can really lean on her fine flat forehand and her vicious two-handed backhand. With her almost unflappable assurance, she just pounds away, swatting one shot after another deep into the corners until her harried, hurried opponent begins to disintegrate. It is now more than three years since Evert's last defeat on clay; that occurred in July 1973, when she lost to Goolagong in the Western Championships. When Evert defeated Mima Jausovec, of Yugoslavia, in the semifinals at Forest Hills, it marked the hundredth consecutive victory in her incredible streak, and after the match, in recognition of this, a number of her admirers presented her with a green-frosted cake on which "Congratulations Chris 100" was inscribed. (The invariable comment by those who attended the ceremony was "The cake should have been made of clay.") It was a little sad, of course, to see Goolagong lose in the final of our Open for the fourth straight time, but it was almost inevitable. At Forest Hills this year, Chris Evert may have played the best tournament of her career.

The Borg-Connors final is likely to be assured of a niche in the annals of tennis, because its outcome was decided by the most galvanic and fascinating tie breaker that has been played in a major championship since the tie breaker made its first appearance in our Open, six years ago, as a means of shortening the boring marathon sets that afflicted tournament tennis. The gallery (and what a mannerly, appreciative gallery watched the final!) was held spellbound throughout the extended tie breaker, and from the stands one could sense the enormous pressure that the players were feeling out on the court. We will get to that presently, but there was more to this hard-fought match between two remarkable young athletes. Whereas Connors had not been pushed at all on his way to the final, Borg had trodden a rocky road. Not only had he been on the verge of elimination by Fillol but in the fourth round Brian Gottfried, one of our more promising players, had won the first two sets from Borg and led him 2–0 in the third. Then, in the quarters, Orantes, the defending champion, at long last showing a few glimmers of his 1975 form, took Borg to five sets. The Borg we saw at Forest Hills did not serve with anything like the stunning power of the Borg we had seen at Wimbledon. There is little doubt that even on the slow Har-Tru he could have served and volleyed effectively had he chosen to use this tactic. Evidently, Borg and Bergelin decided that it would be wiser at Forest Hills to go with a medium-speed sliced service and to concentrate on getting it in. For the rest, Borg depended on out-steadying his opponents from the baseline and passing them, if they came in, with high, looping topspin strokes off his two-handed backhand and his very reliable forehand. However, it was Borg's wonderful physical condition and his poise in the crises, not his shotmaking, that had seen him through to the final. To have a chance against Connors, he would have to raise the standard of his tennis considerably. He did. From the outset, he played with such resolution that Connors had to earn nearly every point he won.

In the first set, for all that, Connors was in control of most of the rallies. He was hitting the ball with absolutely blazing speed—especially with his two-handed backhand, into which he throws so much energy that the force of his swing as often as not lifts both his feet off the ground. Connors, who looks like a junior edition of Pete Rose, of the Philadelphia Phillies, won the first set, 6–4, and punctuated this with one of his jack-o'-lantern urchin grins. In the second set, however, he became a bit complacent, and quickly paid the price for it. In the fourth game, when he made four sloppy errors, Borg broke his serve, and went on from there to take the set, 6–3. The third set started like something out of "Alice in Wonderland." There were six breaks of service in the first seven games. The last of these, which enabled Borg to get back on even terms, was the most surprising: Connors, leading 4–2 and 40–0, made five errors in a row, the last four on balls banged into the net. Then the two men steadied down. From the beginning of the match, neither of them had elected to follow his serve into the forecourt. In what was essentially a baseline duel, Connors had worked on Borg's somewhat vulnerable two-handed backhand and Borg had worked on Connors' somewhat vulnerable one-handed forehand. Now, in the crunch, they stuck to these conservative tactics as the set moved to 5–5, to 6–6, and into the tie breaker.

Let us pick up the tie breaker with Borg in front, four points to two, thanks to three straight errors by Connors. A down-the-line backhand placement by Connors: 4–3. Connors serving the next two points. Driven back by a deep forehand by Connors, Borg nets an attempted passing shot off his backhand: 4–4. Borg goes for another backhand down the line and pulls it off this time. He leads, 5–4. Borg serving the next two points. A brisk rally ends with Connors netting a drop volley, not a very wise shot to play at a time like this: 6–4, Borg. Double set point. Connors fights off the first one with a brave high backhand volley rapped into the clear: 6–5 now. Serve to Connors. He fights off the second set point with a forehand approach shot to Borg's forehand, which slides by for a winner: 6–6. Connors follows with an ace on an American-twist kick serve wide to Borg's forehand: 7–6. Now he holds set point. Borg serving. Connors, under pressure, sails a backhand several feet long: 7–7. Then another error by Connors—an overhit cross-court forehand: 8–7 for Borg. He is at set point for the third time. Connors serving. A forehand whipped down the line draws a short lob from Borg, which Connors smashes away: 8–8. On the next point, after a lob by Borg chases him back behind his baseline, Connors hits a loose smash over the other baseline. He now trails Borg, 8–9. For the fourth time, Borg holds set point. Borg serving. A big chance here. A hard-hit drive by Connors, a weak return by Borg, a perfect smash by Connors. Off the hook again: 9–9. A good rally climaxed by a marvellous shot by

Connors—a backhand taken on the rise and cracked crosscourt for a clean placement; Connors at 10–9 now, at set point for the second time. Connors serving. A fairly long rally on this point. Connors, on the defensive in the early exchanges, plays a deep, forcing backhand that catches Borg slightly off balance. Borg tries to go down the line with his backhand, but the shot is wide. That settles it: 11–9, Connors. Loud exhalation on the court and in the stands.

This definitive tie breaker decided not only the third set but the match, for Borg, in his disappointment, could not regather his hopes or his physical resources, and Connors played a shade the better tennis in the fourth set, to wrap up the match, 6–4, 3–6, 7–6, 6–4. Although for sheer velocity of stroke Connors may have been even more impressive in overwhelming Ken Rosewall in the finals at Wimbledon and Forest Hills in 1974, his conquest of Borg stands, in a way, as the finest victory of his career. He had devised a sound game plan and had executed it superlatively against a tough opponent, never permitting himself to become disheartened by his own bad patches or by Borg's tenacity, displaying immense courage in hitting out hard at many junctures when the loss of a point might have been fatal, and—yes—conducting himself that day like a champion. In many ways, Jimmy Connors still hasn't grown up, but this triumph, which he wanted so badly, could be of inestimable value in helping him shake off one of the longest adolescences in the history of sports.

When Forest Hills was over, one heard on every side what a tremendously exciting tournament it had been. This needs some qualification, I think. There were many rousing matches, such as the men's final, with its stirring tie breaker. However, on quite a few days this year we had the wrong kind of excitement at Forest Hills—excitement akin to that which is generated by a street brawl or an automobile accident. Nastase's compulsive destructiveness in his battle with Pohmann and the crude clowning of Connors in his grudge match with Kodes in the quarter-finals made the tennis that was played on these occasions almost incidental. That is the key to the trouble. The reason that sports have long held such a strong appeal is that they take place in a special world that in feeling and function is quite a bit better than life often is. In this age, in which so much of the spirit of sports is going out of sports, it is not at all pleasant to realize that for many fans the main attraction of Forest Hills this year was not the tennis but the dubious glamour of an "in" spectacle. Watching the great players compete against one another—that is where the excitement should lie.

At any rate, our national championships this year were not a

suitable expression of American tennis. This was the fault not only of
the Nastase-Connors axis and the bellicose crowds (tennis doesn't flourish in an arena atmosphere) but also of the game's governing bodies.
Sometimes it seems that everyone in tennis is preoccupied with making
money and no one is bothering about running the game properly.

THE WIMBLEDON CENTENARY

(1977)

Everyone wanted the tournament celebrating the first hundred years of Wimbledon to be a very fine one—Wimbledon deserved that. Besides, that summer the Queen was celebrating her Silver Jubilee, and Britain wanted something to cheer and to be proud about—such as a banner Wimbledon. As we all know, it is extremely rare when something devoutly wished for actually transpires. The centenary Wimbledon was one of them. It had more than its share of dappled sunshine and exciting matches, like Borg's semifinal against Gerulaitis and his final against Connors. But what really put the icing on the birthday cake was the victory in the Ladies' Singles by Virginia Wade. In her fifteen previous attempts to win at Wimbledon, Virginia, under the stress of the occasion, always found a way to lose. Now, at the perfect time, she found a way to win. London loved it, Britain loved it, the world loved it.

Of all the evocative place names in sport—such as St. Andrews, Green Bay, Madison Square Garden, Holmenkollen Hill, Pauley Pavilion, Fenway Park, the Restigouche, Ascot, Annapurna, Kooyong, Lord's, Old Town, Le Mans, Pebble Beach, Forest Hills, Churchill Downs, Bimini, Wembley, Cooperstown, Aintree, the Solent, Yale Bowl, Saratoga, Stade Roland Garros, Rugby, and Yankee Stadium, to list those that first rush to mind—I do not believe that any holds more significance or rings the bells of memory more loudly and clearly than Wimbledon, the site of the most famous tennis tournament in the world. When you look up Wimbledon in the Encyclopædia Britannica you learn that Wimbledon is a suburb of London situated eight miles from Charing Cross; that Ceawlin, the King of Wessex, defeated Aethelbert, the King of Kent, in that neighborhood in 568 A.D.; and that the district covers five square miles, including the thousand and more acres of Wimbledon Common. There is a passing reference to the All England Club, which conducts the renowned annual tennis tournament—though, almost from the very beginning of the event, it has been the practice to refer to it by the name of its geographical site, much as it is the usual thing to refer to our national tennis championships as Forest Hills, after the village in Queens in which they take place and in which the host club, the West Side Tennis Club, has long been situated. Actually, Wimbledon's official name is The Lawn Tennis Championships, just as the golf competition that we call the British Open is known in Britain as The Open, there having been no other event of that kind in existence when it was inaugurated, in 1860.

The first Wimbledon was held in 1877, four years after the game of lawn tennis was invented, and, accordingly, early this summer Wimbledon celebrated its hundredth anniversary—or cen-teen'-ery, as the British like to say. It was no hollow occasion. The Wimbledon championships are still far and away the most important tennis event in the world. No other sports competition, not even the Masters or the Kentucky Derby, is so meticulously organized or so skillfully presented. Wimbledon is a little like Paris. When you walk down the cobblestone streets of the Île de la Cité or the Île Saint-Louis and gaze across the Seine at the relatively small, exquisitely proportioned, time-yellowed buildings, some of them centuries old, that line the banks of the river, you are overwhelmed by the thought that man could have ever managed to create—and preserve—such a beautiful city. During the fortnight of the championships, when you walk around the grounds at Wimbledon—the Centre Court, surrounded by a dark-green twelve-sided structure, has seats for ten thousand six hundred and fifty-one people and standing room for about thirty-five hundred; the No. 1 Court has seats for fifty-five hundred and standing room for fourteen hundred; and there are thirteen other grass courts, three of which have fairly large stands—it strikes you, similarly, as almost too impressive to be true. Wimbledon has character as well as looks. It not only takes care of officials from all over the globe who carry the proper credentials and wear the right ties, as one expects it to do, it takes equally good care of the patrons whose only badge of distinction is a febrile addiction to tennis. Just as the nabobs can partake of that special Wimbledon treat, strawberries and heavy cream, in their large, ornate marquees, known as the Members Enclosure, so can the average spectator find strawberries and cream of the same quality in good supply at the public refreshment stands. For me, the key to the fact that the people who run Wimbledon really mean to do the best possible job for everyone is the arrangement instituted many years ago for handling the tickets of patrons who cannot stay for the full day's schedule of matches. Since Wimbledon is regularly sold out months ahead (except for a relatively small number of tickets that are kept for sale to the public on each day of the tournament), holders of reserved-seat tickets who leave early are asked to put their tickets in special boxes at the gates, from which they are collected to be sold at a nominal price—around fifty cents—to tennis fans who have hurried from their offices to Wimbledon at the close of the working day and have queued up patiently outside.

So many enchanting players have trod the turf at Wimbledon and so many stirring matches have been fought there that it would take a book about the size of a Britannica volume to begin to cover the tournament's first century. In an article, one can only briefly mention a few of the heroes and heroines who loom largest as one looks back across the decades. For starters, there was that extremely successful brother act the Doherty (pronounced Do-hert'-ee) boys—R. F. (Reggie, also known as Big Do), who won the singles four years in a row (1897–1900), and H. L. (Lawrie, also known as Little Do), who after his older brother's physical stamina had been weakened by bouts of poor health, picked up the mantle and won the singles five straight years (1902–06). The Dohertys, handsome, chivalrous, graceful young upper-class Englishmen right out of "Beau Geste," won the doubles eight times. At the close of his reign in the singles, Little Do was succeeded by the first man from outside the British Isles to carry off the championship—Norman Brookes, an unflappable, saturnine left-hander from Australia, whose chief strengths were a sharp-breaking serve, a natural instinct for volleying, and a tough competitive temperament. Brookes won his second Wimbledon title in 1914, following four straight victories by Anthony Wilding, a tall, superbly conditioned New Zealander, whose sportsmanship and princely bearing on the court recalled the Dohertys. It was a sad day when the news arrived, in May 1915, that Wilding had been killed in action in Flanders.

When the championships were resumed after the First World War, it was all quite different. William Tatem Tilden II, the master of the cannonball service and the all-court game, became in 1920 the first American to capture the men's singles at Wimbledon. In 1930, at thirty-seven, he won his third, and last, title there, the oldest man in the modern era—since the First World War—to win the Wimbledon singles. The nineteen-twenties, of course, also saw the rise of the French Musketeers. Jean Borotra, René Lacoste, and Henri Cochet each won the singles twice, with perhaps the most amazing feat being Cochet's comeback against Tilden in the semifinal round in 1927, when, down two sets and trailing 1–5 in the third, he turned the match around by sweeping seventeen consecutive points, and went on to win. In the nineteen-thirties, two players stood out. The first was Fred Perry, the last Englishman to win at Wimbledon. Champion in 1934, 1935, and 1936, Perry, a magnificent athlete, had possibly the finest running forehand of all time. When he turned professional, he was succeeded by Don Budge, one of a long line of superlative players from California—in his case, Oakland—and the possessor of one of the finest backhands of all time. Budge won back-to-back titles in 1937 and 1938, and then he, too, turned professional.

After the Second World War, the lure of the big money now available on the professional tour led two of the outstanding players of the immediate postwar period—Jack Kramer, from Los Angeles, and Frank Sedgman, from Australia—to go professional within a short time after they consolidated their reputations by winning at Wimbledon. Later on, Lew Hoad and Rod Laver, two more of the marvellous group of internationalists developed at this time in Australia—in full flight, both Hoad and Laver could be positively awesome—also took this step shortly after making successful defenses of their Wimbledon titles. With just about all the top talent now gathered in the professional ranks— Pancho Gonzales, from Los Angeles, had turned pro after only one appearance at Wimbledon as a very young amateur, as had Ken Rosewall, from Australia, in the middle nineteen-fifties, after twice being an unsuccessful Wimbledon finalist—Wimbledon inevitably lost much of its meaning and lustre. It did not recapture them until the arrival of open tennis—open to both amateurs and professionals—in 1968. The first open Wimbledon was carried off, fittingly, by Laver, then the best player in the world. The next year, Gonzales, by that time a graying forty-one, gave the Wimbledon regulars a long-delayed view of his ability and pertinacity when he defeated Charlie Pasarell, from Puerto

Rico, then twenty-five, 22–24, 1–6, 16–14, 6–3, 11–9, in an early-round match that lasted five hours and twelve minutes—the longest match in Wimbledon history. As for the ageless Rosewall, in 1970 he reached his third Wimbledon final (against John Newcombe), and in 1974 his fourth (against Jimmy Connors), a full twenty years after his first.

Of the women champions, the first who bore the mark of greatness was a young English girl now almost totally forgotten—Charlotte Dod, known as Lottie or the Little Wonder. She was only fifteen in 1887, when she won the first of her five Wimbledon titles. When she retired, in 1894, Miss Dod turned to other sports, and became a skating champion, an international field-hockey star, a first-class archer, a prominent Alpinist, and the 1904 British Ladies Golf Champion. In 1905, another phenomenon appeared on the scene—an eighteen-year-old girl named May Sutton, the daughter of an English naval officer who had transplanted his family from Plymouth, England, to Pasadena upon his retirement. A powerfully built, combative young woman with a brutal topspin forehand (hit with a Western grip), Miss Sutton upset the defending champion, Dorothea Douglass, the daughter of an Ealing vicar, 6–3, 6–4, in the Challenge Round. (Until 1922, it was customary for the defending champions in the various divisions to "stand out" while those aspiring to their title played their way, round by round, through what was called the All Comers tournament; then the winner of the All Comers met the defender in the Challenge Round.) In 1906, Miss Douglass defeated Miss Sutton, 6–3, 9–7, but in their rubber match the following year it was Miss Sutton, 6–1, 6–4. After that, Miss Sutton never returned to Wimbledon during her prime, but in 1919, when the championships started up again after the war, Miss Douglass, who had by then become Mrs. Lambert Chambers—and who had accumulated seven singles titles in all—was still going strong at forty, and it was she who, as the defending champion, came up in the Challenge Round against the twenty-year-old French sensation Suzanne Lenglen. In three tremendously exciting sets, during which one player and then the other mounted courageous rallies when they stood on the edge of defeat, Mlle. Lenglen at length prevailed, 10–8, 4–6, 9–7. Thereafter, with the exception of 1924, when she was forced to default because of an attack of jaundice, Lenglen stood in a class apart from her competition, dropping a total of only thirteen games in winning her five final matches. She turned professional in 1926, and with her departure Helen Wills, later Mrs. Moody, became the new queen. Also a Californian (from Berkeley), she won the ladies' championship a record eight times between 1927 and 1938. The four other years, she didn't enter.

Among the women who won the singles at Wimbledon more

than once in the years following the Second World War, in retrospect there is one surprise: Louise Brough. One is apt to forget that Miss Brough, yet another Californian (Beverly Hills), was a four-time champion. Her last victory was scored in 1955, after the enforced retirement, at nineteen, of the luckless Maureen Connolly, one of the most brilliant exponents ever of baseline play, who had won the first of her three straight Wimbledon titles at seventeen. Miss Connolly was a Californian from San Diego. Althea Gibson, a New Yorker, won two Wimbledons (1957 and 1958), and Maria Bueno, of Brazil, won three (1959, 1960, 1964). Margaret Smith, of Australia—she later became Mrs. Court—also won three Wimbledon singles, and the unpredictable Billie Jean King no fewer than six. When she entered this year's championships, Mrs. King, a Californian from Long Beach who has also had great success as a doubles player, needed to win only one more Wimbledon title (which she failed to do) to beat the record nineteen amassed by Elizabeth Ryan, that almost incomparable doubles specialist. Between 1914 and 1934 Miss Ryan—yet another native of Los Angeles—won the women's doubles twelve times and the mixed doubles seven times. The list of relatively recent multiple champions is completed by Chris Evert, the winner in 1974 and 1976. She, of course, is a Floridian.

In the opinion of many students of tennis history, two of the most magnetic figures in the long line of Wimbledon champions appeared on the scene even before the Dohertys—way back in the eighteen-eighties, when the game and the tournament were really in their infancy. These were the Renshaw brothers, Willie and Ernest, and the story of their careers—and especially their long rivalry with an implacable opponent named Herbert Lawford—reads less like fact than like something out of Thackeray with overtones of Kipling. However, before we get to the Renshaws, some even earlier contests and contenders are worth recalling. When the All England Club was founded, in 1868, it was associated solely with croquet, but by 1875, about a year and a half after the invention of lawn tennis, the club was feeling financial strain, and its officers, believing that the solution might well be to ally it with the new and more vigorous game, decided to install some courts. Lawn tennis not only caught on quickly at the club (and elsewhere) but created such interest that within the short space of two years the All England Club decided to stage a lawn tennis championship. In his book "Fifty Years of Wimbledon," published in 1926, A. Wallis Myers, the distinguished English tennis historian, declared that it was Wimbledon that "gave the new pastime a style and status." He added, "Wimbledon was the nursery of the game; it bred the giants of the past, men who, by the exercise of their art, the vigor of their physique, and the force of their personality, inspired countries beyond to accept and pursue the cult of lawn tennis."

Looking back at the first few Wimbledons, one is struck by the rapidity with which certain basic strokes and strategies of the modern game came into being. In the first Wimbledon, there were twenty-two entrants—men who had developed their hand-and-eye coördination at public school or the university by playing court tennis, that intricate medieval game, or racquets, which was an equally aristocratic game, despite its humble genesis, early in the nineteenth century, as a time killer for the inmates of the Fleet Prison, a debtors' prison. Most of these converts to lawn tennis served underhand, and the rest employed a soft, shoulder-high pat. Once the ball was put in play, they were content to exchange soft, looping forehands from the baseline until an error was made. The first champion, Spencer Gore, had other ideas. A tall, agile man who had played racquets at Harrow—which, incidentally, was the first public school to adopt that game—Gore, disdaining the long, polite rallies, elected, whenever he had hit a good hard shot, to rush up to within a few feet of the net and volley the return out of reach of his opponent. In the final, Gore's adept volleying enabled him to defeat W. C. Marshall, a court-tennis player, without much exertion: 6–1, 6–2, 6–4. Their match drew a gallery of two hundred people.

Gore was back the next year to defend his title. In the Challenge Round, he met another graduate of the racquets courts of Harrow—P. Frank Hadow, who was in England on a holiday after spending three years in Ceylon as a coffee planter. Hadow had been introduced to lawn tennis a few weeks before. He liked the game, found he had a gift for it, and sent in his entry for the championship. He won the All Comers by his solid backcourt play and moved on to face Gore in the Challenge Round. When Gore came in to net to volley, Hadow had the perfect antidote: he lobbed the ball over Gore's head for clean winners. After his holiday was over, he went back to Ceylon and his coffee plantations. He did not defend his title the next year, and, for that matter, never again returned to Wimbledon. Many years later, when he was asked how he had hit upon the lob as the riposte to Gore's volleying, Hadow said, "It was only natural enough, though, with a tall, long-legged, and long-armed man sprawling over the net."

Hadow's absence opened the door for J. T. Hartley, a Yorkshire vicar, who had been a court-tennis champion at Oxford. After overcoming an initial distaste for the new offshoot of his first love, Hartley began to play lawn tennis regularly, and at length he made up his mind to enter the championship. He was confident that he would acquit himself respectably, but he did not see himself surviving the quarter-final round, scheduled for Saturday. When he did, he had a problem: he had made no provision for another minister to take over his Sunday duties. With his semifinal match scheduled for Monday afternoon, Hartley caught a train to Yorkshire on Saturday night, arrived in time to deliver his Sunday sermon, caught an early-morning train back to London on Monday, got in at two o'clock, changed trains, and hurried to Wimbledon. He reached the court just in time for his match, but the trip had tired him, and, moreover, in his rush he hadn't had time for lunch. Fortunately, a rain shower forced a temporary halt in play, and during this intermission Hartley had some tea and sandwiches. He returned to the court refreshed and recharged, and mopped up his opponent. He went on to win the final, from Vere St. Leger Gould, an idiosyncratic Irishman.

The following year, 1880, Hartley made a successful defense of the championship. Wimbledon was now beginning to look like Wimbledon. For the first time, two movable grandstands flanked the Centre Court, and there were eleven field courts. There was also a scoreboard in the Centre Court, so that the patrons would be able to follow a match closely even if the umpire's voice was drowned out by the trains of the London & South-Western Railway which rumbled down the tracks adjacent to the club's property. In the Challenge Round that year, Hartley's steady baseline game prevailed, but he did drop the third set to Herbert Lawford, a big, broad-shouldered physical-fitness fanatic who was to play a prominent role during these formative years of lawn tennis. Lawford had been deeply involved in sports at Repton, his public school, and at Edinburgh University. A top-level swimmer, runner, and cyclist, he was twenty-seven when he made his début at Wimbledon, shortly after taking up tennis. He was rather slow in getting around the court, and extremely awkward playing his shots, but he had enormous energy and endless persistence, and, through long hours of practice, improved noticeably year by year. Besides, he possessed one magnificent stroke. This, essentially, was a top spin forehand, which he hit in a highly exaggerated manner: he let the ball drop very low on its bounce, and then, with his powerful right arm and wrist, whipped it up with his racquet and came over the top of it, imparting immense speed to the ball and causing it to duck sharply after it had crossed the net. Few players could cope with this fearsome forehand—"the Lawford stroke," as it came to be called. Everyone in tennis attempted to copy it, but no one came close to matching the effectiveness of its originator. Lawford had one other thing going for him. He loved to compete, and, while he was basically a good sportsman, he was aware that his physical bulk, his strength, his stamina, his walrus mustache, and his fixed, sardonic expression on the court could often intimidate less determined players. In his secret heart, Lawford, in 1880, might have pictured himself defeating Hartley in their next confrontation and going on to enjoy a long and illustrious reign at Wimbledon, and he might well have achieved this had it not been for the Renshaws.

Willie and Ernest Renshaw were twins. They were born in Cheltenham, ninety miles west of London, in 1861, Willie entering the world fifteen minutes before Ernest. They learned their tennis on two courts in Cheltenham, an outdoor asphalt court and an indoor clay court. In 1879, deeming themselves ready for the big time, they sent in their entries for the championship. They got to Wimbledon all right, but at the last moment they decided not to report for their scheduled matches. The panache with which the championship was staged and the huge crowd—at least a thousand spectators were on hand—overawed them, and, remaining in their seats in the stands, they contented themselves with taking notes on the techniques of the players they watched. The next year, they really *were* ready. Members of a well-to-do family, they were able to devote all their time and thought to their tennis, and came on fast. They won the Oxford Doubles Championship, which had been started the previous year and was regarded as the equivalent in doubles of what Wimbledon was in singles play. Then they travelled to Dublin for the Irish Championships, which had also been established in 1879. They won the doubles, and Willie, who was a shade bigger than Ernest and hit the ball with more pace and aggressiveness, took the singles. Great things were expected of Willie at Wimbledon, but he lost in the third round to a good player, O. E. Woodhouse. It had rained all week, and Willie could not find anything like his usual form as he splashed around the waterlogged court. However, as someone must surely have pointed out at the time, Woodhouse had to put up with the same conditions. In the next round, Woodhouse eliminated Ernest. Back to the old practice court.

After practicing intensively that summer and fall, the Renshaws headed south to the Riviera early in 1881 and built themselves a hard sand court on the grounds of the Beausite Hotel, in Cannes. They worked diligently on their tennis that winter, and their successful spring campaign showed it. They won the Oxford Doubles and the Irish Doubles again. (The Renshaws practically invented doubles. They were the first team to use the formation in which one partner stations himself at net while the other serves. They learned to volley expertly and came to net whenever possible. When an opposing team tried to lob them, they were not disconcerted, for through practice they had mastered a revolutionary stroke, the overhead smash.) In Dublin, Willie again won the singles, and he finished his preparation for Wimbledon by carrying off the singles tournament at Prince's, in London. That year, there was no stopping him in the championship, although Lawford gave him all he could handle in their semifinal match before going down, 1-6, 6-3, 6-2, 5-6 (such a score was possible then), 6-3. The Challenge Round was an anticlimax. Hartley, who had not completely recovered from an attack of English cholera, could win only three games in the three sets.

In 1882, the Renshaws, the unbeatable doubles team, were beaten in both the Oxford and the Irish Doubles. An interesting circumstance underlay their defeats. For some time, the players who clung to the baseline game had been trying to persuade the governing body of lawn tennis to ban volleying as detrimental to the sport's best expression, but, although they failed to achieve this, their pressure forced a considerable concession; in 1882, the net, which had been four feet high at the sides, was lowered to three feet six inches, and this made it much easier for the baseliners to pass the volleyers down the alleys in doubles. That was what had happened to the Renshaws when they attempted to defend their doubles titles. In singles play, the lower net at the posts required greater agility and quicker reflexes of the players who loved to patrol the forecourt, as the Renshaws did, but the twins were equal to it. In fact, the period known as the Renshaw Era properly began in 1882. Ernest took the Irish All Comers. His forte was the accurate placement, and he had a finer touch than Willie. In addition, he was faster on his feet. In their informal matches, there was little to choose between them. However, Ernest declined to play Willie in the Challenge Round in Dublin. It was typical of Ernest to defer to his slightly older brother in nearly all matters, and he particularly disliked opposing him in tournaments. At Wimbledon, Ernest was again in splendid form. He outlasted Lawford, 6-4, 4-6, 6-2, 3-6, 6-0, in the fourth round and went on to capture the All Comers. This time, he was induced to meet Willie in the Challenge Round. E. C. (Ned) Potter, Jr., one of the leading authorities on the Renshaws, has written, "It was their first public meeting. Nothing else was talked of in the clubs and drawing rooms but their respective merits. Many bets were placed. In the afternoon, Wimbledon saw the first of the Renshaw crushes. Stately dowagers struggled for places at courtside where they might take a precarious stand on a folding chair. Courtly gentlemen forgot their manners as they elbowed their way among the clerks and shop girls for a better view." Two thousand fans attended the match. Willie won it in five sets—6-1, 2-6, 4-6, 6-2, 6-2

—but many who were on hand left with the feeling that Ernest had possibly thrown the last two sets.

There was another all-Renshaw Challenge Round at Wimbledon the next year, 1883. Ernest's most difficult match in the All Comers had been in the first round, against his old, ever-hopeful rival Lawford. Playing in a heavy wind that bothered both men, Lawford was on the verge of a spectacular triumph when, with the match tied at two sets apiece, he moved to 5–0 in the fifth set. Down to his last gasp, Ernest decided to use a tricky underhand cut serve that he had often fooled with in practice. Not only did it enable him to hold serve but it disconcerted Lawford way out of reason, and his entire game began to unravel. Sticking with his underhand serve, Ernest pulled out the set to win the match. In the Challenge Round, he played just about as well as Willie but went down in five sets: 2–6, 6–3, 6–3, 4–6, 6–3. Some people, knowing how intransigent Ernest was about the importance of being Willie, were not a hundred per cent certain that he had gone all out in the final set. Be that as it may, the tennis world was infatuated with the Renshaws. They were the first genuine Wimbledon heroes, and there is no question that their magnetism was a principal reason that the game underwent a stupendous boom at this time. When you study photos taken of the Renshaws in their prime, you can begin to understand their huge popularity. They were very attractive young men, handsome in a sensitive, delicate way. They parted their dark-brown hair on the side and had rather deep-set eyes, classically straight noses, light mustaches, and longish jaws. Whereas Lawford, the arrant individualist, sometimes showed up on the court wearing a porkpie hat, a striped jersey, tight knickers, and long stockings, the Renshaws favored conservative apparel: long-sleeved white shirts, miniature four-in-hand ties that hung down only three or four inches, and white trousers. As you might imagine, their manners on the court were impeccable. Off the court, they differed somewhat in personality. Willie, who was far more outgoing, frequently appeared in amateur theatricals. Ernest had less self-confidence and stammered.

Beginning in 1884, there was a series of three exciting Challenge Round clashes between Willie and the unsinkable Lawford. Earlier in his career, Lawford had several times enunciated the dictum "Perfect back play will beat perfect volleying," but at this advanced stage of his career he buried his pride and, learning to volley, periodically came thumping into the forecourt after hitting one of his severe forehands. Willie, in top form for their meeting at Wimbledon in 1884, took the first two sets, 6–0, and 6–4. He then began to tire and had just enough left to win the third set, 9–7, and the match. The next year, scrutinized by a taut gallery of thirty-five hundred, who filled the new permanent stands, the two waged perhaps the best of all their duels. In the final of the All Comers, Lawford had defeated Ernest in five hard-fought sets. Against Willie, he dropped the first two sets, 7–5 and 6–2, but, summoning his extraordinary courage and pertinacity and his new adeptness at volleying, he battled his way back into the match. He won the third set, 6–4, and was ahead in the fourth set four games to none with double game point in the fifth when Willie mounted a gallant counter-offensive. He did this by suddenly altering his usual tactics. Volleying only rarely, he stayed patiently in the backcourt and traded ground strokes with Lawford. Gradually, he gained control of their exchanges, pulled up to 5–5, and then won the next two games and the match. In 1886, he started off in the Challenge Round as if he would make short work of Lawford. It took him only nine and a half minutes to win the opening set, without the loss of a game. Lawford dug in and won the second, 7–5. Willie then lifted his game and ran out a very well-played match by taking the next two sets, 6–3 and 6–4. The most valuable result of this historic Challenge Round series—what with Lawford adding a new dimension to his tennis by learning to volley, and with Willie, in effect, doing the same by retreating at intervals to the baseline and attacking from there—was that together the two enlarged the vocabulary of lawn tennis and laid the foundation for the all-court game, which is the game that nearly all the great champions of later eras have played. During the years of these encounters with Lawford, Willie Renshaw reached and then passed his peak. A little over a decade later, Herbert Chipp, a competent tournament player and a sound critic, paid Willie this tribute: "The supreme advantage which, to my mind, William possessed over every other player, past or present, was his power of getting the ball back into his opponent's court with the least possible loss of time. The ball was taken at the top of the bound and forced across the net before the opposing player had well recovered his balance. . . . One never seemed to have any breathing time."

Early in the tournament season of 1887, the whole picture changed. While playing in the Scottish Championships, Willie Renshaw came down with "tennis elbow"—one of the first cases on record. It was felt that it had probably been caused by the heavy overhead smashing that highlighted both his singles and his doubles play. Anyhow, Willie was out for the season. In his absence, Lawford, who was making his tenth appearance at Wimbledon, had his best chance ever to win the championship. One had to be sympathetic to this no longer young man —the "heavy" in the scenario—who had expended so much effort and had harvested so many disappointments in his quest for the championship trophy, which for him was the Holy Grail. But one found one's sympathy also going out to Ernest Renshaw, who had practically made a career of self-effacement. Realizing that perpetuating the Renshaw dynasty was now his responsibility, Ernest buckled down to business. He arrived at Wimbledon fit and serious, and made his way to the All Comers final that would decide the championship that year—with Willie hors de combat, there would be no Challenge Round. Across the net from Ernest in the final, glowering and purposeful, stood Lawford. A terrific match ensued. After Ernest had won the third set, to lead two sets to one, he appeared to be safely home. Then, as frequently happens to a player in any game who has moved out in front and is in sight of victory, Ernest began to play too conservatively. With his exceptional powers of recuperation, Lawford was able to take advantage of this lull to marshal his reserves of strength and to take command. He won the fourth set, 6–4, to draw even, and went on to win the crucial fifth set, 6–4. The old boy had done it—won Wimbledon. Well done indeed!

Lawford's reign lasted only one year. This was not due to the return of Willie Renshaw, although he was back in action at Wimbledon in 1888. Willie's elbow was better, but he was not yet his old self, and was ousted in an early round. No, it was Ernest—shy, stammering Ernest—who stopped Lawford. He really rose to the occasion in the Challenge Round, playing perhaps the most beautiful tennis of his life. From the backcourt he had perfect length off the heavy grass, and when he closed in he hit crisp, imaginative shots that Lawford could not deal with. This time, after Ernest had swept into the lead he did not let up. He dismissed Lawford 6–3, 7–5, 6–0. The Renshaws were back on top. As for Lawford, he was never again a factor in the championship. He had grown too old.

The story of the Renshaws, with its manifold twists and turns, reached its final big moment in 1889, when Willie came all the way back to win his seventh, and last, Wimbledon singles championship—no other man has won the singles more than five times—and when Willie and Ernest won their fifth, and last, Wimbledon doubles championship. (In 1884, the doubles were shifted to Wimbledon from Oxford, where the Renshaws had won them twice.) In the All Comers singles, after defeating Lawford in four sets Willie, up against the young and promising H. S. Barlow, was within two points of losing in straight sets. He managed to reclaim the third set, 8–6. In the fourth set, Barlow held six match points. Willie fought them all off, and at length took the set, 10–8. In the final set, Barlow took the first five games. Willie refused to yield. He called on himself for everything he had, and, reeling off one game after another with dazzling play, capped his incredible comeback by winning the set, 8–6. In the Challenge Round, he faced Ernest, the defending champion, and once again Ernest produced the rather pale stuff he invariably produced when he was playing Willie. The first two sets went to Willie; Ernest took the third, and then subsided quietly in the fourth without winning a game. This marked the close of the Renshaw Era. In 1890, Willie defended his title but was defeated in the Challenge Round by a tall, thin Irishman, W. J. (Ghost) Hamilton. After that, Willie played little competitive tennis, none of it notable. As for Ernest, in 1891, in the fourth round, he met Wilfred Baddeley, who was on his way to the first of his three Wimbledon titles. Ernest scratched out a paltry two games over the three sets. Ernest was then only thirty, yet, like Willie, was merely a tragic shade of his former self. With the Renshaws gone from the Centre Court, interest in lawn tennis entered a decline—some people felt that it had unquestionably seen its best days —but then other heroes came along and Wimbledon began to bloom again.

The Renshaws died young, and under unhappy circumstances. George E. Alexander, of Boise, Idaho, one of the leading scholars of the early years of lawn tennis, recently dug up, at the General Register Office in London, copies of the entries of death of the Renshaws. Ernest was thirty-eight when he died, of the "effects of carbolic acid but whether taken intentionally or not the evidence does not show." Five years later, Willie died of epileptic convulsions. In his will, the game's first great player bequeathed "the first Championship Lawn Tennis Cup won by me at Wimbledon to my sister Edith Ann Renshaw absolutely and without intending or implying any trust." Of course, no one who knows his Wimbledon has ever forgotten the Renshaws. It is wonderfully right that each year the winner of the men's singles receives not only replicas of the two Challenge Cups—the originals are kept permanently at the All England Club—but also a special memorial trophy presented by the members of the Renshaw family.

The fortnight of the centenary Wimbledon started on Monday, June 20th, and ended on Saturday, July 2nd. The first week of play, bringing us to the quarter-finals in both the men's and the women's singles, was rather uneven. There were a good many routine matches, a few bright matches, the usual percentage of upsets (the most surprising one being the expulsion in the third round of the third-seeded man, Guillermo Vilas—the Argentine who recently won the French Championship—at the hands of Billy Martin, a twenty-year-old American, who has done very little since graduating from the ranks of the juniors), and the usual number of unexpected developments, controversial and otherwise. At the top of this last category was the failure of Jimmy Connors, the 1974 Wimbledon champion and the first-seeded player this year, to attend the parade of former Wimbledon champions on the Centre Court on the festive opening day—a ceremony that reached its emotional apex when Elizabeth Ryan, now eighty-five years old, hobbled out on crutches toward the Duke of Kent, the president of the All England Club, and tossed her crutches away as she curtsied before the Duke and the Duchess. Connors, the enfant terrible of contemporary tennis, was practicing at the time about two hundred yards away, testing an injured thumb as he hit some shots with his buddy Ilie Nastase. The list of happier developments included the following: the successful début of fourteen-year-old, ninety-pound Tracy Austin, of California—the youngest (and lightest) person ever accepted for Wimbledon—who won her opening match from Mrs. Elly Vessies-Appel, of the Netherlands, 6–3, 6–3, before succumbing in the next round to Chris Evert, 6–1, 6–1; an affecting performance by Maria Bueno, who, at thirty-seven, reached the third round and played patches of lovely tennis before losing her match with Billie Jean King; the sight of Stan Smith, the 1972 champion, looking more like his old self than he has in years, as he extended Connors to five sets in the fourth round; and some imaginative shotmaking on the part of the uncelebrated Tim Gullikson, the right-handed member of the Gullikson twins, from Onalaska, Wisconsin, who eliminated Raul Ramirez, the Mexican Davis Cup hero, and went on to reach the round of sixteen before losing to Phil Dent, of Australia, in five sets. (Tom, the left-handed twin, who is five minutes older than Tim, was put out by Nastase in the first round. The Gulliksons, the nearest thing to the Renshaws that tennis has seen in quite some time, entered the doubles but were defeated in their first match, in four sets, by the veteran American team of Stan Smith and Bob Lutz.) On Wednesday of the first week, a record crowd of more than thirty-seven thousand was in attendance. Wimbledon galleries are the most international attracted by any annual sports event, and as one makes one's way down the packed walks one hears a constant babble of strange languages and spots an unending assortment of blazers and insignia. I was seated, by the way, between Victor Vassiliev, the bearded representative of *Sovietski Sports*, and Giovanni Clerici, the erudite tennis specialist of *Il Giorno*, of Milan.

By and large, the overall scene at Wimbledon is much the same as it has been for years and years. Outside the grounds, the traditional long queue of tennis enthusiasts lined up to buy standing-room tickets or general-admission tickets or tickets of any kind waits stoically for the gates to open. In the Tea Garden, the main relaxation area, which is

filled with tables, chairs, and large umbrellas, there are numerous refreshment stands, offering sandwiches, salads, pies, cakes, strawberries
and cream, and so on, and, along with those stands, the Champagne and
Pimms Bar, the Wine Bar, the Wimbledon Long Bar, a bookstall, a
souvenir shop, a post office, and, nearby, several Bon Bon Stands, where
one fills one's own paper bag with a variety of hard candies from forty-
five bins—twenty new pence, or thirty-four cents, for a quarter of a
pound. This year, there has been a splendid new addition—a tennis
museum (naturally, it is called simply The Museum), which occupies
part of a new building attached to the eastern rim of the Centre Court
stadium. One noon, before the day's matches got under way, I spent a
reflective and enjoyable hour inching through it. The Museum, as you
might expect, depicts the development of lawn tennis from court tennis
and other early racquet games. It pays a proper tribute to Major Walter
Clopton Wingfield, the inventor of lawn tennis, and then floods us with
memorabilia, such as an exhibit of the intricate and voluminous dresses
the women tennis players of earlier generations were encumbered by,
a replica of an early-twentieth-century Wimbledon dressing room, and
well-selected photographs of the standout champions, accompanied by
descriptions of their deeds. In the center of the museum are two large
glass cases, one filled with life-size wax figures of Suzanne Lenglen,
Fred Perry, and Helen Wills Moody, the other with similar figures of
Willie Renshaw, Dorothea Lambert Chambers, and William T. Tilden
II. At Tilden's feet lies a scattering of the instruction books and the
fiction he wrote, including two of his novels, "It's All in the Game" and
"Glory's Net." My favorite exhibit was a collection of early tennis post-
cards—in particular, one showing an auburn-haired beauty hitting a
forehand drive, with the caption "Love to You from Harrogate." The
only touch that rather disturbed me was that the recordings of snatches
of the early radio broadcasts from Wimbledon, which are piped through
the museum, seemed to contain only English triumphs, like Fred
Perry's conquest of Jack Crawford and Dorothy Round's of Helen
Jacobs. I mentioned this to an old friend, Lance Tingay, who is the
tennis writer for the London *Daily Telegraph*. "Oh, I'm sure you're
wrong about that," he told me, with a smile. "You must have been
preoccupied when the feats of the American and the other foreign stars
were described. I'm absolutely certain that one of Elizabeth Ryan's
victories is given fitting attention."

During the second week, there was an abundance of interesting matches—far more than can be mentioned, unfortunately. However, the
overriding fact was that this Wimbledon Centenary, which everyone

hoped would be a tournament to remember, turned out to be exactly that. In the Gentlemen's Singles, the semifinal match between Bjorn Borg, of Sweden, the defending champion, and Vitas Gerulaitis, of the United States, which Borg won in five sets, proved to be an authentic classic. Don Budge said he thought that it was the best match he had ever seen, and Fred Perry, only a mite more conservative, said he could not remember seeing a better match. This was followed by a first-class final between Borg and Connors—their first meeting on grass. Played under a broiling sun on by far the hottest day of the championships, it consumed three hours and four minutes before Borg pulled it out, 3–6, 6–2, 6–1, 5–7, 6–4. Yet when tennis fans look back on the 1977 championships, what they will remember above all is that this was the year that Virginia Wade, the sweetheart of tennis-playing, tennis-talking, tennis-loving England, at last, in her sixteenth attempt, won the Ladies' Singles. Miss Wade has been one of the top women players in the world for a decade— she won our championship at Forest Hills in 1968 and, later, the Italian and Australian championships—but year after year, instead of rising to the challenge of Wimbledon, she was the victim of attacks of nerves, and, playing miles below her usual standard, always found a way to lose to opponents who were not at all in her class. The knowledge of how keenly her compatriots wanted her to win at Wimbledon only served to impose an increasingly heavy burden on Our Ginny, as she is known in the popular press. What happened this year, consequently, was almost too good to be true. Just when nearly everyone had given up on her—Chris Evert was the odds-on favorite to win the Ladies'—Our Ginny came through, and at the most appropriate time, for this, of course, is the year of Queen Elizabeth's Silver Jubilee, and the Queen herself, making her first visit to Wimbledon since 1962, was seated in the Royal Box.

Let us leave the women for a moment and turn to the men. In the upper half of the draw, Connors made his way to the semifinals, where he met one of the big surprises of the tournament—John McEnroe, of Douglaston, Long Island, a sturdy, athletic eighteen-year-old, who had had to earn a place in the championship field in the qualifying rounds at Roehampton and had then gone out and beaten such established players as Ismail El Shafei, Karl Meiler, Sandy Mayer, and Phil Dent on his way to becoming the youngest player ever to reach the last four of the men's singles. Connors versus McEnroe, which Connors won in four sets, turned out to be a dullish match. McEnroe lacked his customary zest, and Connors played about the same stodgy, fragmented stuff he had got by with throughout the tournament. Connors, however, is respected for his ability to get himself up for a big match, and no one looked for Borg to have an easy time of it in the final, despite his inspired tennis against Gerulaitis in the other semifinal. Borg, who is now twenty-one, changes his game only slightly for Wimbledon: he concentrates on beefing up his serve, for on a skiddy surface like grass a potent serve pays off. At Wimbledon, as at other tournaments and on other surfaces, Borg only occasionally comes to net, preferring to stay at the baseline and wear down his opponent with his heavy topspin forehand and his two-fisted topspin backhand, which are difficult to handle, and with his tireless ability to retrieve nearly everything hit across the net. Borg doesn't go for outright winners often, but when he spots an opening he can sting you with his crosscourt backhand and his down-the-line forehand. Gerulaitis, who was born in Brooklyn and is now twenty-two, has recently improved his game immeasurably. In the preceding years, he was a good enough player to win sizable amounts of prize money, and this enabled him to buy a house, with tennis court, in Kings Point, on the North Shore of Long Island, and to acquire two Rolls-Royces, a Mercedes, and a Porsche. During that period, he was content to embellish his image as a ranking playboy, but on a trip to Europe last year he noticed how zealously players like Borg practiced, and his attitude underwent a marked change. He became a devout practicer, and approached his career far more seriously. The improvement in his game has been sudden and astonishing. He has a stronger first serve now. His second serve, formerly one of his main weaknesses, has come along well. He has bolstered his forehand, though it still does not compare with his sliced backhand, which has always been his most dependable stroke. His forehand volley is surer, and so is his overhead. He now produces all these strokes with fluidity and rhythm, partly because he has practiced them faithfully, and partly because through practice he has sharpened his anticipation and refined his footwork. Today, he is a first-class player, not just an ambitious young man with a flair for the game. This was brought home this spring, when he won his first prestige championship, the Italian Open, and won it on clay, which is not his best surface. In contrast to Borg, he likes to attack whenever possible—to come into the forecourt behind a forcing approach shot. This contrast in the styles of Gerulaitis and Borg set up countless glistening sequences in which one player, seemingly beaten in a rat-tat-tat exchange, somehow got to the ball and improvised an apparent winner only to have the other player, acting purely on reflex, somehow get his racquet on the ball and put it away with an unbelievable stroke. What made the Borg-Gerulaitis match the instant classic it was acclaimed? To begin with, both men were in top form, and that is a rarity. As the match moved on and individual points became more and more significant, both had the guts to play heroic shots in the clutch: raffishly angled, high backhand volleys, soft little half volleys, uncompromising overhead smashes, full-blooded drives that whistled through small openings, lots of deep lobs that had to be chased down—the whole book, in fact. Somehow or other, they sustained this level of play at top speed for the full five sets. Borg deserved to win, because he won the last two games, but Gerulaitis played just as superlatively as he did.

This was a hard act to follow, but the Borg-Connors final, particularly in view of the fact that most finals are anticlimactic, was a tough, bruising, superior match. From beginning to end, the pattern was one of strange fluctuations, with first one man and then the other dominating play. As many people had anticipated, Connors, that natural competitor, came on the court conspicuously abrim with a verve and intensity he had not previously shown in the championships. He was out to gain command of the match quickly, and he did. He won the first set at 6–3, hitting out ferociously, and came within a hair of breaking Borg's service in the third game of the second set. At this juncture, Borg, who may have been still feeling the effects of his battle with Gerulaitis two days before, began to increase the tempo of his play and to become more adventurous, and simultaneously Connors began to miss more frequently, especially with his forehand approach shots. The result was that Borg ran off four straight games, and with them the second set, 6–2. In the third set, with Connors still quiescent and erratic, Borg won five of the first six games, and eventually the set, 6–1, scoring with two blazing aces in the last game. During this stretch—indeed, throughout the final—Borg's serve was his chief strength; one cannot overstate its importance for him. Midway through the fourth set, there was another change. At 4–4, Borg twice stood within a point of breaking Connors' serve for 5–4, but, almost as if he were psychologically unprepared at that moment to win the match, he faltered badly on both points. Following this, Borg began to look a little weary and to play a bit negatively, and Connors, who is never beaten until he *is* beaten, started to rip into his shots with a new surge of confidence. At 5–5, he won eight of the next nine points and took the set, 7–5, to square the match at two sets apiece. Now several other dramatic changes came swiftly. Borg, summoning his reserve strength, started to hit his drives with emphatic topspin again, and swept the first four games of the deciding set. In the fifth game, he was twice within a point of breaking Connors. Tired as he was, Connors fought back brilliantly, and not only saved that game but also carried off the next three games on the strength of some fine, deep approaches and remarkable put-away volleys. Now, just when it appeared that he would probably go on to win, he suffered a spasm of inexplicable carelessness in the critical ninth game, serving a double fault and banging two backhands far out of court. Borg to serve, leading 5–4. Revived by Connors' sudden loss of control—Connors may have simply run out of gas—Borg raced through his service game at love, ending the match with a flourish on an untouchable smash, a hard-hit drive that forced an error, a powerhouse serve that Connors barely got his racquet on, and a backhand down the line, which Connors, who thought that Borg would be going crosscourt, couldn't cope with. The score again: 3–6, 6–2, 6–1, 5–7, 6–4. An absorbing final, played with a most commendable spirit. Borg, by the way, now has a chance to become the first man to win Wimbledon three times in a row since Perry accomplished this in the middle nineteen-thirties.

Back to the Ladies' Singles: Virginia Wade, who is now thirty-one, grew up, and played her first tennis, in South Africa, where her father was the Archdeacon of Durban. Aside from her exceptional athletic endowment—she is recognized as having the best service motion in women's tennis—she is highly intelligent, and took her degree at the University of Sussex in general science and physics. After deciding to make tennis her life, she rose quickly to the international level. Her style of play revealed a rigidly imperious attitude; in losing, as in winning, she insisted on dictating the structure of the match, not always wisely. The last few years, she has worked hard to overcome this tendency. She has tried to learn to make her game more flexible, and to understand that there are many different ways to win points if one thinks and perseveres. During the past year, she decided that, for all the raves she regularly received about her service, it was not doing all that it might for her, so she sought out two American teaching professionals, Ham Richardson and Jerry Teeguarden, to work with her on her toss. She also spent hours on end trying to correct the flaws in her vulnerable forehand. She came to Wimbledon in an uncharacteristically confident frame of mind. She felt that she was "by far the strongest person in the dressing room," and that this was meant to be her tournament.

Miss Wade's first real test came in the quarter-finals, against Rosemary Casals. Miss Casals has always been difficult for her to beat. An acrobatic scrambler, Miss Casals is very likely to cut off an apparently unreachable passing shot with a diving volley, then pick herself up just in time to hustle back and knock off with a leaping overhead smash the lob her opponent has thrown up. Losing points that had looked safely won was what had made Miss Wade's meetings with Miss Casals so exasperating for her. In their match at Wimbledon this year,

Miss Wade was on the ropes several times in the first set, but she stayed in there and managed to win it, 7–5. Then, with games at 2–2 in the second set, she broke Miss Casals' serve twice in a row with a flurry of assertive placements, to take the set, 6–2, and the match. Miss Wade is often given to dithering and stumbling about when she is in sight of victory, and to see her play so effectively against Miss Casals when the chance to win presented itself made one wonder if this really was a "new Virginia." We knew for certain that it was after her semifinal with Chris Evert. In the quarter-final round, Miss Evert had played an almost perfect match in devastating Billie Jean King with the loss of only three games. Theirs is a long and animated rivalry, and Miss Evert was up for the clash. She displayed a diversity of shots we had never seen from her before, including things like sharply angled topspin forehands and a succession of defensive stab volleys in which she guessed correctly each time just where Mrs. King, in charge of the forecourt, would be pasting her volley. Tennis can be an impossible game to understand. Two days later, facing Miss Wade in the semis, Miss Evert, unable to rouse herself from a deep lethargy, may have played the poorest match of her career, and Miss Wade, instead of being overcome by those old Centre Court jitters, was the one who played an almost perfect match. I will bother you with only one statistic: so complete was her control that in the three sets they played Miss Wade only twice hit ground strokes that carried beyond the baseline. That night, the evening tabloids, instead of giving us the familiar front-page headline of "WADE FAILS IN SHOCK DEFEAT," featured variations on "GINNY K.O.s CHAMP." The score, incidentally, was 6–2, 4–6, 6–1. For a time, there was a prospect of an all-English women's final, for in the other semi Betty Stove, of the Netherlands, playing in her thirteenth Wimbledon, was up against Sue Barker, a charming young woman from Devon who has come on fast. It did not happen. Miss Stove—at six feet one, the tallest woman in tennis—was just too crushing with her serve-and-volley game: 6–4, 2–6, 6–4.

The first match each day at Wimbledon begins at two o'clock. At six minutes to two on the afternoon of the Ladies' Final, shortly after the military band in the Centre Court had concluded its rendition of "Land of Hope and Glory," the Queen arrived, wearing a pink-and-white outfit, and proceeded, amid exuberant applause, to the Royal Box. The band struck up "God Save the Queen," and halfway through the anthem the spectators began to sing it softly. Miss Wade and Miss Stove then came out on the court, made their curtsies, and warmed up. Miss Wade did not look nervous as she prepared to serve the opening game, but evidently she was. She did not move as fast or hit the ball as hard as she ordinarily does—a sure sign of tension. In fact, it soon became clear that, like Miss Evert, she was fated to follow a nearly perfect performance with an anguishingly mediocre one. After four deuce points, she did rescue the opening game. She was broken in the fifth game, broke back in the sixth against an equally tight opponent, and was broken again in the ninth game at love. Miss Stove then held service. First set to Miss Stove, 6–4. Subdued groans from the fourteen thousand spectators in the Centre Court. Near the middle of the second set, Miss Wade began to unwind a bit. Her agility improved, and she started to outguess and outmaneuver her opponent. This is essential against Miss Stove, who, once she has ensconced herself at net, is exceedingly hard to pass, because of her tremendous reach. In the eighth game, Miss Wade broke service, thanks in part to Miss Stove's eighth double fault, and then served out for the set, at 6–3. An explosive shout from the encouraged stands. The third set came more easily. Miss Wade won the first four games, mainly on her opponent's errors, for her own shotmaking remained somewhat inhibited. However, now that she had the match for the taking she seized her opportunity firmly and won the last two games with the loss of only two points. Wade, 4–6, 6–3, 6–1. It was a triumph less of flashing strokes and skillfully engineered points than of will, resolution, and determination, but, in a way, this is close to quibbling. The fact of the matter was that Virginia Wade had actually won Wimbledon, and the roars and applause she was accorded by her ecstatic fans on the Centre Court as she was congratulated by the Queen and held aloft the golden salver, the Ladies' Championship trophy, could probably be heard as far away as Putney Bridge.

It was a lifting experience to hear Virginia Wade's thoughts on her triumph: "It was wonderful to win in front of the Queen, but the cheering was so loud it was difficult to hear what she said to me. All I heard her say was 'Well played. It must have been hard work.' I told her that it *was* hard work. . . . I felt I had more incentive this week than I ever had before. Everyone thought I was past it and that I couldn't do it. I wanted to prove that I deserved to be out there among the champions. I felt I belonged—that I was the best player who hadn't won Wimbledon so far. . . . I knew that the most important thing to do today was just to play the best I could and not to let any stray dreams distract me." She said later that she had got through the morning before the match by putting her pillow over her telephone and turning up the volume on a recording of Rachmaninoff's Second Symphony.

Earlier this year, when the spectacular program of events for the Queen's Silver Jubilee was being planned, many people held the view that, times being as parlous as they are today, the British public would hardly be in a mood for pomp and circumstance, reviews and tattoos, fireworks and festivities. These fears proved to be groundless. The Queen's great personal popularity carried the day, and the Silver Jubilee has been a colossal success. Then the Centenary Wimbledon came along, and Virginia Wade, with her victory, added that extra, unexpected contribution that really sets a celebration aglow. When the happy spectators in the Centre Court, following the presentation of the championship trophy to Our Ginny by Her Majesty, spontaneously began to sing "For She's a Jolly Good Fellow," I'm sure I wasn't the only American present who did not know for certain whether it was Virginia Wade or Queen Elizabeth II they had in mind.

THE INCREDIBLE
TENNIS EXPLOSION

(1977)

The early autumn of 1977, when the tennis boom was approaching the end of its first decade, seemed the right time to reflect on that phenomenon. It was not an easy subject to research: It called for some hard statistics, and they have never been one of tennis' strong suits. Another thing: As one leaned back and calmly reviewed the game's ten-year expansion (and the varied and astonishing reasons behind it), the whole explosion still seemed incredible.

In the second act of Arthur Miller's "Death of a Salesman," a significant scene takes place when Willy Loman, the salesman—he has just lost his job—calls in at his neighbor Charley's office to borrow some money. In the reception room, he meets Charley's son, Bernard, who is killing a little time before travelling down to Washington. The stage directions note that "a pair of tennis racquets and an overnight bag are on the floor" next to the chair Bernard is sitting in. Throughout his boyhood and young manhood, Bernard, in Willy Loman's mind, had been a drab bookworm—nothing at all compared to Willy's older son, Biff, who had been a glittering high-school football star and had been plied with scholarships by several large universities. Things have changed drastically, however. Biff, in the throes of a tragic psychological confusion brought on by his crushing disappointment in his father, never went to college, and has floundered around without purpose since his glory days in high school. Bernard, on the other hand, is now a lawyer and has obviously matured well. In his conversation with Willy in the reception room, we learn that Bernard is going to Washington to argue a case. (He doesn't mention that he will be arguing it before the Supreme Court, but his father does later.) When Willy asks him if he is going to play tennis in Washington, Bernard answers that he will be staying with a friend who has a court. The tennis racquets are, in a way, Bernard's oriflamme. Where Biff is lost, Bernard, the drab bookworm, has grown up into a solid, quietly assured young man who is on the right track and will almost certainly enjoy a happy and fruitful life.

When "Death of a Salesman" opened on Broadway, in February 1949, Miller's use of the tennis racquets as a symbol of Bernard's changed status was remarkably successful, for in those days tennis was associated predominantly with the well-to-do, well-bred, well-educated set. It definitely connoted the good, privileged life. Today, I should imagine, the racquets would not illustrate Miller's point quite so effectively, since the position of tennis has changed a great deal in this country during the intervening years. It has become an authentic major sport, played by a wide cross-section of the population, and, according to a Harris Survey taken a few years ago, it is now exceeded in spectator popularity only by football, baseball, and basketball. Back in 1949, nevertheless, tennis was not exactly static. It was growing annually at an estimated rate of five per cent in terms of sales, players, and courts, and it continued to do so throughout the nineteen-fifties and into the nineteen-sixties.

In 1968, with the advent of open tennis the tennis boom, which had long been predicted, suddenly broke like a tidal wave. It far surpassed anyone's anticipations, to put it mildly. Now, as the boom is approaching the close of its first decade, one sees on every side evidence of the deep indentation it has made in American life. For example, when I walk to Grand Central Station, a few blocks away, at the close of the working day, it is rare that I do not pass two or three persons carrying tennis racquets, and frequently I pass six or seven. The tennis racquet is now accepted as standard equipment, like the briefcase or the shopping bag. On my way to the station, I pass Feron's, one of the oldest tennis specialty shops in New York. It now sells not only tennis balls, racquets, and apparel but all sorts of knickknacks—ice buckets decorated with a color photograph of the Forest Hills marquee, thermos bottles designed to look like larger versions of the cans of tennis balls put out by the leading manufacturers, tennis drinking glasses, tennis scarves, tennis address and telephone books, tennis aprons, and mailboxes adorned with a drawing of a cute little puppy chewing on a tennis ball in front of a net. There is nothing singular about Feron's. Another thing: When I enter Grand Central, I am very much aware that up above, occupying what was originally office space in the section of the terminal building that fronts on Vanderbilt Avenue, is the Grand Central Racquet Club, which charges the highest fee I know of for renting either of its two courts—forty-five dollars an hour in prime time. Wherever one travels, be it in the city, the suburbs, or the rural stretches, one runs into an astonishing abundance of relatively new tennis facilities, ranging from public courts built with public funds to elegant private clubs with outdoor and indoor courts, saunas, bars, and pools. Nearly all of them are seething with activity. In a word, there has never been a sports explosion in this country to compare with the tennis explosion.

Since we live in an age in which most sports have official bureaus of statistics, which regularly provide us with the information that a certain major-league baseball player has just broken the record for most total hits in a career by a switch-hitter or that a certain pro football player has just tied the record for most unassisted tackles during one game by an outside linebacker, it comes as rather a shock to discover that tennis, almost alone among the big sports, has never kept adequate records. I mention this because statistics, while never telling all of a story, can be a tremendous aid in helping one to understand some of its salient aspects. In any event, thanks to the assistance of a number of people who have been deeply involved in tennis for many years, I have been able to assemble some fairly hard figures and some informed estimates that I believe will serve to bring out the awesome proportions of the tennis boom.

o According to *Tennis Industry,* a monthly trade journal published in Miami, a reliable pre-boom census taken in 1960 placed the number of tennis players in the United States at slightly over five and a half million. In 1970, when the A. C. Nielsen Company, the well-known market-research firm, was first called in to conduct a tennis survey, it found that about ten million Americans played the game "from time to time." By 1976, according to a Nielsen study for that year, there were twenty-nine million tennis players in the country. This figure seemed a trifle exuberant to many people. The Nielsen field hands, they felt, must have counted anyone who had played any tennis at all that year, be it only a single set of doubles at a company outing. They believed that a much more accurate figure was 19,272,660, which the 1976 Nielsen report indicated to be the number of Americans who played tennis more than three times a month. (Six per cent of our players, the report informed us, were children under twelve, twenty-four per cent were teen-agers, thirty-five per cent were men, and thirty-five per cent women.)

o The best estimate of the number of tennis courts in the United States today is around a hundred and fifty thousand—more than twice the total before the boom. In the late sixties and early seventies, when tennis really began to grow, four to five thousand courts were built each year for individual owners, schools and colleges, towns and cities, clubs and resorts. Last year, somewhere in the neighborhood of eleven thousand new courts were built. This year, the figure is down a bit, because, beginning last autumn, our economic inflation began to affect tennis, and, for the first time since 1968, the boom started to taper off.

o The tabulations of Alfred S. Alschuler, Jr., one of the directors of a Chicago company called Tennis Planning Consultants, indicate that this year Americans will buy close to a hundred and fifty-seven million tennis balls—three times as many as in 1970. To keep up with the constantly increasing demand, in 1972 the General Tire & Rubber Company, one of the three large American manufacturers of tennis balls, doubled its production by opening a new plant in Phoenix, Arizona. Two years later, it opened another plant, in Ireland, and a year after that added one in Jonesboro, Arkansas. Still trying to keep up, it then expanded the facilities at its main plant, in Jeannette, Pennsylvania. It is difficult to obtain dependable figures on the production and sale of tennis racquets in this country. However, statistics on how many racquets have been imported each year during the nineteen-seventies are available. Until recently, about eighty per cent of the wooden-frame racquets sold here were made abroad (most of them in Taiwan, Pakistan, Belgium, and Japan), and, according to Alschuler, between 1970 and 1974 their number rose from two million three hundred thousand to nine million four hundred thousand. For 1976, Alschuler estimated the total gross sales of the tennis industry—balls, racquets, sneakers, clothes, court construction, club memberships, tennis camps, and so on —at a billion and a quarter dollars. Many people in the game think this is on the conservative side, and that two billion dollars would be nearer the mark.

o Counting day camps, there are now about five hundred tennis camps across the country.

o In 1968, *World Tennis,* our oldest tennis monthly magazine, had reached a circulation of forty-nine thousand five hundred. At present, its circulation is three hundred and twenty-five thousand.

o In 1960, there were approximately fifty indoor-tennis clubs in the United States. Today, there are some fifteen hundred indoor clubs, and around two million people play indoor tennis.

o Before the coming of open tennis, the men's amateur tournament schedule was limited to about fifteen substantial events a year—the players received their money under the table—and professional tennis consisted principally of several tours that wended their unpublicized, dusty ways around the globe. Once or twice a year, the pros convened to see who was playing the best tennis. Nowadays, there is at least one tournament of consequence every week of the year, and some weeks there are as many as five going on simultaneously, on several continents. (The tennis explosion has been a universal phenomenon, although in no other country has it been as tremendous as here.) Before 1968, there was no women's professional tennis to speak of. It has now become a thriving, many-sided business that offers astounding financial rewards.

o The vast increase in televised tennis has had an incalculable influence on the growth of the game. Of the total time allotted to sports in 1971 by the three commercial national networks, only two per cent went to tennis. By 1976, when televised tennis hit its peak, the figure was up to thirteen per cent. That year, counting the events telecast by the Public Broadcasting Service, a nonprofit national network, some seventy tournaments were covered, compared to seven in 1971. (Bud Collins, the informed and adroit commentator who is affiliated with both PBS and the National Broadcasting Company, appeared on nearly sixty telecasts in 1976 and was on the air at least a hundred and seventy-five hours.) Oh, it has been quite a change! Some Sundays the past few years, there have been three different television programs devoted to tennis at the fans' fingertips—more air time in a single day than the game was accorded over a full year prior to 1968. At that time, if I remember correctly, tennis coverage usually began and ended with abbreviated broadcasts from Forest Hills on the final two days of the championships. Speaking of championships, the Columbia Broadcasting System is said to have agreed to pay the United States Tennis Association between seven and eight million dollars for the rights to telecast the indoor championships (held in Salisbury, Maryland), the clay-court championships (in Indianapolis), and the climactic national championships (in New York City) this year and the next two years, a nice little hike from the 1973 contract whereby the U.S.T.A. (then the U.S. Lawn Tennis Association) received a million dollars for the rights to televise the championships at Forest Hills for three years. Previous to that, the U.S.L.T.A. had received a hundred thousand dollars a year for those television rights.

The tennis boom, as you may have gathered, has been an uncommonly complicated affair. I would, however, like to comment briefly on some of the aspects of the boom that have struck me as especially interesting, including several that I feel haven't received the attention they deserve.

To begin with, the tennis boom has been unique as sports booms go in that persons of both sexes and of all ages have been a part of it. At least a third of the recruits have been middle-aged or past middle age—an unprecedented occurrence, since earlier in this century most Americans had come to accept the injunction that when a man reached forty he should stop shovelling snow and cut out other strenuous physical activities that could lead to harmful overexertion. The person who probably did the most to disprove this bromide was Dr. Paul Dudley White, the Boston heart specialist who was called in by the White House after President Eisenhower suffered his heart attack in 1955. The next winter, the President, then sixty-five, went back to playing golf, for he had recovered well from his attack, and Dr. White was firmly of the belief that nothing promotes good health better than sensible exercise, even for people who are getting on in years. Americans were impressed by Dr. White's prescription whenever they saw a photo of President Eisenhower swinging a golf club or of Dr. White, no spring chicken himself, bent low over the handlebars of his bicycle. While tennis had always been listed among the "lifetime sports," along with fishing, golf, and shuffleboard, during the past decade it has shown itself to be emphatically that. In answer to popular demand, for some time now the U.S.T.A. has operated a series of tournaments for men sixty and over, sixty-five and over, seventy and over, and seventy-five and over. This past September, it established singles and doubles championships for men eighty and over.

Tennis also gained many new adherents, both before the boom and during it, from the repeated advice of medical leaders that it was not healthy to permit oneself to become fat. Playing a vigorous sport like tennis was one of the most agreeable ways to lose weight, and for this reason women, in particular, gravitated to it in numbers. Everybody likes to look good, and many women, once they had slimmed down a bit, discovered that when they wore a tennis dress it made them feel active, attractive, and "part of the scene." As a result, many of them started wearing tennis dresses when they went to the supermarket or performed other routine chores. Moreover, many women who didn't play the game began to wear tennis dresses around town simply because they found they looked nice in them. Before the tennis boom, it had been de rigueur at most tennis clubs for the players to dress only in white. During the boom, this changed, and outfits of all hues became permissible, but a lot of players, both newcomers to the game and people who had grown up with it, nevertheless preferred to wear white, and for the first time in many years white became an "in" color for women away from the court as well as on it. On the other hand, many men and women were all in favor of tennis outfits that came in different colors and patterns. They looked forward eagerly to sporting their persimmon outfit, say, in the first round of the club championship, and then, if they won, breaking out that spangled Euphrates-bronze number for their second-round match. In the opinion of Ed Fabricius, the public-relations director of the U.S.T.A., for some of the recent converts to tennis the acceptability of colored outfits has had a deeper meaning: it signifies that tennis no longer belongs to the people who wear only white and are members of the old, uppity clubs.

It is important, I believe, to stress that the flowering of tennis into an egalitarian passion didn't happen overnight—that the ground had been carefully prepared for it over a considerable period. In the nineteen-fifties, pockets of tennis enthusiasts, out of sheer love of the game, got local group-instruction programs started on school and public courts here and there around the country, and a national society called the Lifetime Sports Education Project attempted to do the same thing on a broader scale. In 1960 and 1961, the U.S.L.T.A. became interested in these efforts, and a joint committee, the U.S.L.T.A.-A.A.H.P.E.R. (the American Association of Health, Physical Education, and Recreation), was established. However, transforming this imposing amalgamation of initials into a functioning organization was a long process. It wasn't until 1972 that the U.S.L.T.A. ultimately set up an Education and Research Center (with one paid employee) in Princeton, New Jersey, under the direction of Eve Kraft, a local resident, and John Conroy, the University's tennis coach, with whom she had initiated a series of small, informal tennis classes back in the fifties which had evolved into a successful pilot program of group teaching. Today, the Education and Research Center, which produces numerous publications, distributes films, and holds regional teaching workshops, has a staff of eleven paid employees and receives adequate funds from the U.S.T.A. But the main point is this: the invaluable contribution made by the Princeton unit and other such units in the nineteen-sixties and afterward was in getting the tennis pro from the private club together with the physical-education instructor. The tennis pro had something definite to offer: he knew the game. The P.E. instructor also had something definite to offer: he or she might not know enough about tennis to teach people how to hit a slice service or a topspin drive, but whereas most tennis pros were at home only when teaching an individual pupil, the P.E. instructor knew how to take sixty people onto a tennis court and conduct a controlled, educative hour of group instruction. "All of the successful grass-roots programs have depended on this cross-ventilation between the teaching pros and the P.E. teachers," Mrs. Kraft told me a while back. "The two disciplines augmented each other perfectly. The P.E. teachers were able to start group tennis instruction in many of our schools and public parks, and they interested countless young people in the game. Which reminds me—the other important service that units like ours provided was showing people the right procedure to get their local town councils to grant their schools and parks the funds to build the new courts that now were necessary." The Princeton Community Tennis Program, which Mrs. Kraft began twenty-two years ago, continues to be a model of how to teach an individual sport to large groups of players. This year, in the Princeton area, two thousand residents, young and old, took regular lessons from a staff of a hundred and fifty instructors.

The expanded television coverage of tennis acted as a powerful supplement to individual and group instruction, since it is exceedingly beneficial for players of all levels to observe the game's champions in action and to study their methods. Lamar Hunt, the head of World Championship Tennis, and NBC deserve the credit for originating the first series of national tennis telecasts. On eight Sundays in the winter and spring of 1972, NBC carried the final match of that week's W.C.T. tournament. On May 14th that year, the final of the W.C.T. championship was televised, and this was particularly fortunate. It enabled an audience that had swelled to over fifty million to watch what many tennis scholars regard as the finest match ever played—the unforgettable five-set duel between Laver and Rosewall. One veteran head of sales for a prominent sporting-goods company believes that this one match turned a million people who had watched the telecast on to tennis. About a year and a half later, on the night of September 20, 1973, another enormous television audience was at its sets for the hundred-thousand-dollar challenge match—winner take all—between Bobby Riggs and Billie Jean King, which was held in the Houston Astrodome. A crowd of 30,492 spectators, a record for a tennis match, was on hand, and they saw some very good tennis—practically all of it played by Mrs. King, who was completely in control, winning 6–4, 6–3, 6–3. Mrs. King's stunning triumph had the effect of further increasing the already sizable army of women tennis players. Within a comparatively short time, however, the hundred-thousand-dollar purse Mrs. King had won began to look like peanuts. In April 1975, Jimmy Connors, who comes from Illinois, and John Newcombe, of Australia, met in a televised challenge match in Las Vegas, and Connors, the winner, earned two hundred and fifty thousand dollars plus a healthy percentage of the match's total gross—not bad pay for about three hours' work. Last March, though, Connors surpassed this. He defeated Ilie Nastase in Puerto Rico in a televised challenge match that was advertised as a two-hundred-and-fifty-thousand-dollar, winner-take-all confrontation. Not long afterward, however, word leaked out that the financial structure of the match had been slightly misrepresented, and that Connors had been guaranteed five hundred thousand dollars and Nastase a hundred and fifty thousand. This was bad business. Television has done a great deal to help popularize tennis, but I trust we are all somewhat wiser now than before this put-on and more aware that as we enter the Age of Very Big Sport we must be extremely vigilant. Already a good deal of the spirit of sport has gone out of sport, and if we let ourselves nod off the national associations will become superannuated and the big money will control sports.

The appreciable income that a tennis player of tournament calibre can currently accumulate has not been lost on our aspiring young athletes. (For starters, last year the six top-ranked American men each collected over two hundred thousand dollars in prize money alone.) Many teen-agers, of both sexes, with an aptitude for athletics have dropped the other sports they were connected with in favor of pouring their energy into tennis, which they look upon as a gravy train that will keep on rolling for a good many years to come. Still, the large majority of teen-agers who have taken up tennis have done so simply because they were smitten by the game. (They also prefer the informal atmosphere of a small tennis club or tennis-and-swimming club to the stiffness that prevails at many country clubs.) The tennis boom has provided this group with a pantheon of heroes and heroines they can identify with and admire. In this general connection, for some reason that defies understanding, tennis, from its beginnings, had been regarded in certain circles as a prissy, decorous, almost effeminate game. The only explanations of this nonsense which occur to me are that tennis is not a contact sport and that a lot of wealthy people who speak in overly refined accents had long been associated with it. Surely if a person has watched two competent players in action for the better part of a set it must be obvious to him that tennis is an unusually taxing game, requiring exceptional coördination. In any event, as the public became acquainted with handsome, rugged fellows like Borg and Newcombe and came to appreciate the artistry and appeal of young women like Chris Evert and Evonne Goolagong, the old Fauntleroy stigma that tennis had long had to put up with was removed once and for all. I am reminded of the similar service President Eisenhower performed for golf. For years, whenever I walked through Grand Central Station carrying my golf bag, there were always a couple of guys who had to sing out chidingly, "Play a good game, Reginald," or something along that line. This stopped abruptly when Eisenhower's fanatic love of golf became known. If Ike, a down-to-earth, regular fellow, liked golf—so went the thinking—the game had to be all right.

Golf has played a much more influential role in the growth of tennis than is generally understood. Several years before open tennis arrived, golf began to undergo some injurious modifications. At most golf clubs, the bulk of the players—men who scored in the high 80s, in the 90s, and often in three figures—took it into their heads to approach the game like the touring tournament pros they saw on television: they started to take three minutes to study a putt and then two minutes more to hit it. Since these club players in time went in for the same exquisite dawdling before executing every shot from tee to green, it wasn't long before it took them—and everybody else—five hours to play eighteen holes. Now it takes five and a half hours. During the period in which this slowdown was taking place, at many clubs riding in a golf cart replaced walking as the accepted method of getting around a course. The chief result of this innovation was that no one got much exercise unless he was a demon for replacing divots. These distortions of the game displeased a number of golfers, and many of them reacted by playing less golf and more tennis than before. It made a lot of sense. A five-and-a-half-hour round ate up your whole Saturday or Sunday. In an hour and a half on the tennis court, you could get infinitely more exercise—indeed, a real workout. There were other reasons that people who had previously played neither game turned to tennis. In many areas, it was next to impossible to get into the desirable golf clubs; after the golf boom of the fifties and sixties, these clubs had long waiting lists. The new tennis clubs, granted, possessed less prestige than the old country clubs, but at least there were memberships to be had, and as the tennis boom kept booming the people to whom social status was of some concern decided that a well-run tennis club took care of their needs sufficiently. Besides, tennis clubs were much less expensive than golf clubs. Consider the difference in the entrance fees. An ivied golf club might set a new member back as much as ten thousand dollars, but it took only seven hundred and fifty dollars to join one of the better tennis clubs. There was a wide disparity, too, between the annual dues at golf clubs and at tennis clubs, to say nothing of miscellaneous expenses; as a rule, a golf club cost a member three times as much. One could understand why. A fairly large staff and expensive machinery were needed to maintain the hundred and fifty acres, or more, that the eighteen holes occupied, but a couple of men could maintain sixteen clay-type or composition courts without much trouble.

As the tennis clubs gradually acquired a personality of their own, an important change took place. In many communities, families began to spend more time at the tennis club, since the kids liked hanging around the club as much as the adults did, and the two groups somehow didn't get in each other's way. Many unanticipatable things happened to make the operation of the clubs work out well. For example, on weekday afternoons, when the cost of renting a court was the lowest, the housewives, having planned their day accordingly, took over in numbers. At first, Saturday and Sunday nights presented a headache— the clubs were deserted because their members, as they always had, drove into town to eat dinner or catch a show. This gradually altered. Three or four couples at indoor clubs started the practice of renting a court for a few hours on Saturday night. This soon was taken up by many other members, as was a related form of entertainment: twenty couples would band together to rent the entire club for a New Year's Eve party or some other gala occasion. As more and more clubs added indoor courts, the tennis club became the year-round focus of its members' social life.

No one was really surprised when an increasing percentage of boys and girls of junior-high and high-school age developed into capable players. This seemed only natural when one took into account the early age at which they had started tennis, the immense amount of time they spent playing and practicing, the many hours of instruction they received, and the ardor engendered by being involved in an "in" game. It was a mystery, though—and it still is to me—how so many men and women over forty who had never played tennis in their youth and who apparently possessed not a particle of athletic talent somehow managed to learn to play respectable tennis. For years before the boom, I had seen such people stepping onto tennis courts and finding that it was beyond their powers to run to the ball and hit it. I had assumed that they faced up to the facts after a few dismal sessions of endlessly whiffing the air, and thereafter concentrated on swimming or bridge or whatever it was they were good at and enjoyed. How is it that in recent years so many of these same hopeless cases have fared so much better? The only possible answers, I should think, are improved instruction and many more hours of practice. One particular day comes to mind—a day I spent some five years ago in Bretton Woods, New Hampshire, where Rod Laver and Roy Emerson were running a tennis camp for adults which consisted of a series of seven-day clinics, the campers arriving on Sunday and leaving the following Saturday. About forty players of various degrees of skill were attending the camp at the time of my visit. Laver, who is not notably outgoing by nature, did not seem to be relishing his teaching chores, but Emerson, an eminently gregarious man, was patently having a very good time, even though he spent most of the morning session working with the poorest players. There was one outstandingly sad case, who I thought would prove to be too much even for a man as patient and resourceful, and as adept at teaching, as Emerson. She was that classic type—a woman in her early forties who seemed utterly devoid of eye-and-hand coördination and could not make contact with the ball no matter how slowly it was hit to her. Emerson delegated the rest of his pupils to an assistant and began working with the woman himself. He stood at the net and had her stand at the opposite service line, and tossed a dozen balls underhand so that they bounced up softly for her. She didn't hit one. He crossed to her side of the net and, standing twelve or fourteen feet away, repeated the procedure. Same story. He called over a young assistant to handle the ball tossing, and, moving behind the woman and holding her arm, tried to transmit to her the movement, the feel, that goes into the forehand stroke. She ticked one or two balls on the frame of her racquet the first time they tried this. They kept repeating the exercise, and halfway through the third batch of balls tossed by the assistant she began to hit some of them on the face of the racquet. Two hours later, I checked to see what further progress, if any, she had made. She had rejoined the group made up of the least advanced players—it is essential to divide a class into different groups according to their relative ability, so that the novices do not suffer humiliation—and, somehow, she was hitting every other ball on her racquet strings with what vaguely resembled a tennis stroke. I saw her again late in the afternoon after Emerson had given her a little more individual attention and when her group was preparing to call it a day. She was still very unsure of herself, but every so often she delivered a nice-looking forehand with a suspicion of timing. I couldn't believe my eyes. I have an idea that before her week at tennis camp was over, this woman had been exposed with some success to the elements of the serve, the backhand, and the volley, and that she had returned home with a sufficient knowledge of the fundamentals and just enough confidence to undertake playing tennis with her friends, to go on improving, and to become in time a passable doubles player who genuinely enjoyed the game. By the way, most of the older people who have taken up tennis in the past decade have approached it with a wonderfully sensible attitude. They have not tried to serve like Arthur Ashe or paste a forehand like Greer Stevens. They have been content to get the ball back over the net with the most dependable stroke they can devise, and they have been quick to grasp the wisdom of Hazel Hotchkiss Wightman's adage: If you can return the ball successfully three times in a row, you will probably win the point.

One of the happier repercussions of the boom among people past the blush of youth was the formation of the Tennis Grand Masters, in 1973, by Alvin Bunis, of Cincinnati, a former tournament player, who had retired from the scrap-iron business in 1972 at the age of forty-nine. Three years before that, following a match against the ageless Gardnar Mulloy in the National Senior Grass Courts Championships, an idea had struck Bunis: Wouldn't it be marvellous if one could assemble the older champions, like Mulloy, who were still able to play excellent tennis? After his retirement, he set out to do this. En route, he evolved three fundamental requirements for any player who wished to compete in a Grand Masters tournament: the player had to be over forty-five; he had to have won a national or a major championship; and he had to be able to play at a level that would be of interest to a critical gallery. In 1973, Bunis held an experimental tournament at the Town Club, in Milwaukee, banking heavily on such old horses as Frank Sedgman, Vic Seixas, and Tom Brown to carry the load. The tournament went extremely well. Later that year, he interested Mulloy, Pancho Segura, and Sven Davidson in his project and also consolidated the format that the Grand Masters still adheres to for all its tournaments: on Friday, a field of eight players meets in four singles matches; on Saturday, two doubles matches and the singles semifinals are played; on Sunday, the two finals take place. The following year, 1974, was an encouraging one. The troupe was booked for several ten-thousand-dollar tournaments. (This meant that the least any player received was seven hundred and twenty-five dollars.) Many long-established tennis clubs, like Merion and Pebble Beach, which did not have the physical plant or the wherewithal to take care of Connors and company, were delighted at the chance to present, at popular prices, Sedgman, Seixas, Davidson, Torben Ulrich, and other stars of an earlier era who had come out of the woodwork when word got around about the Grand Masters. "The big thing about our tournaments is the quality of the tennis," Bunis said not long ago. "Our fellows can't blister the ball the way they used to, but everything is relative, and the spectators aren't all that aware that the pace of play has slowed down. What they do notice is the players' beautiful execution of their strokes and the way they move an opponent around to set up a winning stroke. The Grand Masters, I believe, is the only group of middle-aged professional athletes still playing a strenuous physical game, and this gives their galleries a terrific lift."

In 1975, when Almaden Vineyards contracted to underwrite eleven tournaments, the Grand Masters really arrived. Each year since, they have played several other tournaments in this country and have performed overseas in such countries as Australia, Denmark, England, Italy, South Africa, Sweden, and Saudi Arabia. In 1975, incidentally, Sedgman's prize money came to seventy-five thousand dollars, the second-highest amount ever collected in one year by this extraordinary athlete, who roughly a quarter of a century ago won one Wimbledon Championship, two Australian Championships, and two United States Championships.

Whenever I think of the tennis boom, I think of one man in particular, John Gardiner, who, among his multiple enterprises, owns and operates the famous tennis ranches in Carmel Valley, California, and Scottsdale, Arizona, that bear his name. Gardiner epitomizes the enormous change that the tennis boom has wrought in the lives of hundreds of men and women who had been connected with the sport for years and who had the good fortune and the necessary intelligence to ride the wave when it eventually broke. I first met Gardiner in 1951, when he was the tennis pro at Pebble Beach. A likable, outgoing, ambitious young man from West Philadelphia who had attended Pennsylvania State Teachers College and had taught tennis at summer camps in the Poconos, he had decided to settle on the West Coast when he got out of the service after the Second World War. Gardiner, who has the sun-whitened blond hair and clear blue eyes that are so common among tennis players, was beginning at that time to get a little heavy, and one gathered that he had long since given up any dreams of becoming a tournament player and would be devoting all of his time to teaching. His domain at Pebble Beach was not grand. It consisted of only three courts. They received a fair amount of play, and Gardiner gave a good number of lessons, but he was filled with a sense of great insignificance. Few people who lived in the neighborhood—the Monterey Peninsula—were really into tennis. Many of them talked and lived golf, and this wasn't unusual, considering that the course at Pebble Beach may be the finest in the world and that only a few miles away were the Monterey Peninsula Country Club and the dramatic and fascinating course at Cypress Point. When the conversation wasn't about golf, it was about horses, for many residents of the peninsula were all wrapped up in jumping, trail riding, and hunting. Gardiner found it difficult to get the youngsters he taught tennis to concentrate primarily on that game—their other interests seemed to take precedence. "That was frustrating, and so was developing a sound, comprehensive system of teaching tennis," he once told me. "There weren't many first-rate instruction books. You had to go way back to Bill Tilden's 'Match Play and the Spin of the Ball.' The current stars didn't tell you much." The desire to learn all he could by observing the top players in action led Gardiner to take off part of two years in the middle nineteen-fifties to work on the staff of Jack Kramer's professional tour.

In 1957, Gardiner made the decision that was to change the course of his career. While still holding on to his job at Pebble Beach, he purchased, with the assistance of friends, a tract of twenty acres— beautiful land, on which stood a low-slung country house with a swimming pool—near the village of Carmel Valley, fourteen miles inland from the coastal highway. He built three tennis courts and added some cottages, and John Gardiner's Tennis Ranch opened for business. For a while, it showed more promise than profit. For example, in the summer of 1958, when Gardiner ran his first tennis camp at the ranch—fourteen campers paid a fee of three hundred dollars for the three-week session —he lost nineteen thousand dollars. At the same time, he had the feeling that he had hit on an idea with a future. His camp, by the way, wasn't the first tennis camp. As far as one can ascertain, that distinction belongs to Jean Hoxie, an able and dedicated tennis teacher who established a summer tennis camp in the middle nineteen-forties in Hamtramck, Michigan. However, since most of Mrs. Hoxie's campers were kids from the Hamtramck area who returned home after each day's sessions—the other campers lived with Mrs. Hoxie in her home—it was basically a day camp, and Gardiner thinks that his was the first tennis camp that operated along the same lines as a regular summer camp. Today, twenty years later, Gardiner's tennis camp in Carmel Valley holds three three-week sessions, each attended by a hundred and twenty campers, and the tuition is eight hundred dollars. The camp currently has sixteen courts, a teaching staff of eight professionals and twenty-two college players, along with all the newfangled teaching equipment, from videotape-replay machines to computerized ball machines. A few years ago, Gardiner opened a second summer camp for boys and girls at Sun Valley, which has also fared very well.

I spent some time at Gardiner's Tennis Ranch in Carmel Valley in August 1959, when the camp was in its second season. Gardiner was pleased by the camp's growth and its prospects, but whenever we talked about the programs for adults he had been trying to get started at the ranch, his mood changed abruptly and he became somewhat gloomy. "Look, I'm not trying to make all the money in the world," I remember him saying one evening. "At the same time, we're raising a family now, which takes money, and I must admit I'm a little unhappy about how much better golf professionals do than we tennis professionals. When you drop into their big shops, they're selling their members new golf bags, new golf balls, new clubs, new gloves, new golf shoes, new umbrellas, new golf hats, new rain clothes—you name it. On top of that, they're now in the clothing game. They've got racks and racks of slacks and skirts, endless piles of blouses and sport shirts and shorts and sweaters. They pick up another bundle from renting their fleet of golf carts. Golf—that's the perfect game to get into. In tennis, your merchandising possibilities are so limited. There's only so much equipment and clothes a player needs. But the crux of the matter is the difficulty you have getting more adults to play tennis. Anybody can play golf. A man can be in his sixties and way out of condition, but that's no trouble—he can rent a cart. He may have the worst golf swing in the world, but he can still make contact with the ball, and somehow he hits some surprisingly good shots. The same is true of women golfers. Tennis is entirely different. To play it well enough to derive some pleasure and satisfaction, you must be in good enough physical shape to do quite a lot of running. Then, in order to hit the ball and keep it in play, you have to have some athletic ability. Most boys and girls who are exposed to tennis learn to play a creditable game. That's why our tennis camps have done well, and most people who learned tennis when they were young will go on to play it all their lives. But adults who have no previous tennis background often find the game too hard to learn when they're middle-aged and slowing down. That's the problem." If I remember correctly, during this period, apart from local members who were drawn to the ranch because of its charm and good food, and who played a lot of their tennis there, the prosperity of the project depended to a large degree on special package deals, such as five-day slim-down-and-shape-up clinics—tennis, saunas, massage, relaxation, and rest—aimed at youngish matrons from the San Francisco area. One can understand why Gardiner occasionally envied the golf entrepreneurs.

Gardiner made his next big move in 1967, just before the tennis boom erupted. It was a definite gamble. With some friends of his, he bought fifty-three acres on Camelback Mountain, in Scottsdale, Arizona, which had originally been developed as a tennis club by the movie stars John Ireland and Joanne Dru, who were husband and wife. They hadn't been able to make a go of it, nor had the club's next three owners. Gardiner and his associates built twenty-five courts at John

Gardiner's Tennis Ranch on Camelback. They also built forty-one condominiums, called casitas, priced between fifty and sixty-eight thousand dollars. By this time, it was clear that many people were interested in investing in a condominium at a golf resort or a skiing resort. But would anyone buy a condominium at a tennis resort? The answer was quick in coming. Within fourteen months, all the condominiums had been sold. In 1970, when Camelback expanded, there was a change: no new condominiums were built, but twelve new single-family houses, called casas, six of them with their own pool and tennis court, went up. The most expensive casa cost more than half a million dollars, but the most interesting probably is the one that belongs to Ken Rosewall, who teaches at Camelback's clinics. Rosewall's tennis court is situated on the roof of his house.

The season at the Camelback ranch extends from autumn through early spring. The heart of the operation is the seven-day clinics. They are held over a thirty-three-week span and have been going on since 1968–69. Each Sunday, an average of eighty tennis enthusiasts— the exact size of each weekly clinic depends on the accommodations that are made available by the owners' rentals of their casitas and casas —converge from all over the world on the Camelback ranch for what Gardiner likes to refer to as "a purposeful vacation." Thirty-six professionals, each a graduate of Gardiner's nine-week training course, make up the teaching staff. The cost of a week's clinic at Camelback for two people runs to around fourteen hundred dollars, and the annual gross of the clinics is now over two and a half million dollars. Additionally, the Carmel Valley ranch now holds twenty-five weekly clinics in the autumn and spring, and Gardiner is also involved in adult camps in Sugar Bush, Vermont (strictly a summer proposition); Dillon, Colorado; Port St. Lucie, Florida; and Century City, a part of Los Angeles.

Gardiner deserves his success. Aside from his obvious ability as a businessman, he has appreciated from the start that "we're only as good as our product, which is teaching tennis." Ninety per cent of his instructors are college graduates; many of them found there was a shortage of jobs in education and turned to tennis. Gardiner believes in an uncomplicated, uniform system of instruction—hence the nine-week training course—and he is certain the higher the number of balls a player gets to hit, the better his chances of improving his game. When we talked this past summer, I think he became most animated when describing how the girls and boys at his summer camps get eighty-two hours of instruction and play seventy-five matches during their three-week session. Gardiner has a lot on his mind these days, but he makes sure he still does some teaching himself.

A NEW ERA BEGINS:
FLUSHING MEADOW PARK

(1978)

*On Tuesday evening, August 29th, the first matches in the 1978 United
States Championships were played at the U.S.T.A.'s new home, the
National Tennis Center in Flushing Meadow Park, outside New York
City. It will be some time before the new facility is finished and has had
the time to settle down. Then we will be able to judge whether or not
it has fulfilled the hopes that everybody in tennis has for it. As the
revised stadium rose at Flushing Meadow Park, we were all surprised,
I believe, at learning that it was the first stadium specifically built for
a major tennis event since Roland Garros went up outside Paris in 1928.*

Last year, months before the national championships took place at the
West Side Tennis Club, in Forest Hills, Queens—the men's singles and
women's singles had been played there without interruption since
1924, the doubles since 1970—the United States Tennis Association
made it known that in 1978 the championships would be shifted to a
new site: Flushing Meadow Park, also in Queens, where, pursuant to an
agreement with the New York City Department of Parks and Recrea-

tion, the U.S.T.A. would build, operate, and maintain a sixteen-acre National Tennis Center that would be used exclusively by that organization sixty days a year but whose facilities (twenty-seven outdoor courts and nine air-conditioned indoor courts) would be open to the tennis-playing public on a rental basis the rest of the time. As is generally appreciated, particularly by people who live in or near New York City, nowadays it takes about three times as long as first projected, not to mention many times the amount of money originally estimated, to build or remodel a sizable architectural project in this city (*vide* Yankee Stadium). Consequently, when the U.S.T.A. announced that it would, in effect, be burning its bridges behind it, there was considerable concern as to whether the new stadium—a renovation of the Singer Bowl, which was built for the 1964–65 World's Fair and renamed the Louis Armstrong Stadium in 1973—would be completed in time for this year's championships. For starters, the plans for the new stadium required the approval of no fewer than nine municipal agencies.

In dealing with this Sargasso Sea of red tape and the countless other problems, the U.S.T.A. has had one major asset going for it: its incumbent president, William Ewing (Slew) Hester, Jr., of Jackson, Mississippi, the scion of a family of Copiah County politicians and the first U.S.T.A. president from the Deep South, knows a great deal about the business of business. Because of his experience as the young president of a trucking company, he was assigned by the Army during the Second World War to work with the famed Red Ball Express, the transportation outfit that operated with such marked effectiveness in northern France. Subsequently, he has been, successively, the sales manager of a glass-container-manufacturing company, the executive vice-president of a truck and air-conditioning distributorship and then of an oil company, and from 1962 on an independent oil producer, or wildcatter. At sixty-six, Hester, a sturdily built, ruddy-complexioned, direct man who has been a fine tennis player since boyhood, has an impressive background in tennis administration. He has headed the Mississippi Tennis Association and the Southern Tennis Association, and, as a man who loves a challenge, he was single-handedly responsible for pushing through in his hometown a big-time tennis club that now has twenty-six courts. He was also the force behind the establishment of an annual seventy-five-thousand-dollar professional tournament that is held in Jackson. It was his confidence and aggressiveness that lay behind the U.S.T.A.'s decision to leave Forest Hills, which had its limitations as the home of the American Championships, and to create a National Tennis Center.

This past spring, after the harsh and protracted winter, I found myself wondering from time to time how the work on the new center

was progressing. No word about it had come from the U.S.T.A. head-quarters, in Manhattan. In talks with some of my friends who are associated with tennis, I discovered that they were similarly concerned. Early in May, just as we were making plans to go out to Flushing Meadow Park to see what the situation was, the U.S.T.A., in a most uncharacteristic move (it has never been known for its penchant for public relations), sent out a letter announcing that there would be a bus expedition from Manhattan to the new center the following week for tennis writers and editors and other people connected with the game, in order that we could see what had been done so far and be brought up to date on the general state of affairs. There was little doubt in our minds that this junket was the brainchild of the U.S.T.A.'s new public-relations director, Ed Fabricius, who joined the organization last year. In any event, at ten-forty-five on the morning of May 10th, about thirty of us climbed aboard a chartered bus at the rear entrance, on West Fifty-eighth Street, of the Essex House. Fabricius was on hand, as were half a dozen other persons from the U.S.T.A., including Mike Burns, the executive secretary, and Hester, who had flown up from Mississippi. From the beginning, the atmosphere was easy and convivial, as it usually is when people who haven't seen each other for some time get together again. Then, to top things off, as the bus started up and headed toward the East River Drive a uniformed waiter began to make his way up the aisle serving Bloody Marys or coffee and Danish pastry. This created such pleased astonishment that as the bus swung off Grand Central Parkway, and, passing Shea Stadium, moved down the leafy streets of Flushing Meadow Park toward the heart of the new tennis center, the euphoria was almost tangible. The weather unquestionably had something to do with this. The sun was out, and there were patches of bright blue in a lightly clouded sky—a perfect day for a trip into the comparative country.

It should be stated immediately that the structure we found ourselves facing upon debarking from the bus was essentially the old Louis Armstrong Stadium. At that point, the general mood turned to one of disappointment: we had expected to see much more progress. We filed into the stadium and made our way to the east end of the stands —actually, the northeast end—and found seats on the weatherworn wooden benches in that unaltered section of the stadium. The work crews below were raising such a din that various people who attempted to address our group could not be heard, and it was decided to wait seven minutes or so until it was twelve o'clock, when the workmen had their lunch break. During that interval, I slowly took in the complex scene in front of us. The best way, I think, to describe what it looked

like then and what we were told it would look like when it was finished
is to begin with the matrix, Armstrong Stadium. The main problem it
posed for those charged with turning it into a larger and more modern
stadium that would be particularly suited for tennis is that in shape it
was a long oval. As many as five courts could easily have been laid out
in its center, but that wouldn't have been desirable. For one thing,
there is no need for that many courts in the stadium of a tennis complex,
and, for another, the spectators at one end of the oval would from time
to time have found themselves too far away from the court in use to
have a good view of the action. Ideally, a tennis stadium should have
only one court, and the stands should rise at a steep pitch, to give the
spectators the feeling they are right on top of things. The Centre Court
at Wimbledon is built that way, as is the *Cour Centrale* at Stade Roland
Garros, in Auteuil, outside Paris, where the French Championships are
held. (At Forest Hills, there is room in the stadium for two, or even
three, courts, but the stadium nevertheless works out very well, because the stands do rise at a properly abrupt angle.) At the new tennis
center, an excellent solution, as we could see, had been hit upon last
autumn for dealing with the problems presented by Armstrong Stadium: it was decided to divide the long oval into two separate areas, by
erecting a new stand, which would stretch across its width—thus creat-
ing a large sub-stadium, to be known as the Stadium Court, with a
seating capacity of almost twenty thousand, and a smaller sub-stadium,
which would be called the Grandstand Court and would accommodate
approximately six thousand people. It was further decided that the
existing walkway, some ten feet above ground level, that ran around the
periphery of the oval, connecting the two areas, would be retained. This
would enable spectators who had tickets for the Stadium Court to
saunter over, when the urge struck them, and watch the match going
on in the Grandstand Court. It was decided that, at least for the time
being, separate tickets would not be sold for the Grandstand Court. I
mention this because the contiguity of the two courts is somewhat like
the setup at Wimbledon, where the attractive No. 1 Court (which has
seats for fifty-five hundred and standing room for fourteen hundred) is
physically connected to the Centre Court (which has seats for almost
eleven thousand and standing room for thirty-five hundred), but at
Wimbledon separate tickets are sold for the No. 1 Court and, as a result,
there is relatively little space available to take care of the people who
make their way there from the Centre Court or the thirteen field
courts, hoping to find a spot to watch a favorite player or a specific
match.

I should emphasize that on that distant day back in May when we had our first look at the new stadium, work on it hadn't proceeded very far. We could see from our position, which looked down on the Grandstand Court, where a wooden shack was serving as the temporary field office for the construction company, that the new foundation was about completed. Another thing—most of the structural-steel frame-work was up for the new dividing stand, which would be thirty-two rows high and extremely steep. By tournament time, the front of this new stand formed the east side of the Stadium Court, and a huge press box was perched at the top. (The back of this stand, which serves as the west side of the Grandstand Court, has no seating facilities—at least for the time being. By the way, except for refinishing and painting the wooden benches, it was decided to leave the Grandstand Court end of the stadium unchanged for the first championships.) As for the Stadium Court, the plan was more intricate. It called for a rim of new boxes— eight rows deep on the sides of the stadium and four rows on the ends —to replace the lower rows of old concrete benches. It also called for the remainder of the old stadium, the top of which was forty feet above the ground, to be used. From that point upward, new rows would be constructed of precast concrete slabs supported by structural steel. At the date of our visit, only about a quarter of the twenty-five-foot con-crete slabs had been hoisted into place by the crane then occupying most of the floor of that court.

One thought of all the work that lay ahead and wondered when the renovation would be far enough advanced for the playing surfaces to be laid in both courts. The type of surface selected, we learned, was a rubberized acrylic cushion, on an asphalt base, called DecoTurf II. It has two valuable properties going for it. First, it is an all-weather com-position that requires practically no maintenance. Second, its speed— basically, this type of court is slower than grass but appreciably faster than clay—can be adjusted by changing the composition of the texture layers, the two layers that lie beneath the top two layers, which deter-mine the color. (All in all, the DecoTurf II surface of the courts at Flushing Meadow Park is composed of eight layers.) The courts would be a soft green—a welcome relief after three summers of gazing at the depressing dark-gray hue, tinged with dark green, of the Har-Tru courts that were installed at Forest Hills when the grass was removed in 1975. Much more significantly, since healthy grass apparently cannot be maintained in the industrial areas of our country, it would seem that a composition court, responsive in a sensible degree to both the serve-and-volley paragons who flourish on grass and the patient baseline artists who are toughest on clay, might be the proper surface for our championships. Surely there are enough tournaments played on clay or clay-type courts as it is: the Italian and the French Championships, of course, and also the United States Clay Court Championships—a tournament that was instituted in 1910 and to which we have paid insufficient attention in recent years. Ellsworth Vines, George Lott, Frank Parker, Bobby Riggs, Pancho Segura, Pancho Gonzales, Vic Seixas, Tony Trabert, Arthur Ashe, and Jimmy Connors have all won the men's clay-court singles at least once, and, way, way back, William T. Tilden II won it seven times.

On the day of our spring outing, while the construction crews were having their lunch Hester gave a short, frank talk. In it, he touched on the huge amount of work that lay ahead, but his mood was essentially optimistic. Afterward, he answered a few questions. "When do I think the surfaces will be down on the two stadium courts? Probably around August 27th. That's a couple of days before the championships start. This year, as long as we have someplace for the spectators to sit and courts for the contestants to play on, we'll be very satisfied. Next year, we can start to make this the outstanding tennis center we think it's going to be."

He was asked about the planes from nearby La Guardia Airport, which fly low over Flushing Meadow Park.

"The takeoff pattern's into the west today, so it's fairly quiet," he said. "When the takeoff pattern is into the southeast, we'll get lots of noise. The southeast-to-northwest runway—that's the best alternative takeoff strip for us."

He ended by saying, "We're going to be ready for August 30th, the opening day of the tournament. We'll solve whatever the problems are, and we will play."

Hester then introduced the architect, David Kenneth Specter; a representative of the Monsey Products Company, the manufacturers of DecoTurf II; and Bill Talbert, who would be returning to his old job of tournament director after a two-year absence. Each of them answered a batch of questions, and afterward we strolled down the walkway to the embryonic Stadium Court to get a better look at it. The architect came over and informed us that there would be an elevator up to the press box, and, now that we could see for ourselves that the east wall of the Stadium Court had an alpine incline to it, this was good news, in a way. At the same time, we wondered why they had to stick the press box up that high, reducing the players on the court below to the size of toy soldiers and making it almost impossible to get the feel of a match. Well, at any rate, we concluded, it was better than the press box at Forest Hills, with its underwater gloom. And, to be honest, I suppose that in this era of Very Big Sport, in which television calls so many of the shots, the old orthodox press corps can be pretty hard to please—sometimes rightly so, of course.

The bus trip back to Manhattan went quickly, perhaps because there was so much to think about—for example, the lanes of sycamores and pin oaks we had seen, which, along with lush fields of grass, could, if intelligently used, make every summer day at Flushing Meadow Park a Renoir Sunday in the country. But what one thought about most was all that had to be done in a mere three and a half months if the show was to go on. Just before I got off the bus, I turned around and said to Hester, who was sitting a couple of rows behind me, "It's going to be awfully close, isn't it?"

He smiled broadly and easily. "Very close," he said. "But I've got three phones on my desk back in Jackson, and whenever a problem comes up I'll hear about it just as soon as the construction manager does. I think we'll make it. We'd better."

As we know now, the new stadium was finished in time. There was no chance to take care of all the trimmings, but there were courts for the players to play on and seats for the spectators to sit on. In fact, all things considered, the 1978 championships went very well indeed.

Surprisingly, the new stadium at Flushing Meadow Park is the first to be built as the home of a major tennis championship since Stade Roland Garros was opened, in 1928. The oldest tennis championship, to be sure, is Wimbledon, which was originally staged on the lawns of the All England Croquet Club, covering three and a half acres on Worple Road, in the Borough of Wimbledon, some eight miles southwest of the heart of London. This croquet club had been organized in 1868, when that insidious Victorian pastime was at the peak of its popularity. Croquet remained the only game available to the membership at Worple Road until 1875, when the men directing the club, worried about its declining financial health, made the bold move of allocating the major share of the club's acreage to two new games: lawn tennis, which had been invented in 1873 by Major Walter Clopton Wingfield, and badminton, which had been developed by the British Army in India. In 1877, the All England Croquet Club staged the first Lawn Tennis Championship, open to all amateurs. The championship was a definite success, and so were the subsequent Wimbledons—it early became the custom to refer to the tournament by its geographical site—and within a relatively short time the grounds at the club were given over exclusively to tennis courts. Larger and larger crowds, enchanted by the skill and the personalities of the Renshaw twins and the Doherty brothers and later by such colorful foreign invaders as Norman Brookes (of Australia), May Sutton and Maurice McLoughlin (of the United States), and Anthony Wilding (of New Zealand), turned out to watch the matches at Wimbledon. No stadium was built, but, to accommodate the ever-growing number of spectators, the capacity of the stands on the four sides of the Centre Court was periodically increased. (The renowned Centre Court received that name simply because it was situated at the center of the other courts.) At length, when Wimbledon was resumed following the First World War, the officers of the All England Club, realizing that the crush at the championships had been going on far too long, decided that after the 1921 tournament the club would be moved from Worple Road to a much more commodious tract of land, on Church Road, also in Wimbledon. There they laid out an ample number of field courts and erected the present Centre Court in an imposing twelve-sided wooden stadium, which was painted dark green. The stands were covered by a roof, but the court area, naturally, wasn't.

Nearly all the Wimbledon regulars hated to leave the old grounds on Worple Road. Their feelings were eloquently expressed by A. Wallis Myers, the tennis correspondent of the London *Daily Telegraph*. The opening sentences of his book "Twenty Years of Lawn Tennis," written in 1921, after the last championship had been held at Worple Road, go as follows:

> I must begin these reminiscences on a note of sadness. Wimbledon is passing! Not the institution which the world knows as the lawn tennis championships, but the ground hallowed by the history of the game—a history shoemarked on its courts. It is rather a tragic thought, this uprooting of a shrine saluted for two-score years and more by every disciple of lawn tennis in this country and by many a pilgrim from distant lands.

Myers, however, was quick to point out that the move had been imperative for almost a decade and that "the pent-up waters burst their bonds in 1919 and 1920." He continued:

> Nearly four times as many seats, I was told, could have been sold for the last championship meeting. I know not how many spectators, prepared to stand, stayed away because they knew that not even a ferret could squeeze through the Centre Court crowd. On the morning of the Tilden-Patterson match last July, having an engagement to play a private game with Commander Hillyard [the secretary of the All England Club], yearning for a little exercise to relieve his secretarial cares, I had to pick my way over the bodies of those who, for several hours before and still to come, were waiting for the gates to open.

I would like to digress for a moment, for this last excerpt suggests a brief, light comment. Myers belonged to an era in which a good many of the people who covered sports were gentlemen writers. As a Commander of the Order of the British Empire, a sharp-featured man who often chose to pose for the camera with his pipe cradled between thumb and forefinger, and a very useful doubles partner (if not a player of championship calibre, which he frequently managed to imply that he was), Myers wished to be thought of as a real insider, and he found it hard not to drop names like Commander Hillyard's. As a result, in reading him one continually runs into passages like this:

> I shall never forget Gore's successful defense of his title in 1909. His challenger was Ritchie who, in a domestic year, by dint of fine victories over Roper Barrett and Dixon, seemed destined to have his name enrolled among the elect. I had been Ritchie's guest on his house-boat at Laleham-on-Thames the night before this match. Motoring to Wimbledon on the great day, something went wrong with the car. It was nothing very serious, but the owner had to use his right arm vigorously to restart the engine. I remember expressing some distress at the incident at the time. Did this little contretemps have any effect on the challenger when, with the match and title seemingly in his grasp, he found himself being slowly overhauled by the holder? Rarely did tide turn so completely.

I hasten to add that many contemporaries of Myers also wrote in this manner but that few, if any, of them wrote as well as he did when he had sufficient time and a sense of purpose. An example of Myers at his best is his account of the historic final of the 1919 Wimbledon Ladies' Singles, between the aging British heroine Dorothea Lambert Chambers and the young French marvel Suzanne Lenglen, which Lenglen won, 10–8, 4–6, 9–7. It is as full of vitality today as it was sixty years ago. I should think that Myers was the most influential tennis writer in the world during the decade before the First World War and the decade after it, and certainly few people knew and loved both the Wimbledon of Worple Road and the Wimbledon of Church Road, the site of the game's first true stadium, as deeply as he did.

Early in the nineteen-twenties, improved tennis facilities began to go up in the capital cities of the various Australian states, in response to growing interest in the game in that country as new stars of international standing—most notably, Gerald Patterson and James O. Anderson—rose to take over where the veteran Brookes was leaving off. White City, in Sydney, was typical of this improvement. The New South

Wales Lawn Tennis Association, seeking a headquarters with room for future expansion, bought a twelve-acre plot on Rushcutters Bay, which was two miles from the center of town and had formerly been the site of an amusement park called White City. The N.S.W.L.T.A. saw no reason to change that name as it went about constructing its plant, which in time consisted of thirty-seven grass courts and half a dozen hard courts. White City replaced the old Double Bay Grounds as the site of the state championships and—when it was New South Wales' turn in the national rotation—of the Australian Championships and Davis Cup competitions. Until 1954, the permanent grandstands erected around the two center courts seated about eight thousand. Then the north stand was extended to bring the seating capacity up to ten thousand, and, that December—when tennis fever was at its height in Australia, because the United States team was challenging for the Davis Cup at White City—temporary extra rows, reaching high into the sky in a sensational way, were added at the top of the stands. On the first day of the match, at least 25,578 spectators—that was the official count, but there were probably even more people wedged in—peered down at the players. This is still the largest crowd ever to watch a tennis match held outdoors.

Kooyong, which is the leading club in Melbourne—the second-largest city in Australia and the capital of its second most important state, Victoria—has a similar history. Founded in the early nineteen-twenties, Kooyong, which became the headquarters of the Victorian Lawn Tennis Association, succeeded a site with another wonderfully evocative name, Warehousemen's Grounds—now called Albert Grounds—as the locus of the state championships and also of the big national and international events when it was Victoria's turn to hold them. (As it happened, the first Davis Cup Challenge Round held in Australia had been played at Warehousemen's Grounds, in 1908.) Kooyong, which covers more than seventeen acres of a leafy suburb about four miles from the center of Melbourne, started with temporary stands around its two center courts. Then, in 1927, it undertook the construction of the lower part of an oval concrete stadium. This accommodated about four thousand, and additions made in 1934 and 1953 brought its seating capacity to about twelve thousand. Whenever Kooyong has been chosen as the host for a Davis Cup Challenge Round, more rows have been added at the top of the stands, as at White City. A crowd of twenty-two thousand turned out, for example, on each of the three days of the 1953 Challenge Round, when Lew Hoad and Ken Rosewall were the heroes of a thrilling Challenge Round.

Besides Kooyong, which has put on five Challenge Rounds, and

White City, which has put on four, as well as one final round (after the Davis Cup format was changed, in 1972), there are three other prominent Australian centers of tennis which should be mentioned. They are situated in Adelaide, Brisbane, and Perth, the capital cities of the states of South Australia, Queensland, and Western Australia, respectively. The one in Adelaide, which is operated by the South Australian Lawn Tennis Association, and which borders on the War Memorial Drive, is commonly referred to either as Memorial Drive or simply as the Drive. It currently has thirty-four grass courts, of which thirty had been established by 1922. It was not until 1939, however, that the first stands in what became the club's "stadium area"—it is built around two courts —went up. These courts are now enclosed by a quadrangle of stands— three of them permanent—which normally holds sixty-five hundred spectators but, if necessary, can be extended to take care of as many as twenty thousand, as it did during the 1956 Challenge Round. Four Challenge Rounds in all, the first in 1952, have been held at the Drive. Another three have been staged at the Milton Tennis Courts—Milton is a suburb of Brisbane—which is where the top events are played in Queensland. The history of the Milton club goes back to 1895, when two grass courts were built on a reclaimed dump. Queensland was a primitive place in those days, and for years there were no grandstands for the spectators; the conveniences supplied by the club began and ended with hitching rails for horses and buggies. Today, Milton has eleven grass courts, eleven granite courts, and thirteen all-weather courts of acrylic on a concrete base. Four rather modest wooden grandstands enclose two grass courts in the stadium area, but, again, when the situation warrants it the stands can be added on to, dramatically. For example, seating for some nineteen thousand people was provided in 1958, the first time Brisbane was accorded the honor of holding the Davis Cup Challenge Round. As for Perth, that handsome city by the Indian Ocean, the outdoor competitions are held at the Royal King's Park Tennis Club. The setup there is rather unusual. The Western Australian Lawn Tennis Association owns only the three center grass courts, which are bordered by concrete grandstands with a seating capacity of ten thousand. The Royal King's Park Tennis Club owns the other twenty-two grass courts and leases them to the W.A.L.T.A. when they are required for a big competition like the national championships. Perth has never been selected for a Davis Cup Challenge Round, but preliminary Cup rounds have been played there—such as that dreadful (for us) interzone final in 1960, in which the highly favored American team, after leading two matches to none, was eliminated by Italy.

To sum up, despite the intense tennis ferment that began in the

nineteen-twenties and reached its peak in the nineteen-fifties and
-sixties, Australia has invested in only one permanent modern tennis
stadium—the one at Kooyong. As a rule, the island continent has chosen
to do things its own way, erecting grandstands around the center courts
of its leading clubs and then, on the big occasions, adding row upon row
upon row with steel and wood until an uncommonly large crowd of
unawed Aussies, perched almost in the clouds, can be taken care of. (I
might note that in the opinion of Harry Hopman, the perennial non-
playing captain of the Davis Cup teams during the great Australian era
after the Second World War, Memorial Drive and Royal King's Park
have the best grass.)

The year after the new Wimbledon opened its Centre Court, to an
impressed and delighted public, saw the completion of another major
tennis stadium that was designed from the outset along the lines of a
classic stadium. This structure, which had a seating capacity of fourteen
thousand, went up at the West Side Tennis Club, which by that date—
1923—was situated in Forest Hills. Today, when logjams in the construction business are chronic, it seems impossible that a horseshoe-
shaped concrete stadium a hundred and ninety-five feet long and a
hundred and forty-five feet wide and rising thirty-nine rows above a
ten-foot wall that separated the viewing area from the playing area
could ever have been built in four months, but it was. Work on it started
on April 9th and was so near completion on August 10th that the first
Wightman Cup team match—the top American women players versus
the top British women players—was put on there with a gallery of five
thousand on hand. If the stadium at Forest Hills has always been a
first-class place to watch the great players, much of the credit must go
to the architect, Kenneth M. Murchison, and the engineer, Charles
Landers. Both were members of the West Side Club and, as such,
appreciated the qualities a tennis stadium should have.

The decision to build this stadium was the winning ploy in a
series of tactical maneuvers that the West Side Club, led by the ambitious and astute Julian Myrick, made over a dozen years or more, with
the object of making the club the venue of the most important tennis
events held in our country. An abbreviated review of the club's climb
to power might be useful. The West Side was formed in 1892, and took
that name because the grounds it rented were situated on Central Park
West between Eighty-eighth and Eighty-ninth streets. There was room
for five courts. In 1902, it moved to a larger plot, on 117th Street, near
Morningside Drive. Six years later, it was on the move again—this time,
to 238th Street and Broadway, where it rented two blocks of un-

developed land and built a clubhouse, twelve grass courts, and fifteen clay courts. In 1912, informed that the lessor—the Van Cortlandt Estate —wished to sell the property, the club, after a conscientious investigation of possible new sites, bought a parcel of roughly ten acres in Forest Hills from the Sage Foundation Homes Company. At seventy-seven thousand dollars, this was a steal, especially when one took into account the sylvan retreat that Forest Hills was in those days. Frederick Law Olmsted, the landscape architect, had laid out a boulevard and a main street, between which ran narrow, curving side streets. He had also planned pleasant small private parks accessible through gates in the back gardens of the residents' neo-Tudor stucco and half-timbered houses. What made this Eden even more desirable was that it was only fourteen minutes from Manhattan by electrified train.

If the addition of the West Side Tennis Club substantially enhanced the allure and value of the community of Forest Hills, it worked the other way around, too. Back in 1911, when the club was still situated on 238th Street, the energetic Myrick and his friends had engineered its selection by the U.S.L.T.A. (in those days, of course, and until 1975, the U.S.T.A. was still the U.S.L.T.A., the United States Lawn Tennis Association) as the site of the Davis Cup interzone final between the United States and Great Britain. Crowds of more than three thousand had come out on each of the three days of the match, which the United States won, 4–1. In 1913, the club again put on the interzone final. The American team beat Australasia (Australia and New Zealand), 4–1, this time and then sailed to England, where it edged out Great Britain, 3–2, at Wimbledon—the first American triumph in the Challenge Round since 1902, two years after the Davis Cup competition was inaugurated. In 1914, our team defended the Cup at the West Side Club's new home in Forest Hills. In a thrilling clash, highlighted by the famous match between McLoughlin and Brookes, Australasia won back the Cup, by the score of 3–2. On each of the three days, over twelve thousand well-mannered but superbly responsive fans filled three wooden bleachers, a special section in front of the clubhouse, and every available foot of standing room. No gallery even half that size had ever turned out to watch the tennis at the Newport Casino, where our national championships had been held since they were instituted, in 1881.

The Casino, designed by McKim, Mead & White, had been commissioned in 1880 by James Gordon Bennett, Jr., the publisher of the New York *Herald.* A graceful potpourri of shingled buildings, the Casino was rather European in its architectural style and in its social style as well. From the point of view of tennis, the trouble with Newport was that the people who attended the championships did so less to see the matches than to be seen. Besides, a turnout of four or five thousand spectators for the finals was the most that one could hope for at Newport, and this hardly compared with the roaring twelve thousand who had come out daily to Forest Hills for the Challenge Round of 1914. Accordingly, in February 1915, at the annual meeting of our national tennis association, it was voted to transfer the men's championships from Newport—which had been their home for thirty-four years—to Forest Hills. (The women's singles championship, which had first been played at the Philadelphia Cricket Club, in 1887, continued to be played there through 1920, after which it was shifted to Forest Hills.) The men's singles and doubles were duly held at Forest Hills through 1920—except in 1917, when our championships were cancelled because of the war. At the meeting of the U.S.L.T.A. in the winter of 1921, however, much to the chagrin of the West Side Club, that venerable Philadelphia institution the Germantown Cricket Club was able to mobilize a majority of the votes and was awarded the men's championships for 1921, 1922, and 1923. During those years, the West Side Club had to make do with the women's championships and the Davis Cup Challenge Rounds as its top features. Large, exuberant crowds turned out for the Challenge Rounds in 1921 and 1922, and this fact was not lost on Julian Myrick (who was in an excellent position to notice it, since he was the U.S.L.T.A. president from 1920 through 1922). He was sure that an era of unprecedented popularity and prosperity lay ahead for tennis, and this feeling led him in 1922 to make on behalf of the West Side Club a shrewd and bold proposition to the U.S.L.T.A.: the club would build a stadium comparable to Wimbledon's if, in return, the U.S.L.T.A. would guarantee that the men's singles, the men's doubles, or the American team's most important Davis Cup match would be played at Forest Hills annually during the next ten years, starting in 1923. This was the trump card, all right. The men's singles returned to Forest Hills in 1924 and remained there, along with the women's singles, through 1977.

Forest Hills hoped to become another Wimbledon, but it never did. It never came close, in fact. Had there been a true meeting of minds between the West Side Tennis Club and the U.S.L.T.A., such as existed between the All England Club and the Lawn Tennis Association (they interlock so cohesively that it is hard to detect where the authority of one leaves off and that of the other begins), our championships might have reached a much higher level of function and flavor than they ever did reach (and they might still be lodged at Forest Hills). As it was, an abiding acrimony grew up between the two organizations, for each was convinced that the other was not carrying its proper share of the load and was carrying off more than its rightful share of the profits. Consequently, both bodies let matters that needed scrupulous attention drift into limbo. For one thing, the public was never properly taken care of. There was no parking space available for anyone except the players, the officials, the club members, and dignitaries; the refreshments available to the public were well below the expected standard; the lavatories and the other public facilities became archaic. The only people who were in a position to enjoy the championships—apart from the tennis itself—were the members of the West Side Club and the relatively small, élite corps of tournament regulars (such as the ladies and gentlemen of the media) who also had the run of the clubhouse area and could eat, drink, socialize, and relax there. However, as I have noted, the members of the West Side Club in recent times became quite unhappy with their share of the pie. They were justifiably outraged when, a few years ago, the club's official representative somehow agreed to a new contract with the U.S.L.T.A., under which the association would receive all the proceeds from the sale of the lucrative television rights to the championships, while the club would receive not one cent. As for the U.S.L.T.A., with tennis booming on all sides, it was eager to have a home of its own. In 1977, when it was able to work out the deal with the City of New York which assured it of having such a home at Flushing Meadow Park, it lost little time in arranging to leave Forest Hills.

With the exception of Kooyong, the one tennis stadium constructed by a major tennis power in the fifty-five-year interval between the building of the stadium at Forest Hills and the creation of the new stadium at Flushing Meadow Park was Stade Roland Garros, which came into being in 1928. Up to that time, the French had used the courts at the Stade Français, in Saint-Cloud, and those of the Racing Club, at Croix Catelan, in the Bois de Boulogne. These were good facilities, but in the summer of 1927 France's position in the world of tennis underwent a spectacular change. That year, the Four Musketeers—René Lacoste, Jean Borotra, Henri Cochet, and Jacques Brugnon—successfully completed their quest for the Davis Cup, which had started in 1922 and had gradually gathered the emotional commitment of a crusade, by defeating the American team, at Germantown, three matches to two. The French Tennis Federation felt that this glorious achievement merited an appropriate gesture of recognition, such as a new stadium. Besides, after working so hard to become the world's dominant tennis nation, the French fully intended to keep the Cup as long as the Americans had—seven years

—and there was a need for a stadium to accommodate the large galleries that would be cheering the team on. The federation was able to obtain a subsidy from a grateful government, and work on the new home of French tennis began at once. Al Laney, of the Paris *Herald,* describes, unforgettably, in his book "Covering the Court" what went into building Roland Garros and the unique atmosphere it possessed from the outset:

> As might be expected, they [the French] came up with the most attractive tennis ground in the world. They chose a tree-shaded spot on the edge of the Bois de Boulogne not far from the Auteuil race course, and, where other tennis plants had been planned from a purely utilitarian point of view, this one was laid out with an eye to preserving as much of the natural beauty of the site as possible and even adding to it.
>
> Some of the courts were hidden among spreading trees behind an old, old house which was itself partly concealed by growing things. I seem to remember that there were eight courts but, turning the eye backward and inward, I can actually see and count only seven. I have known any number of people who went regularly to the matches in those days who cannot recall for certain where three of the courts were situated. How different from Wimbledon or Forest Hills, where they march like soldiers in rows side by side.
>
> The old house was carefully preserved as a clubhouse for eating, drinking, and dressing purposes; and they left plenty of room for strolling about, sitting at tables, and ordering things brought in glasses, tall and small. Everywhere there were flowers, informal and unofficial.
>
> They surrounded one of the khaki-colored courts with poured concrete stands and, although about as many could be seated as in the other places for watching tennis, it seemed much smaller. Its architecture was simple. Just a plain stand along each side and each end of the court and all running together at the corners to form an oblong box with no top. This simple arrangement managed somehow an informal quality that made the people seated in it seem very near the players and the players nearer one another. The arena effect of Wimbledon and Forest Hills was entirely lacking.

To add one more short segment from Laney's loving recollection of Roland Garros:

> The crowds at Wimbledon were much larger, about as cosmopolitan, and just as "dressy" too, if you disregard the ever-present models the

leading dressmakers always send to such places to parade the new frocks like showgirls in a Ziegfeld revue. Everything seemed to combine, however, at Auteuil to produce something unique in sports, and I am wondering if the catalytic agent may have been gaiety. The French knew how to be gay in those days.

They were now on top of the tennis world, likely to remain there for years, and war was still a small, remote cloud on a distant horizon. Year followed pleasant carefree year as the summertime came round again and we all went to Auteuil for the French Championships, the interzone matches, and the challenge round. There was for me always the faint feeling that I was entering upon a setting for a musical comedy and that all the people wandering about chattering in a dozen languages were extras carefully chosen and costumed to form a background against which the main actors would perform.

The men charged with selecting the playing surface for the courts at Roland Garros took that responsibility with the utmost seriousness. Borotra, Lacoste, and Cochet—all the Musketeers except Brugnon, who was the doubles specialist—had by this time proved themselves sufficiently expert on grass to win the singles championship at Wimbledon. All three—especially Lacoste, who had won our singles championship in 1926 and 1927, and who defeated Tilden in the match that really clinched the French victory in the 1927 Challenge Round—had also performed well on American grass. Nevertheless, on the European continent clay is the native surface for the tennis player—he grows up on it—and a clay-type composition was decided on for Roland Garros. In Lacoste's opinion—he was kind enough to answer a letter I wrote him this summer asking a number of questions—the courts at Roland Garros were probably made of the same compound of materials as those at Saint-Cloud. "They are not En-Tout-Cas courts which, I believe, are more porous and made of thicker particles [of crushed stone]," Lacoste wrote. "Until the last two or three years, I consider they were made of too small particles and for this reason they were very slow when wet and they were too hard in dry, hot weather." This fits in perfectly with the story that has circulated for years as to why the French wanted terribly slow courts at Roland Garros and how they made sure they got what they wanted. From the day the French began their all-out attempt to capture the Cup, they understood that their efforts would be doomed unless they learned how to beat the mighty Tilden. This meant, above all, learning how to handle Tilden's wicked cannonball serve—or, more specifically, how to wear him down so that after a set or two his cannonball would start to lose its velocity and accuracy, and Tilden thus would become less commanding and more vulnerable. They succeeded so well that in time Cochet and Lacoste were able to defeat Tilden on grass, the surface on which his serve was at its fiercest. Tilden was aging, but, for all that, the French, after winning the Cup, continued to fear him, and with good reason. While they appreciated that he was somewhat less dangerous on clay, which is much slower than grass, at Roland Garros they took no chances and deliberately built courts that were extremely slow when wet. This is the first part of the story that has come down to us. The second part is that the French did not rely on a felicitous rainstorm to dampen the center court before a Tilden match at Roland Garros. No, they went out the night or the morning before and hosed down the court. And yet on that very slow court, in the Challenge Round of 1928, Tilden, using spin and guile instead of sheer power—it was a windy day and called for a departure from his usual strategy—played one of the finest matches of his career, outlasting Lacoste in five sets. However, there is no doubt that the clay at Roland Garros was a critical factor in the French teams' continued success in defending the Davis Cup. They had set out to retain the Cup for as long as the United States had just retained it, and they almost did. They held it for six years—until 1933, when the Musketeers had grown old, and Fred Perry, a bounding young Englishman who had become the best player in the world, led the British team to victory in the Challenge Round.

The rise of the French and their period of supremacy constitute one of the most captivating chapters in sport. Their breakthrough depended on all four of the Musketeers, but chiefly on Lacoste, who though he was the youngest member of the team was its leader, inasmuch as he had one of the most acute tennis minds of all time. He was the man who figured out how to go about beating Tilden. His suggestions to his teammates on how to alter their tactics in the course of difficult matches were invaluable. When he was still in his teens and was just beginning to come on as a player, Lacoste started his career-long practice of entering in notebooks, as he sat in the stands, his observations on the strengths and weaknesses of the players he would be facing in tournaments, along with his thoughts on the most efficacious way to blunt their best weapons. In my letter to Lacoste this summer, I asked if he would give me a few examples of the sort of things he had jotted down in those famous notebooks. He complied with this request, and the paragraph in which he did is so fascinating that it simply has to be quoted:

What I wrote in my notebooks were just short remarks about the best tactics or shots against different opponents. For instance, for returning Tilden's service I had noted: "Very short firm swing." To beat Johnston I had noted: "Aggressive sliced shots with full swing." Against Borotra I had noted: "Accurate crosscourt passing shots." Against Cochet I had noted: "Fast drives with some topspin."

When a man has the ability to hit the ball as well as Lacoste did, and, in addition, has such a talent for analysis, he is almost certain to become a great champion.

During the summer, in the weeks before the 1978 Open Championships got under way, I made two trips into the fastnesses of Queens. The first, early in July, was to Forest Hills. Lamar Hunt, the head of the promotional organization called World Championship Tennis—its annual tournament season finishes in May—had contracted with the West Side Club to put on an invitational event the week after Wimbledon. I went out on the Wednesday evening, because Ken Rosewall was playing Vitas Gerulaitis, and one never knows how many more opportunities there will be to see Rosewall in action. Gerulaitis won in straight sets, but the quality of play was rewardingly high.

I made my second trip—another visit to Flushing Meadow Park —on the twenty-fifth of August, the Friday before the start of the tournament, which had been moved up to the night of Tuesday the twenty-ninth. I had learned about this change when, the day before revisiting the new National Tennis Center, I had telephoned Slew Hester in his office on Capitol Street in Jackson. "We just had to do it," he explained in his unique manner of speaking, in which a strong Mississippi accent is fused with a vigorous delivery. "We got such tremendous coöperation from the construction men, the union officials, the city employees—from everybody—that I wanted to be sure they all had a chance to see some tennis played in the stadium they helped build. That's why we went and scheduled a couple of matches for Tuesday night—it made it possible for us to give two tickets to everyone who had worked with us to get the job done. We had some obligations to pay back. Funny thing, I had no idea that so many of the hardhats were interested in tennis, but when we put on a tournament for them early in August something like two hundred out of a total of three hundred and fifty workmen showed up." Hester cleared his throat, and lowered the volume of his voice a few decibels. "The new tennis center, as you may have heard, has overshot the six million dollars we'd estimated it would cost," he continued. "It will come close to ten million. We spent the money out of necessity. We had a date to meet, and the only way we could do it was by paying overtime money—plenty of overtime money. The biggest headache for us was that the unions' contracts with the builders expired at the end of June. After that, many of the unions went out on strike against the contractors. We went directly to the heads of the unions, and we were able to avoid any harmful strikes at the new stadium. Hy Zausner, who was my deputy, did a hell of a job, and we kept moving along. By late July, we had the seats in the stadium. We started installing the courts the first week in August, and they were finished and lined on Friday, August 18th. I hear that Connors came out and played on them that weekend." A pause for a chuckle. "You know, you never stop running into problems," he went on. "For example, in June we discovered that the Parks Department's power supply would be inadequate for our needs, and we had to build our own power station. Day before yesterday, the damn sewage pump blew. That's fixed now. We're ready. That's the big thing. We're ready to go."

On the morning of my visit to Flushing Meadow Park, a gray and foggy day, the first thing I did was inspect the Stadium Court. I could hardly believe what I saw. It was much larger than I had visualized it back in May, and much handsomer: roughly rectangular in shape, and gleaming brightly on three of its four sides with sixteen rows of seats with blue backrests just behind the courtside boxes, then twelve rows of silvery aluminum benches without backs, and then sixteen rows of benches with red backrests. On the fourth side—the new stand—there was a slight variation on this scheme: no silver benches. As I slogged my way to the top of the stadium, I stopped for a moment to watch a workman who was sticking numbers on the individual seats, but all the critical work had obviously been finished some time before. From the top, I gazed down and around incredulously at what had been accomplished since our group visit in May. Then, collecting myself, I studied the Grandstand Court—it has a red-and-blue color motif—and, after inspecting the DecoTurf II surface in the Stadium Court, I strolled around and looked at the field courts and at the white-and-yellow striped tents that would house food concessions or luncheons and dinners put on by big companies. I then poked around the headquarters building, where the space occupied by the nine indoor courts would be used as hospitality centers during the championships by other companies entertaining clients and guests over the twelve days of the tournament. Everywhere I walked, people were bustling around, and, even when an airplane was not screeching overhead, there was such a hubbub that it was hard to hear yourself think. At the trailer that served as the office of the construction company, I had the good luck to run into

Hy Zausner, Hester's deputy. He suggested that we might be able to converse more easily if we sat inside his car, which was parked nearby. Zausner, a calm, soft-spoken white-haired man who is in his seventies but doesn't look even sixty, is as astonishing in his own way as Hester. He is best known to the public as the founder of the Port Washington Tennis Academy, a nonprofit enterprise in Port Washington, Long Island, which he started in the mid-nineteen-sixties. Before that, Zausner had spent the bulk of his working hours in the cheese business, but he somehow also found the time to build shopping centers, and this activity, which brought him into contact with contractors and subcontractors and the rest of the people involved in the complicated world of real estate and getting things built, made him the ideal person to serve as Hester's right-hand man—the man who was always on the premises. From May through August, Zausner and Hester talked on the telephone anywhere from five to ten times a day. Zausner's experience in the building game was particularly valuable when the members of seven unions—the electricians, the engineers, the plumbers, the carpenters, the bricklayers, the bricklayers' helpers, and the teamsters—went on strike. He also showed a gift for improvisation. For example, when it rained on the day scheduled for the construction workers' tennis tournament, he had the event switched to the Port Washington Tennis Academy, where it was played on the thirteen indoor courts.

When we left Zausner's car at the end of our chat, I asked him about one major problem that we hadn't touched on—the terrible shriek the airplanes made as they took off from La Guardia and flew directly over the stadium or very close to it. "I don't know the answer," he said. "We've been talking for some time with the men in charge at La Guardia to see if they'll be able to use other runways during our afternoon and night sessions. We'll just have to wait, and hope that they'll be able to find a solution." As Zausner walked back to the trailer, five people converged on him from different directions.

At the Tuesday-night session that had been added to the United States Open Championships, Tracy Austin, the fifteen-year-old phenomenon from Rolling Hills, California, won her first-round match with the loss of only one game, and Bjorn Borg, the current Wimbledon champion and the player seeded No. 1 in the men's singles, quickly dispatched Bob Hewitt, the veteran doubles star from South Africa. It was a rather boring evening, for the tennis was mundane and most of the time was given over to speeches by officials and politicians which reminded one that Americans are notoriously poor public speakers: they do not take the trouble to organize their remarks and wander on and on. Once this prologue was dispensed with, the United States Open really got under way on Wednesday. There were no upsets, but a couple of matches were much closer than had been expected. For example, Gerulaitis, the fourth-seeded player, barely edged past an unknown young Frenchman, Pascal Portes, 7–5, 7–5, and Ashe, attempting a comeback after a prolonged heel injury, had to fight off three match points before winning, 4–6, 7–6, 6–1, over Ross Case, of Australia. (Until the fourth round, the men's matches consisted of only three sets. From that point on, they consisted of five—as they ordinarily do throughout championships played on hard courts or on grass, since shorter rallies are produced than on clay and less time per set is required.) However, the subject of most conversations on the opening day, and on the ensuing days as well, was, of course, the National Tennis Center. If the opinions of the people I talked with were representative, the large majority were not merely pleased with the Stadium Court but somewhat overwhelmed by its grandness. Most of them were also happy to find that the field courts were not massed in long parallel rows but dispersed over the grounds south of the stadium. As for the surface of the courts, the consensus was that the DecoTurf II played well, but a number of contestants and observers felt that it had been made to play a bit too fast, which militated against the clay-court virtuosos, and they also thought that the ball bounced too high on it. Gerulaitis, who replaced the Har-Tru surface of the practice court at his home, at Kings Point, Long Island, with DecoTurf II, remarked that his court was discernibly slower than the ones at Flushing Meadow Park, and he predicted that they would favor the serve-and-volley experts—especially those who got in a high percentage of their first serves. Nevertheless, all of us noted that in many matches the players engaged in long, patient rallies from the baseline. No, the surface, while probably a shade too fast, had been a good choice. The new stadium's most serious problem was not underfoot but overhead—the planes taking off from La Guardia. Planes take off into the wind, and when the wind was out of the southeast, as it was on quite a number of days, planes flying low over the stadium created such a nerve-racking roar that the players either paused momentarily or, if a point was already started, had to continue it under painfully distracting conditions.

During the twelve days of the championships, there were four extraordinarily fine matches. The first of these, a fourth-round match played on the evening of Labor Day, was between Guillermo Vilas, the almost too intelligent poet-athlete from Argentina, who was the defending champion, and Butch Walts, a big, broad-shouldered man of twenty-three who, after a couple of years at the University of

Southern California, joined the Phoenix Racquets, of World Team Tennis, two years ago and has built a reputation as one of the most thunderous servers in the game. In winning the first two sets, Walts demonstrated that he can do a few things besides serve. He hung in pertinaciously on extended rallies and won many of them at crucial junctures by running around his backhand and sending blistering forehand drives into the open corner of the court. Vilas took the next two sets, and seemed to have the situation under control, but Walts, to everyone's surprise, surged back and won the fifth set with some big, brave hitting. The scores: 6–4, 7–6, 4–6, 6–7, 6–2. The second outstanding match brought Jimmy Connors, seeded second, up against Adriano Panatta, of Italy, in the fourth round the next afternoon. Full of spirited thrusts by both players, this not only was the most exciting men's match of the tournament but may well have decided the final outcome of the men's singles, and, for that reason, I think it may be best to put it aside for the moment and return to it later. As for the two other memorable matches, both involved Pam Shriver, a sixteen-year-old, seeded sixteenth in the women's singles. Tennis people have been talking about Pamela Howard Shriver, of Lutherville, Maryland, for just about a year now. Their enthusiasm over her prospects is noteworthy in itself, considering that never before have there been so many stunningly talented young women players—to name just a few, Tracy Austin, of course, Anne Smith, Linda Siegel, Kathy and Barbara Jordan (who play No. 1 and No. 2 on the Stanford women's team), Maria Fernandez, Bettina Bunge, and Caroline Stoll, all of whom are Americans, and two promising Czechs, Hana Mandlikova and Hana Strachonova. Unlike most of the members of her age group, Shriver plays "the big game," and plays it with flair. She has the physical equipment to do so. A reed-slim girl, she is six feet tall, but she has such sound athletic coördination that there is no hint of gawkiness about her; rather, she moves swiftly and gracefully over the court. She has a lot going for her: a fast, controlled serve with marvellous wrist action; an exceptional feel for the forecourt, which she plays effectively not only because of her reach but because she has good anticipation and reflexes; adequate ground strokes, although she hits both her backhand and her forehand with underspin, and so lacks the pace that flat or topspin drives would give her; a sanguine attitude, from what one can see; and, finally, she is very pretty—bright, expressive eyes, curly light-brown hair, and the sort of wide smile that the movie queens of the nineteen-thirties and -forties used to flash. While big things were expected of her, it was thought that it would take her another year or so to arrive. For example, she has yet to defeat Tracy

Austin, although they have met nine times, and at Wimbledon this year, when she was on the verge of beating Sue Barker, an established player, and thus establishing herself, she failed to cash in on three match points. Oh, yes—she uses a Prince racquet, which has a bigger face than conventional racquets, and her coach is Don Candy, the former Australian internationalist.

At Flushing Meadow Park, Shriver, playing more confidently each round, made her way to the semifinals in the second quarter of the draw by defeating Candy Reynolds, Sharon Walsh, Jeanne Evert (Chris' younger sister), Kerry Reid, and Lesley Hunt. Virginia Wade, last year's Wimbledon champion, had been expected to march through this quarter but had been eliminated in the third round, and it was Shriver instead who faced Martina Navratilova, this year's Wimbledon champion, on the second Friday of the tournament, under a cold gray sky. Navratilova, a twenty-one-year-old Czech who defected to this country three years ago, is a good-sized, sturdy, strong athlete, and she has improved her serve-and-volley game to the point where this year she has come to be recognized as the No. 1 woman player in the world. This rise to the top was abetted by Chris Evert's decision to take a long vacation from competition, and when the two met in the final at Eastbourne, just before Wimbledon, and then in the final at Wimbledon, Navratilova, displaying a new assurance under stress, pulled out two tough three-set matches. Against Shriver, Navratilova, a left-hander, was in good fluid form from the opening game, holding her hard-hit serve with little or no trouble. The astounding thing was that Shriver, far from being rattled by playing the biggest match of her career on the Stadium Court, rose to the occasion. Sometimes she can be too emotional under tournament pressure, but that day she was in complete control of herself, concentrating well and playing the pivotal points with courage. For instance, in the tenth game, serving at 4–5, she fought off two set points—the second with a gorgeous backhand volley angled crosscourt—and went on, after wasting three game points, to hold service. In the twelfth game, she survived two more set points for Navratilova. This knotted matters at six games apiece and brought on a twelve-point tie breaker to decide the set. Though Shriver was clearly in an inspired mood, I must admit that I was still bowled over when she went on to win the tie breaker, seven points to five. The winning shot was a backhand that she took on a high bounce and slashed down at Navratilova's feet as she came hurrying in to volley the return. Navratilova could not handle it, and the ball skidded off the frame of her racquet and into the bottom of the net. First set to Shriver, 7–6.

By this stage of the proceedings, the spectators in the Stadium

Court fully appreciated how formidable a tennis player young **Pam Shriver** could be, but I don't think that many of them believed she would be able to keep it all together and go on to win the match. She did, though. She took the second set, 7–6, after another tie breaker—seven points to three—and that was it. What made her victory still more amazing was that the second set was twice interrupted by rain—halted for forty-eight minutes the first time and for thirty minutes the second. Usually, it is the more experienced player who benefits from a stoppage of play. During the first interruption, I retreated to the press box and began discussing this matter with a tallish, reserved man in, I should say, his early forties who happened to be standing beside me. It became evident that he knew quite a bit about Shriver, and when I mentioned this to him he said, "I guess I should. I'm her father." Pam, I learned, is the second of three children—all daughters. Mr. Shriver is in the insurance business. He had come up from Baltimore that morning on the train, and during the match he had been so nervous that he had changed his seat to one in a thinly populated section near the top of the stands, where he could suffer in private. Although he realized that it was unfortunate that the rain had come when his daughter was playing so well, he thought that she might still win the match. "Pam can handle a lot of pressure," he said. "She knows her own mind, for sure. You ought to be around some of the times when she and Don Candy go at each other." As it turned out, Pam Shriver wavered badly only once in the second set, tossing away three match points in the tenth game. In her session with the press after the match, she was all ease and high spirits. Had the rain delays bothered her? "No," she said. "If I had crowded myself with how I should play Martina's serve, or when I should come to net, and all the other things, the waits might have bothered me, but I told myself just to go out and play my best shots. That kept me loose." She was amusing at times. When someone asked her how she stood in her matches with Tracy Austin, she grimaced and muttered, "Next question." And when she was asked how she planned to play Evert in the final, she said, "Just like I played Martina today. I'll come to net as often as I can. That's my game. Can you see me trying to hit ground strokes from the baseline with Chris!"

On my way out of the interview room, I saw Mr. Shriver again, looking far more relaxed. I remarked on his daughter's nice sense of humor. "Gets it from her mother," he said.

The Evert-Shriver final took place on a bright, sunny afternoon. The wind was coming out of the south, and so we were treated to a fine irritating display of low-flying commercial aircraft. There was considerable drama inherent in this match. Evert is now a grown woman of twenty-three, but one remembers as if it were yesterday her first appearance in the championships, in 1971, when *she* was sixteen, a slim kid with a ponytail. That year, she revivified a dullish tournament, knocking off players of the calibre of Mary Ann Eisel, Françoise Durr, and Lesley Hunt before being stopped in the semis by Billie Jean King. This year, on her route to the final, in the lower half of the draw, she defeated Donna Ganz, Caroline Stoll, Regina Marsikova, Tracy Austin (7–5, 6–1), and Wendy Turnbull. In the final, Evert got off fast, whipping her forehand and two-handed-backhand drives deep and hard. Halfway through the set, however, she unconsciously let down a fraction, and, before she knew it, Shriver, who was beginning to play as effectively as she had against Navratilova, got back into the match in the eighth game: after fending Evert off at game point with a beautiful half volley hit with touch, she broke Evert's serve with two untouchable overhead smashes. Games 4–all. After this, Evert picked up the pace again, and, coming to net behind severe drives more frequently than she usually does and putting away her volleys decisively, she took the set, 7–5.

During this set and the next, by the way, Shriver served as well as any woman player I have ever watched. She was both powerful and accurate. When she was serving to the deuce court, she often cut loose with acutely angled slices that pulled Evert far out of position, and when she was serving to the ad court she whacked bona fide cannonballs down the center line. Moreover, she played first-class all-around tennis and, in particular, came up with some wonderfully acrobatic volleys as she ranged along the net. The quality of her tennis in the second set made it imperative for Evert to reach for everything she had. She began to whistle very low drives down the sidelines, keeping Shriver back or passing her cleanly on many of her forays into the forecourt. When the situation suggested it, she threw in deceptive lobs or hustled in to net herself to volley or smash. When Evert calls on her full vocabulary, including some strokes she has acquired only in recent years, you know that she knows she is in a match. The ninth game was the key game in this set. Shriver, serving at 4–4, went quickly to 40–love on a serve and smash, a serve and volley, and an error by Evert. Evert answered with three daring winners: a forehand return of service right down the line, a crisp volley, and a fast forehand drive that Shriver couldn't get to. After saving another game point, Evert summoned two more of her best: a forehand return of service that whistled down the line like a rifle shot and, at break point, another punishing return of service that Shriver could not handle and volleyed into the net. Evert, 5–4 in games, was serving for the match. Shriver was not conceding anything. In the tenth game, she had three chances to break back, but Evert stubbornly held her off and, at length, took the game, set, and match. In my opinion, it was the best women's final in our championships since the one in 1963 between Maria Bueno and Margaret Smith. Shriver, instead of turning to jelly in the crunch, as many had thought she might, had been magnificent, forcing Evert to come up with the finest sustained shotmaking she has produced in quite some time. In doing so, Evert won her fourth straight United States Women's Open title—a feat previously performed only by Molla Bjurstedt (later Mrs. Mallory) and Helen Jacobs. Shriver, it goes without saying, was a revelation. No one can be sure whether, as she moves into her late teens, she will retain her naturalness and sang-froid. A few girls do, but many become self-conscious as they grow older. I have a feeling, however, that the self-possession Pam Shriver showed us is an intrinsic part of her makeup, and that she will go on to become a truly great player.

Let us go back now to the match between Connors and Panatta. Its importance lay in the fact that it roused Connors to life. Up to then, his tennis had been well below his best standard, and he would clearly have to do something about this if he was to have a chance of defeating Borg, his arch-rival, in the final. From the outset of the tournament, everyone seemed to take for granted that these two—Borg coming through the upper draw, Connors through the lower—would ultimately battle it out for the title. Connors was thought to have a good chance of winning, because he was playing on a surface that was ideal for his game—a hard court on which the ball bounced high and so allowed him to release every last ounce of power into his shots. (He often leaves the ground with both feet as he swats the ball.) On the other hand, Borg, who is most at home on clay but has adjusted well to grass, has no fondness for hard courts, so it was agreed from the start that if we did have a Borg-Connors final it would be a far different story from their final at Wimbledon this year, in which Borg, playing possibly the best and most aggressive tennis of his career, dominated an enigmatically docile Connors, 6–2, 6–2, 6–3. In any event, Connors' first serious test came in the fourth round against Panatta, a twenty-eight-year-old Roman. They had previously played eight matches, with Connors winning six of them. Last year, they split two matches: Connors was the victor in the World Championship Tennis championship in Dallas after losing to Panatta in the W.C.T. tournament in Houston. That week in Houston was about the only good one Panatta enjoyed in 1977. The year was a terrific comedown for him. In 1976, he had won both the Italian Open and the French Open, and from 1970 through 1975 he had been the national champion of Italy. By far the most talented of the Italian players of this decade, Panatta, who stands well over six feet, is an extremely handsome, dark-haired man with something of the look of a huskier Alain Delon. When he is in top form, he can be spectacularly good, and since he has a theatrical nature and the ability to establish contact with the thousands who throng the Foro Italico, in Rome, and the other Italian tennis centers, it is not difficult to see why he has been a national idol, admired no less lavishly than the ranking Italian movie stars. In this country, except for that one big week in Houston, Panatta has never played anything like the tennis he is capable of—nor did he at Flushing Meadow Park, in taking the opening set from Connors, 6–4. Connors won the second set, 6–4, and added the third, 6–1. He was not particularly sharp, but there was no need for him to be—not the way Panatta was lumbering around the court seeming merely to be going through the motions. One was reminded that if at times Panatta has swept his fans into delirious rapture, there have also been times when he has disappointed them so bitterly that, shouting at the top of their lungs, they have pelted him with every abusive term they could think of. Panatta incites these extremes of love and hate because on his good days his bravura talent is so thrillingly apparent, while on his off days, sulky and sluggish, he often gives the impression that he isn't trying at all. In the fourth set, with no advance intimation, Panatta began to "read" Connors much more quickly, to move to the ball more rapidly, and to play some splendidly imaginative shots. He broke Connors' serve, to lead 3–1, and went on to overwhelm him with the power of his hitting. His serve, which up to this point had been nothing special, suddenly became exceedingly heavy and much faster. Connors could not cope with it. Encouraged, Panatta, erupting like Vesuvius, showered brilliant placements all over the court. He won the fourth set, at 6–1, to even the match at two sets apiece. Connors was in deep trouble, and realized it. He tried to fight back, but Panatta would not be diverted. Continuing to keep Connors off balance with the velocity of his shots, he got to 5–3 in the deciding set. At this desperate moment, Connors made a great stand. Putting more punch into his serve, he held it at love: 4–5. He decided then to rip into every shot, and went on to break Panatta at thirty. This made it 5–5. Connors, we were then reminded, is a strange young man. Delighted by the sterling tennis he had managed to muster just when he needed it, he threw off his cloak of restraint for the first time during the tournament, and, from then on, whenever he came up with an exceptional winning shot—and he came up with quite a few— he reverted to his old act: he strutted cockily around the court; he threw punches at the sky effusively; and, arching his back and tilting his head far back, he walked along the baseline as if he were treading a tight-rope. Most times in the past, many of us have felt that Connors' purpose in parading these antics was to show up his opponent and glorify himself. Not this day. Unmistakably, he was simply exhibiting for himself alone the joy he felt at playing such sensational stuff when nothing less would have done. Sensing now that he could win the match that had seemed lost, he served another strong game, to go ahead 6–5. Then Panatta, who has so often been accused of quitting when the going gets rough, showed us something. Down love–40, he got in two very heavy first serves and a good second serve to rub out the triple match point that Connors had held. Fighting hard, he saved one more match point, but then, at ad in and with a chance to pull out the game, he played an unsure point and lost it. Deuce for the third time. It was then that Connors came through with the shot that won this intense duel. After serving well, Panatta held control of the rally and, commanding the forecourt, stung a wicked crosscourt forehand volley that looked like a sure winner. Racing far out of court—beyond the doubles alley—Connors somehow got his racquet on the ball and hit a line-drive backhand that barely cleared the head of the net-cord judge and came back onto the court, landing two feet inside the left sideline. Match point for Connors, for the fifth time. Panatta missed with his first serve. Gambling on catching Connors off guard, he banged his second just as hard. It was long by an inch or two. Double fault. Game, set, and match, Connors. In victory, he did something I had never seen him do before. He came trudging to net, as did Panatta, and they threw their arms around each other. It gave this wonderful match just the right epilogue. Since I have in the past been as annoyed as anyone by Connors' rudeness on court, I should like to repeat that, as I saw it, there was nothing belittling or malicious in the mugging and strutting with which he garnished the eleventh-hour rally that saw him sweep the last four games. He is just an odd duck, Jimmy Connors, and there is no doubt whatever that he plays his best tennis when he is dramatizing himself all over the premises in his own eccentric fashion. As for Panatta, he was cheerful and placid in defeat. It was understandable. He would have preferred to win, but he had finally played a superlative match in America, and he was happy about that.

The Panatta match behind him, Connors advanced to the final with straight-set victories over Brian Gottfried, from Florida, 6–2, 7–6, 6–1, and John McEnroe, the feisty nineteen-year-old Long Islander, 6–2, 6–2, 7–5. His one lapse came in the third set against McEnroe, when he permitted himself to drowse and fell behind 1–5 before snapping awake and reeling off six straight games. In the other half of the draw, Borg reached the final by defeating Hewitt; Heinz Gunthardt, of Switzerland; Bernie Mitton, of South Africa; Harold Solomon, from Florida; Raul Ramirez, of Mexico; and Gerulaitis, a close friend, with whom he had practiced on Gerulaitis' court in Kings Point. Despite his reservations about the hard courts at Flushing Meadow Park, Borg had dropped only two sets—one to Mitton and one to Ramirez—but the sparkle that his tennis had had at Wimbledon was unquestionably missing. As is his custom, he kept most of his thoughts to himself. On more than one occasion, he avowed that a first-class tennis player should be able to win on clay, grass, and hard courts, and, with his deep-set pale-blue eyes as expressionless as usual, he said that if he and Connors met in the final Connors would be difficult to beat, since the court suited his style of play. On the morning of the final, everyone I talked with was keyed up at the prospect of seeing these old rivals—Borg is twenty-two, Connors twenty-six—going at it again. Some mentioned that, inasmuch as Borg had won five of their last six matches, he would probably win this one in spite of his lacklustre form. Others felt that Connors had begun to look like the unstoppable player of 1974, when he carried off both Wimbledon and Forest Hills. You can imagine the magnitude of the letdown when, shortly after noon, the report began to circulate that Borg had developed a blister on the thumb of his racquet hand. He had first noticed it the previous evening, after his match with Gerulaitis. In May, Borg had come up with a blister on that thumb before his semifinal match in the W.C.T. championship and had been forced to default. The word was that he would not default today, but one could not help thinking that the true story might well be that the blister was more than an ordinary blister and that Borg had elected to play only because a sportsman does not default in the final round of a major championship —it means too much to the championship.

The final went on, and it was, inevitably, an unfortunate anticlimax. There is no point in describing it in detail. Suffice it to say that Connors broke Borg's serve in the fifth game to win the opening set, 6–4, and that he won the second and third sets, at 6–2, 6–2. Connors did not drop a service game. Indeed, Borg at no time held a break point on Connors' serve.

It was impossible not to feel sympathetic toward both finalists. After the match, Borg behaved exactly as everybody knew he would. He referred to his ailment as "just a blister," and denied having taken an injection to deaden the pain. In avoiding any alibi, he was adhering to the highly admirable code one associates with the Australian stars: if you have an injury, you do not play; if you play, then you do not have an injury. The fact is that Borg had an infection beneath the callus on his thumb, and it hurt so much that he had been injected with a pain-killing drug, Marcaine, three hours before the match. He preferred to speak of how effectively Connors had played, how Connors had kept attacking the ball. Borg's injury was hard on Connors, too. Over the last four years, he had lost six of seven finals at Wimbledon and Forest Hills. He wanted terribly to turn things around, and at Flushing Meadow Park, from the Panatta match on, he was taking the ball so fast on the rise and hitting it so solidly that there was a very good chance he might have dominated a healthy Borg. There is nothing more to say except to congratulate both men—two of the most gifted athletes of this era —and to hope that they will be confronting each other in the years ahead on many bright afternoons when each is at the peak of his game and raring to go.

A few wrap-up thoughts on the National Tennis Center. Except for the unlucky twist of fate that rendered the Connors-Borg final so much less than the pièce de résistance it might well have been, the first championships at Flushing Meadow Park were eminently successful. The stadium was ready, and, given the race against the calendar occasioned by the move from Forest Hills, that was all that anyone could have reasonably expected. Accordingly, while many tennis hands, old and young, noted quite a few shortcomings in the new venue, they let them pass; there would be plenty of time to attend to them before the 1979 championships. Their only concern now is that the U.S.T.A. follow through conscientiously, so that the tennis center will fulfill its immense potentialities. First of all, I gathered during the championships, they would like the center to have more of the flavor of tennis about it. For example, they think that a tennis museum in the headquarters building would be an appropriate feature. Conversely, they see no reason for the commercial note that is struck by such policies as allowing signs with the names of a shampoo manufacturer, an insurance company, a car-rental service, and so on to appear, within television range, at the portals of the Stadium Court. The desideratum is the atmosphere of a fine tennis club, such as Wimbledon has. They believe that more lavatory and other comfort facilities should be provided. With the center a sort of island off by itself, they think that a much greater variety of food and drink should be available, especially since many patrons who attend the afternoon sessions stay on for the evening sessions, and they would be happy if at this international event there were restaurants serving the cuisines of different nations. A diet largely composed of frankfurters and knockwurst can pall. They expect that next year adequate seating accommodations will be set up at each of the field courts used in the tournament, and they would consider it a definite step in the right direction if more individual courts were spread over the center's green acres, in the manner of Roland Garros. They have strong reservations about a proposed plan of adding a tier of luxury "sky boxes" at the top of the stands in the Stadium Court—this could impair the court's appealing design —but they would like to see the seating capacity of the Grandstand Court increased. Last but most important, they feel that Flushing Meadow Park can never be an American Wimbledon unless some way is found to avoid the abrasive disturbance caused by aircraft taking off from La Guardia. (One wit suggested that the U.S.T.A. buy La Guardia.) And, yes, they realize that an excellent start has been made, and they have an inkling that Slew Hester and his associates are completely aware of what has to be done to make the National Tennis Center all that it should be.